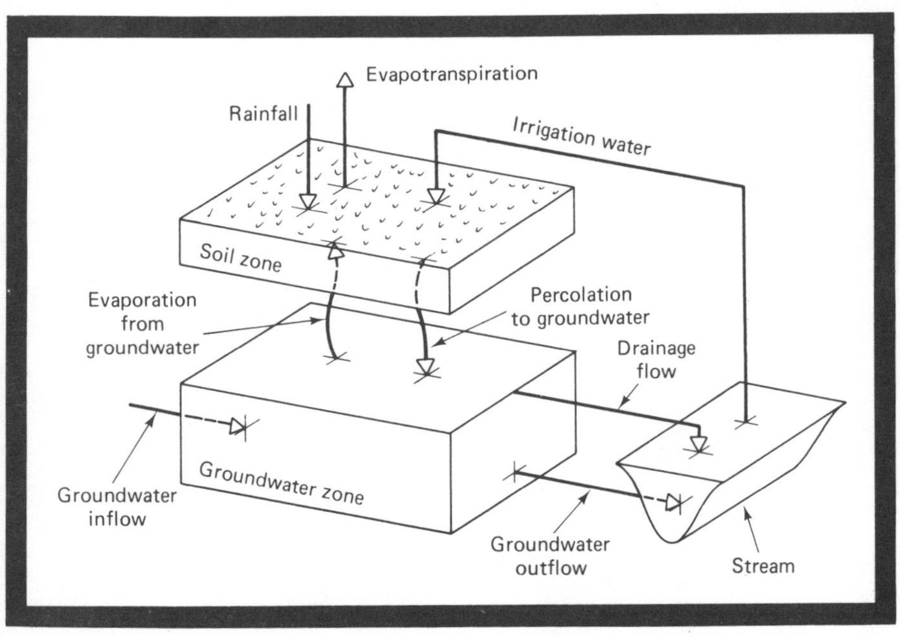

Representation of a typical irrigation cell in the detailed simulation model *(Figure 7-4)*

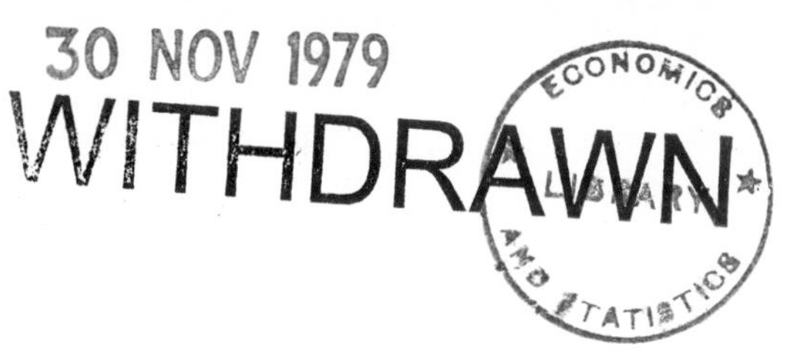

Applied Water Resource Systems Planning

DAVID C. MAJOR
ROBERTO L. LENTON

PRENTICE-HALL, INC., *Englewood Cliffs, New Jersey 07632*

Library of Congress Cataloging in Publication Data

MAJOR, DAVID C.   (date)
Applied water resource systems planning.

Includes bibliographies and index.
1. Water resources development—Planning—Argentine Republic—Colorado River watershed (Río Negro Province) I. Lenton, R. L., joint author. II. Title.
TC437.C6M34   333.9′1′009827   78–12735
ISBN 0–13–043364–0

Prentice-Hall Series
in Environmental Sciences
GRANVILLE H. SEWELL, *Editor*

Editorial/production supervision by Chris Moffa
Cover design by Saiki and Sprung
Manufacturing buyer: Gordon Osbourne

Printed in the United States of America

10 9 8 7 6 5 4 3 2 1

PRENTICE-HALL INTERNATIONAL, INC., *London*
PRENTICE-HALL OF AUSTRALIA PTY. LIMITED, *Sydney*
PRENTICE-HALL OF CANADA, LTD., *Toronto*
PRENTICE-HALL OF INDIA PRIVATE LIMITED, *New Delhi*
PRENTICE-HALL OF JAPAN, INC., *Tokyo*
PRENTICE-HALL OF SOUTHEAST ASIA PTE. LTD., *Singapore*
WHITEHALL BOOKS LIMITED, *Wellington, New Zealand*

CONTENTS

PREFACE

This book is an introduction to applied water resource systems planning. It is based on a study of the Río Colorado, Argentina. The study, a cooperative effort of the Ralph M. Parsons Laboratory for Water Resources and Hydrodynamics of the Massachusetts Institute of Technology and the State Subsecretariat for Water Resources of Argentina, had three principal objectives: to adapt modern water resource planning techniques to Argentina; to train Argentine professionals in the use of these techniques; and to apply the techniques to a particular river basin in Argentina, the Río Colorado. The latter objective is the focus of this book. The methods used in the study—multiobjective investment criteria and mathematical modeling techniques—are primarily those that have developed on the basis of the work of the Harvard Water Program. We are indebted to the distinguished members of this program for their pioneering efforts. The book is designed for use both as a text in upper-level water resource systems and related courses, and as a volume in the working libraries of water resource professionals and those in related fields. Our suggestions for the use of the book in teaching, based on our experience at MIT, are given in the Introduction.

We are grateful to our co-authors for their help and encouragement. All of the material in the book, with the exception of the Introduction, some descriptive sections in Chapter 1, the theoretical material in Chapters 2 and 3, the conclusions in Chapter 12, and minor parts of other chapters, is based on the reports and working papers, in English and Spanish, of the MIT–Argentina project. The authors of the original material are listed as the authors of the corresponding chapters in this book. In writing each chapter, we have revised and edited, sometimes extensively, the original material and in some cases have rewritten the material entirely. Where chapter authors are not given—that is, for the Introduction, Chapters 1, 4, 12, and Appendix A,—we have written the chapters. All of the authors are pleased to acknowledge the help and assistance of: Peter S. Eagleson, Head of the Department of Civil Engineering at MIT while the study was undertaken; Donald R. F. Harleman, Director of the Ralph M. Parsons Laboratory for Water Resources and Hydrodynamics at MIT; Frank Satlow of the MIT Press; Joseph Connolly and Carol van Aken of the Office of Sponsored Programs at MIT; Paul

Kirshen and José Córdova for helpful reviews of the manuscript; and Randall Hogan for assistance in preparing graphs. We also wish to honor the memory of the late Arthur T. Ippen, Institute Professor at MIT, Professor Harleman's predecessor as Director of the Parsons Laboratory and, it is fair to say, the teacher of each of the authors. The following officials of the Argentine government assisted, through advice and criticism, in the study:

Dr. Guillermo Cano, former Secretary of State for Water Resources, Argentina;

Ing. Juan Dalbagni, former head of the Dirección Nacional Sectorial de Desarrollo de Recursos Hídricos of the State Secretariat for Water Resources, Argentina;

Ing. Antonio P. Federico, former Subsecretary of State for Water Resources, Argentina;

Ing. Enrique Aisiks, former Advisor to the Secretary of State for Water Resources, Argentina;

Ing. Jorge Simonelli, former Secretary of State for Water Resources, Argentina;

Dr. Alieto A. Guadagni, former Secretary of State for Water Resources, Argentina;

Ing. Ennio Pontussi, former coordinator for the Comisión Técnica Interprovincial del Río Colorado, Argentina; and

Ing. Aquilino Velasco Díaz, head of the Dirección Nacional Sectorial de Desarrollo de Recursos Hídricos of the State Subsecretariat for Water Resources, Argentina.

We wish to thank also the many colleagues of these officials from the national and provincial governments of Argentina who provided advice and assistance, as well as, in particular, Ing. Luis Urbano Jáuregui, the Subsecretary of State for Water Resources, Argentina, during the writing of this book.

For the financial support that enabled us to complete the book, we wish to thank the Office of the Dean of the School of Engineering at MIT; the Office of the Provost of MIT; and the Department of Civil Engineering at MIT.

David C. Major
Cambridge, Massachusetts

Roberto L. Lenton
New Delhi, India

INTRODUCTION

This is a book on applied water resource systems planning techniques and their application to the Río Colorado, Argentina. The purpose of the book is to demonstrate the application of techniques that have been well developed in theory and used, for the most part, individually in practice, but that have rarely been applied in the integrated way in which they were used in the real planning study described here. We have attempted to bring together the principal features of the Río Colorado study in such a way that the methods and lessons of the study will be useful not only to students and specialists in water resources planning but also to those in the many related fields—urban and regional planning, geography, agricultural engineering, systems analysis, environmental studies, and others—whose practitioners are concerned with water planning.

The goals of the Río Colorado study, which was part of a broader contract to bring modern river basin planning methods to Argentina, were (1) to illustrate these methods by an application, and (2) to enable decision-makers to understand the physical, economic, and social trade-offs involved in the choice of a development scheme for the river (the allocation of the waters of which has been a long-standing source of controversy in Argentina) and thus to assist them in choosing among alternative development plans.

The book is organized into three parts. Part One, Chapters 1–4, provides the background to the study; a description of the Río Colorado and its development sites; our methodology, including the use of multiple planning objectives and our approach to mathematical modeling; and an overview of the system of models used to generate development programs for the Río Colorado.

Part Two, Chapters 5–8, contains descriptions of each of the four principal mathematical models used in the study: the system of three models used to generate program alternatives for the Río Colorado, and a fourth model used for data generation and model verification.

Part Three, Chapters 9–12 and Appendix A, contains the parameter inputs to the models, the model results, and interpretations of the work.

USING THE BOOK AS A TEACHING AID

A fundamental reason for writing this book is to make available to teachers and students material that we have found of value in our teaching at MIT. We expect that those teaching courses in water resource systems analysis, urban and regional planning, resource economics, project evaluation, geography, and systems and planning more generally will find the work useful.

We describe first the use that we recommend for the book in courses in water resource systems analysis, then outline its application in courses in resource economics and project evaluation, and then suggest its relationship more generally to other courses.

The typical modern course in water resource systems analysis, by which we mean a course that explores the ways in which systems analysis techniques can be used in water resources planning and design, includes the topics shown in Table 1. As an example, the course Water Resources Systems I offered by the Department of Civil Engineering at MIT has in recent years followed the outline in the table. In Table 1, we have indicated the number of weeks that might be devoted to each topic and have listed the parts of the book that might be assigned as reading in connection with each topic. For a course with this type of outline, the instructor might well give an overview of the nature of the issues addressed by water resource planners at the start of the semester by covering Chapter 1 of the book, before lecturing on the remaining course topics that emphasize systems analysis tools for dealing with such issues.

The text could also be used with good results in a course dealing more specifically with "Case Studies in Water Resources Planning," which could follow the Río Colorado study completely, and which perhaps also could describe other case studies by way of contrast and comparison.

For courses in resource economics and project evaluation, the book could appropriately be used both in the applied sections of the course, as well as in conjunction with theoretical sections for those who prefer to teach the theoretical material with suitable applied examples at each point. Supposing that such a course is based on texts such as those by Howe (1971), Maass, Hufschmidt, Dorfman, Thomas, Marglin, Fair (1962), Major (1977), Marglin (1967),

Table 1 Use of the Book as a Text in a Typical Water Resource Systems Course

Weeks	*Topic*	*Corresponding Book Chapters*
2	Introduction to fundamentals of project evaluation; multiple objectives; design criteria; overview of optimization and simulation	Chapter 2 Planning Theory: Multiobjectives Chapter 3 Planning Theory: The Role of Mathematical Models in Water Resources Planning Chapter 4 Planning for the Río Colorado: An Overview Overview of remaining chapters
4	Introduction to the use of optimization techniques in water resource systems design	Chapter 5 The Mathematical Programming Screening Model
4	Introduction to the use of simulation techniques in water resource systems design	Chapter 6 Simulation Analyses: The Basic Model Chapter 7 Simulation Analyses: The Detailed Model
2	Introduction to dynamic planning problems in water resources	Chapter 8 The Mathematical Programming Sequencing Model
2	Case studies	All chapters, but especially: Chapter 1 The Río Colorado Basin Chapter 9 Economic Parameters Chapter 10 Engineering and Cost Parameters Chapter 11 Outputs of the Models Chapter 12 Perspectives on the Case Study Appendix A Model Choice and Development

and UNIDO (1972), Table 2 gives a list of those topics in conjunction with which we think the book can be used.

For students in such courses, an excellent exercise for a term paper or seminar presentation would be to choose one or more theoretical investment criteria from Maass et al. (1962), Major (1977), Marglin (1967), or UNIDO (1972) and to make an analysis of what we have done both in terms of the theory and in terms of what the student feels to be the appropriate standards for success in applying the theory in a real planning operation. A more ambitious project is to compare and contrast the entire methodology of our study —multiple objectives and the use of several mathematical models together to analyze a planning problem—with the basic methodology used in another river basin case study or other resource planning study.

The book can also be used in courses in geography, urban and regional planning, and systems and planning. To make the book accessible to students and teachers in these related fields as well as to the specialist in water resources, we have written each chapter in such a way that, we hope, the nonspecialist can obtain a good sense of the material contained in the chapter

Table 2 Use of the Book in Courses in Resource Economics and Project Evaluation

Topic	*Corresponding Book Chapters*	
Planning setting: a developing region	Chapter 1	The Río Colorado Basin
Multiobjectives: choice of objectives and use in planning	Chapter 2	Planning Theory: Multiobjectives
	Chapter 3	Planning Theory: The Role of Mathematical Models in Water Resources Planning
	Chapter 4	Planning for the Río Colorado: An Overview
	Chapter 5	The Mathematical Programming Screening Model
	Chapter 11	Outputs of the Models
Benefit and cost accounting	Chapter 4	Planning for the Río Colorado: An Overview
	Chapter 9	Economic Parameters
Project sequencing	Chapter 8	The Mathematical Programming Sequencing Model
	Chapter 11	Outputs of the Models
	Appendix A	Model Choice and Development
The role of modeling methods in resource planning	Chapter 3	Planning Theory: The Role of Mathematical Models in Water Resources Planning
	Chapter 12	Perspectives on the Case Study
	Appendix A	Model Choice and Development

without necessarily reading the details that will be of interest to the specialist in water resources. The linkage of parts of the book to specific topics will depend on the specific nature of the course in each case. The suggested topics given for courses in water resource systems analysis and resource economics and project evaluation will provide guidelines.

HISTORY AND ORGANIZATION OF THE STUDY

The study was done by members of the Water Resources Division of the Department of Civil Engineering, Massachusetts Institute of Technology, for the State Secretariat (later Subsecretariat) for Water Resources of the Republic of Argentina. The study began in September, 1970, and the results were presented in a series of reports to the State Secretariat that were completed in 1973. An agreement on a development plan for the Río Colorado based on the results of the study was reached by Argentine officials in 1976; this agreement is described in Chapter 12. The funding for the study came primarily from a prefeasibility loan of $400,000 from the Inter-American Development Bank to Argentina, with supplementary funding from the State Secretariat. The project team was composed both of MIT personnel and of a group of six young Argentine professionals who came to MIT for the duration of the contract period. The disciplines represented on the project team included economics, systems analysis, water resources engineering, and agricultural engineering.

The contract had three main objectives: to adapt modern water resource systems planning techniques to Argentina; to train selected Argentine professionals in the use of these techniques; and to apply the techniques to a particular river basin in Argentina, the Río Colorado. It is the work done to fulfill the third objective of the contract that is the basis of this book. The background of the contract is as follows.

During the 1960s, particularly in the United States and particularly as a result of the work of the Harvard Water Program [Maass et al., 1962], new methods of water resource planning were developed that can be divided into two main areas: mathematical modeling techniques, and multiobjective investment criteria. Both of these areas have now begun to receive fairly widespread acceptance, though perhaps not sufficient application, in water planning in the United States. Their recognition abroad has been less extensive, relatively speaking, and it was to bring these new methods to Argentina that the MIT–Argentina program was undertaken. The contract was developed through the personal experience, contacts, and explorations of the first State Secretary for Water Resources of Argentina, Dr. Guillermo Cano, who, prior to accepting this position, was a member of the United Nations staff in New York. When the opportunity arose to introduce new developments in water resource planning for use in the context of the programs of the newly formed State Secretariat, he invited a group of MIT faculty members to Buenos Aires, and this led to the study described in this book.

PARTICIPANTS IN THE PROJECT

A large number of persons participated in the project, including the faculty members responsible for the project, graduate and undergraduate students at MIT, the Argentine professionals who were appointed as visiting research engineers at the Ralph M. Parsons Laboratory for Water Resources and Hydrodynamics for the duration of the contract, and research and technical support staff. In addition, members of the Secretariat participated on a regular basis during visits to Argentina by MIT staff and during several visits to the United States by Argentine staff, and a counterpart working group was formed by the Argentines during the second year of the contract.

Table 3 lists those who participated in the study and those who participated in the preparation of this volume.

PROJECT REPORTS

The final reports of the project are listed here. For readers interested in further detail, Table 4 lists the chapters of the book based in substantial part on particular project reports, and gives the numbers of the reports.

Table 3 Participants in the MIT Río Colorado Project

MIT Faculty	*Argentine Government Trainees*	*MIT Graduate Research Assistants*	*Other MIT Graduate and Undergraduate Students*	*Administrative Assistants*	*Editorial Assistants for* Applied Water Resource Systems Planning
Frank E. Perkins	Marcos Elinger	Jay Hellman	Edward Hammond	Erika Babcock	Leslie Chow
John C. Schaake, Jr.	Tomás Facet	Jared Cohon	Richard West	Pat Dixon	Debra Knopman
David C. Major	Roberto Lenton	Donald Evans	Mark Daskin	Diane Pasquale	Victoria Murphy
David H. Marks	Javier Pascuchi	Anders Haan	Joseph Lee	Elba Rosso	Kathleen Wallace
Brendan M. Harley	José Suarez	Richard Laramie	Malcolm Petroccia		
Walter Grayman, PhD	Juan Valdés	Edward McBean	Glen Speckert		
Project Manager		Darío Valencia	Charles Ward		
		Guillermo Vicens			
		Eric Wood			

FINAL REPORT

Volume I. Planes Para el Desarrollo Integrado del Río Colorado, Parte I, II, III, November 1972.

Volume II. Formulation and Evaluation of Alternatives in the Design of Water Resource Systems, November 1972.

OTHER PROJECT REPORTS

1. Cohon, Jared L., Tomás B. Facet, Anders H. Haan, and David H. Marks, "Mathematical Programming Models and Methodological Approaches for River Basin Planning," Ralph M. Parsons Laboratory for Water Resources and Hydrodynamics, MIT, January 1973.

2. Evans, Donald H., Brendan M. Harley, and Rafael Bras, "Application of Linear Routing Systems to Regional Groundwater Problems," Ralph M. Parsons Laboratory for Water Resources and Hydrodynamics, MIT, Technical Report No. 155, September 1972.

3. Grayman, Walter M., "Río Colorado Data Report," Ralph M. Parsons Laboratory for Water Resources and Hydrodynamics, MIT, November 1972.

4. Harley, Brendan M., Juan Valdés, Marcos Elinger, John C. Schaake, Jr., and Guillermo Vicens, "A Model for the Detailed Simulation of River Basin Hydrologic Processes and for Water Resource System Evaluation," Ralph M. Parsons Laboratory for Water Resources and Hydrodynamics, MIT, July 1973.

5. Hellman, Jay John, "Migration in a Developing Country: A Systems Study: The Stimulation and Retention of Agricultural Migrants," Ph.D thesis, Department of Civil Engineering, MIT, September 1972.

6. Laramie, Richard L., and John C. Schaake, Jr., "Simulation of the Continuous Snowmelt Process," Ralph M. Parsons Laboratory for Water Resources and Hydrodynamics, MIT, Technical Report No. 143, January 1972.

7. McBean, Edward A., Roberto L. Lenton, Guillermo J. Vicens, and John C. Schaake, Jr., "A General Purpose Simulation Model for Analysis of Surface Water Allocation Using Large Time Increments," Ralph M. Parsons Laboratory for Water Resources and Hydrodynamics, MIT, Technical Report No. 160, November 1972.

8. McBean, Edward A., and John C. Schaake, Jr., "A Marginal Analysis-System Simulation Technique to Formulate Improved Water Resources Configurations to Meet Multiple Objectives," Ralph M. Parsons Laboratory for Water Resources and Hydrodynamics, MIT, Technical Report No. 166, February 1973.

9. Pascuchi, Javier, "Macroeconomic Aspects of Water Resources Planning in Argentina," Ralph M. Parsons Laboratory for Water Resources and Hydrodynamics, MIT, November 1972.

10. Pascuchi, Javier, "Métodos para la Estimación de los Beneficios del Riego," Ralph M. Parsons Laboratory for Water Resources and Hydrodynamics, MIT, September 1972.

11. Suarez, José, "Iteración Económica en Mercados para la Electricidad," Ralph M. Parsons Laboratory for Water Resources and Hydrodynamics, MIT, September 1972.

12. Valencia, Darío, and John C. Schaake, Jr., "A Disaggregation Model for Time Series Analysis and Synthesis," Ralph M. Parsons Laboratory for Water Resources and Hydrodynamics, MIT, Technical Report No. 149, June 1972.

13. Vicens, Guillermo J., and John C. Schaake, Jr., "Simulation Criteria for Selecting Water Resource System Alternatives," Ralph M. Parsons Laboratory for Water Resources and Hydrodynamics, MIT, Technical Report No. 154, September 1972.

Table 4 Project Reports on which Individual Chapters are Based

Chapter No.	*Report No.*
5	1
6	7
7	4
8	1
9	9, 10, 11
10	3
11	Final Report

A NOTE ON PLACE NAMES

We have followed the practice of using local place names for Río Colorado sites throughout the book. (We have departed from Spanish usage in capitalizing *Río* when used as part of a name, e.g. Río Colorado). A list of names of development sites on the Río Colorado is given in Table 11A-32, together with English translations of the site names. In some cases, where we have aggregated small irrigation areas into a single area for modeling purposes, we have assigned a name to the larger area, as is the case with Mendoza Zone I. In other cases, we have used a short version of the full name of a place. For example, we refer to Valles Interiores de Caleu-Caleu as Valles Interiores or Valle Interior.

UNITS

Throughout the book we have used the metric system of units. Table 5 shows the principal units employed, their equivalents in the English system of units, and their most common multiples or submultiples.

Table 5 Units of Measurement Used in the Book

Type of Measurement	*Unit*	*Equivalent*	*Multiples or Submultiples*
Length	m	1 m = 3.28 ft	1 km = 1000 m
Area	ha	1 ha = 2.47 acres	1 km^2 = 100 ha
Volume	MCM	1 MCM = 810.7 acre-feet	1 MCM = 10^6 m^3
Flow	m^3/sec	1 m^3/sec = 35.31 cfs	
Power	MW	1 MW = 56880 Btu/min	1 MW = 1000 kW
Energy	GWh	1 GWh = 3.412 × 10^9 Btu	1 GWh = 10^6 kWh 1 GWh = 10^3 MWh
Temperature	°C	°C = (°F + 32) × $\frac{5}{9}$	

REFERENCES

HOWE, CHARLES W. *Benefit-Cost Analysis for Water System Planning.* Washington, D.C.: American Geophysical Union, Water Resources Monograph 2, 1971.

MAASS, ARTHUR, MAYNARD M. HUFSCHMIDT, ROBERT DORFMAN, HAROLD A. THOMAS, JR., STEPHEN A. MARGLIN, and GORDON MASKEW FAIR. *Design of Water-Resource Systems.* Cambridge, Mass.: Harvard University Press, 1962.

MAJOR, DAVID C. *Multiobjective Water Resource Planning.* Washington, D.C.: American Geophysical Union, Water Resources Monograph 4, 1977.

MARGLIN, STEPHEN A. *Public Investment Criteria.* Cambridge, Mass.: MIT Press, 1967.

UNIDO (United Nations Industrial Development Organization). *Guidelines for Project Evaluation.* New York: United Nations, 1972.

Part I

Background, Description, Methodology, and Overview

CHAPTER ONE | THE RIO COLORADO BASIN

This chapter provides an overview of the Río Colorado basin and describes the potential reservoir, irrigation, power, and interbasin diversion sites along the river. The chapter has four sections: a general description of the Río Colorado and its economy, and descriptions of each of the three main regions—the upper, middle, and lower basins, and the project sites contained in each. This chapter is the first of four that introduces the factual and methodological background of the study.

THE RIO COLORADO: AN OVERVIEW

The Río Colorado rises from snowmelt runoff in the Andes and flows in generally easterly directions for about 1,100 km through arid country to its mouth in the Atlantic, about 125 km south of the grain exporting port of Bahía Blanca. The mean annual flow of the river in its lower reaches is about 130 m^3/sec. Although the Colorado is a small river, the distribution of water in Argentina is such that, aside from the giant group of rivers forming the Plate Basin, the Colorado is one of the largest rivers in the country. The river is largely undeveloped at present, and the population of the basin proper is probably not more than 50,000 persons. The basin itself is a fairly narrow strip along the river, but the Río Colorado is linked economically, and can be further linked through development, with adjoining areas and with the country as a whole. Decision-making on the allocation of the waters of the river is made complex because it flows through or borders on five of Argentina's 22 provinces: Mendoza, Río Negro, Neuquén, La Pampa, and Buenos Aires provinces.

Figure 1-1 is a map of the entire basin and Figures 1-4, 1-5, and 1-7 are maps of each of the main regions showing the project sites in them. Details on the project sites described in this chapter are given in Grayman (1972) and the references cited therein for each site; the sources of information used to locate projects on the basin and regional maps are summarized in Chow, Lenton and Major (1977).

The Río Colorado is hydrologically a relatively simple entity. The Colorado is formed at the confluence of its two main tributaries, the Río Grande and the Río Barrancas, and then flows to the Atlantic with only two minor tributaries through a zone of sparse rainfall. The profile of the river is shown in Figure 1-2. The flow pattern of the river has a peak in December (at the end of the southern hemisphere spring) and a minimum occurring between April and August (Figure 1-3). The basin can be related by man-made transfers to rivers to the north and to the south. To the north, exports of water are possible to areas in the old wealthy province of Mendoza, which has as a principal industry the growing of wine grapes in irrigated areas. To the south, imports to the Río Colorado are possible from points in the Río Negro basin.

The principal purposes of development on the river at present are for creating and enlarging irrigation areas and for producing hydroelectric energy. The river is not now regulated, although water is diverted for irrigation at several sites. The only substantial long-established irrigation area is at Pedro Luro near the mouth of the river. Several new areas are under development further upstream. Irrigation uses are primarily consumptive uses of water; and the flows not consumptively used carry salts when returned to the river. (Thus, the development of irrigation sites upstream has both quality and quantity consequences for the use of the river downstream.) Although the production of hydroelectric power is a nonconsumptive use of water, the necessity to maintain heads or to discharge water during non-growing seasons for the production of power can lead to conflict between power production and the use of water for irrigation.

The river is an exceptionally interesting case from the point of view of decision-making, because each of the five riverine provinces has interests somewhat different from those of the others and from those of the national government. Because some of the riverine provinces or some areas within them have few resources aside from the river; given the historic importance of irrigation to many areas of Argentina; and given the plans that the separate provinces have for development that would, if all were brought to fruition, require water in excess of the capacity of the river, the decision problem is of great practical as well as theoretical interest.

The basin has three topographic subregions: the western mountainous area, the central tablelands, and the plains of the east, which we refer to as the upper, middle, and lower basins. A consequence of their expanse and terrain is a wide range of climates. Average annual temperatures in the upper basin are below 0°C, whereas the climate in the central and eastern regions is considerably milder, with mean annual temperatures typically between 10°C and 15°C.

Precipitation is abundant (approximately 1,000 mm/year) in the mountainous parts of Mendoza along the Chilean border and in the Neuquén highlands, where most of the precipitation falls as snow during the winter. Near the confluence of the rivers Grande and Barrancas, the average annual precipitation decreases rapidly to 200 mm, a value characteristic of much of the central region. Further east there is a gradual increase, reaching 400 mm/year along the Atlantic coast. Another important hydrologic characteristic is the frequent and substantial oscillation in mean annual rainfall; measurements of more than 200% and less than 50% of the average have been recorded (ITALCONSULT, 1961, p. 14).

Population centers in the basin are small. The largest, according to the 1970 census (República Argentina, Censo Nacional de Población, Familias, y Viviendas, 1970: Localidades con 1,000 y Más Habitantes) are Pedro Luro, in Buenos Aires province, with a 1970 population of 2,641 (a slight decrease from the 1960 value of 2,882) and in Río Negro province, the new development area of Catriel, with a 1970 population of 5,322, up from 707 in 1960.

Even where cattle breeding is most extensive, land in the area of the Río Colorado has not, at least until recently, been used to its full potential, and in some areas, particularly in the central subregion, as much as 50% of the land has not been utilized (ITALCONSULT, 1961, p. 54).

The basin has to be seen economically in the context of the riverine provinces themselves. The two most highly developed of these are Mendoza and Buenos Aires provinces. Both have diversified economies. In the other three provinces, agriculture and mining are the sectors that make the largest single contributions to provincial product. In Neuquén, economic activity revolves around mining and oil drilling. La Pampa primarily supports cattle raising, and Río Negro is an agricultural region (ITALCONSULT, 1961, pp. 50–51).

The riverine provinces have long been interested in the development potential of the Río Colorado. The most notable recent expression of this interest began in 1956 (Velasco n.d.) when the government of the province of La Pampa invited representatives from the other four riverine provinces to meet to discuss the utilization of the river. At the meeting that resulted from this invitation, the provinces agreed that they had the right to regulate the use of the river according to interprovincial agreement, and they agreed also to set up the Interprovincial Technical Commission of the Río Colorado (COTIRC: Comisíon Técnica Interprovincial del Río Colorado), formed in 1957.

A second conference was held in 1958, at which the provincial govern-

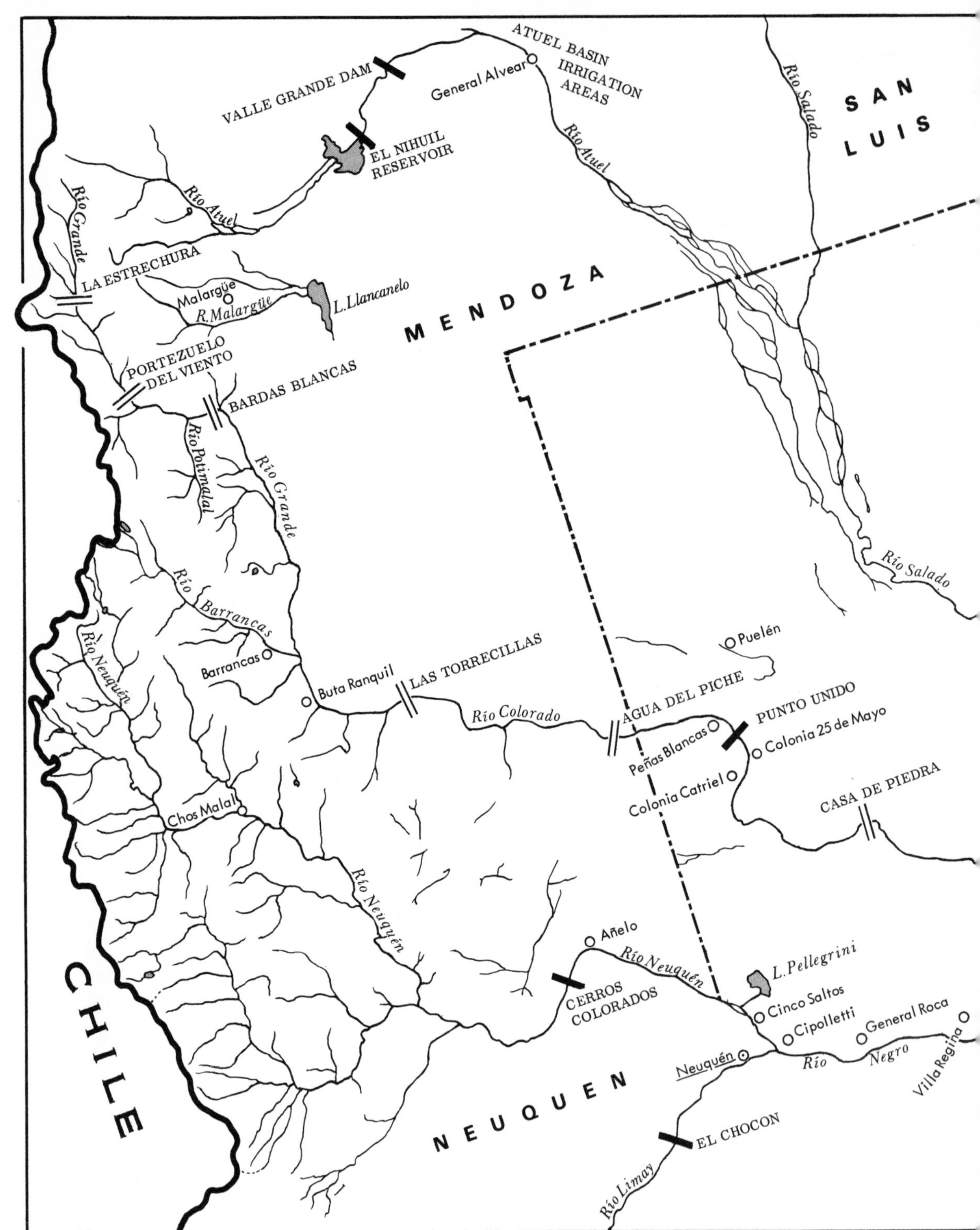
ATUEL BASIN
IRRIGATION
AREAS
General Alvear
VALLE GRANDE DAM
EL NIHUIL
RESERVOIR
Río Salado
SAN
LUIS
Río Atuel
Río Grande
Río Atuel
LA ESTRECHURA
Malargüe
R.Malargüe
L.Llancanelo
MENDOZA
MENDOZA
PORTEZUELO
DEL VIENTO
BARDAS BLANCAS
Río Potimalal
Río Grande
Río Salado
Río Barrancas
Río Neuquén
Barrancas
Buta Ranquil
LAS TORRECILLAS
Puelén
AGUA DEL PICHE
Río Colorado
PUNTO UNIDO
Peñas Blancas
Colonia 25 de Mayo
Colonia Catriel
CASA DE PIEDRA
Chos Malal
Río Neuquén
Añelo
Río Neuquén
L. Pellegrini
CERROS
COLORADOS
Cinco Saltos
Cipolletti
General Roca
Villa Regina
Neuquén
Río
Negro
CHILE
NEUQUEN
EL CHOCON
Río Limay

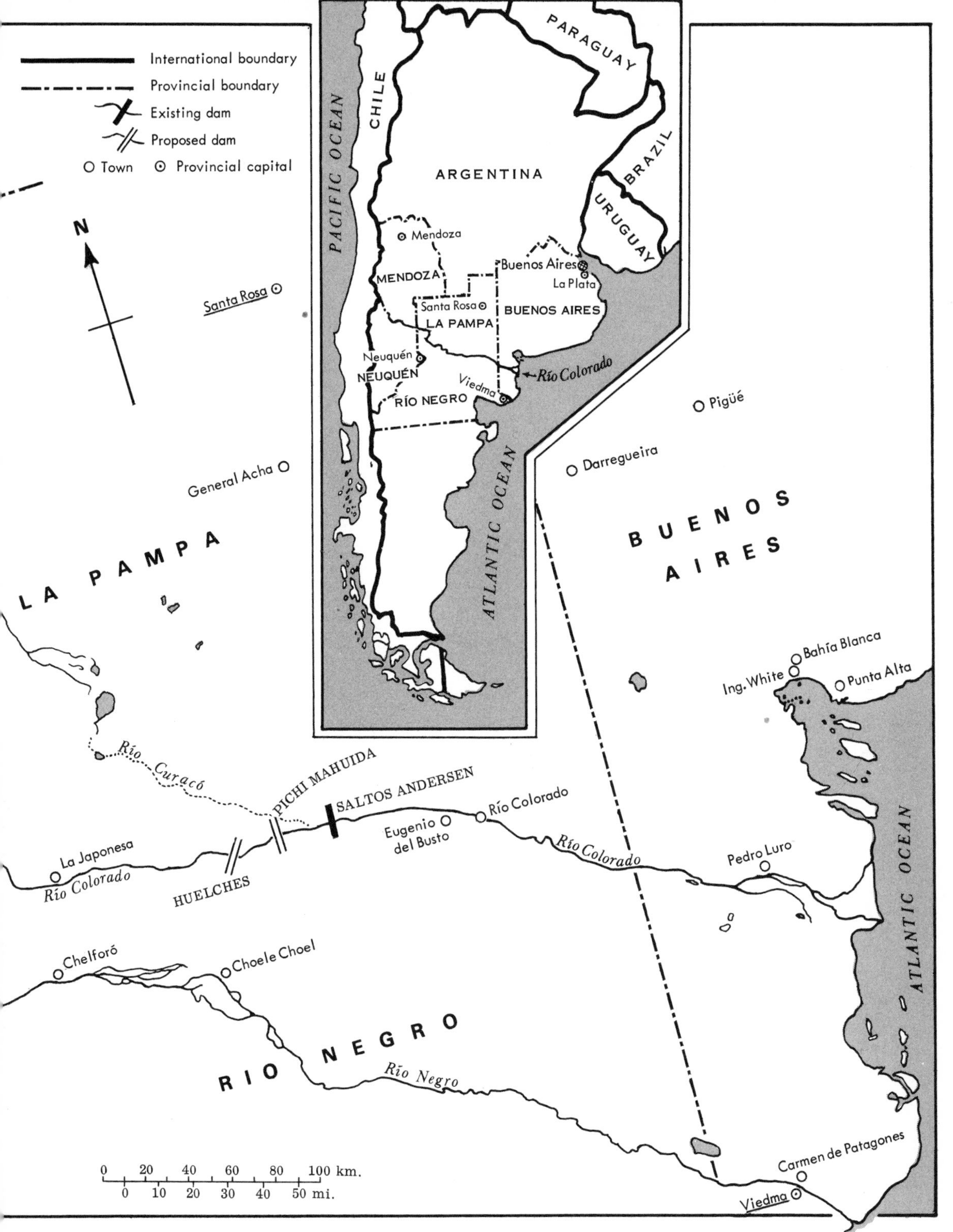

Figure 1-1
Map of the Río Colorado Basin.

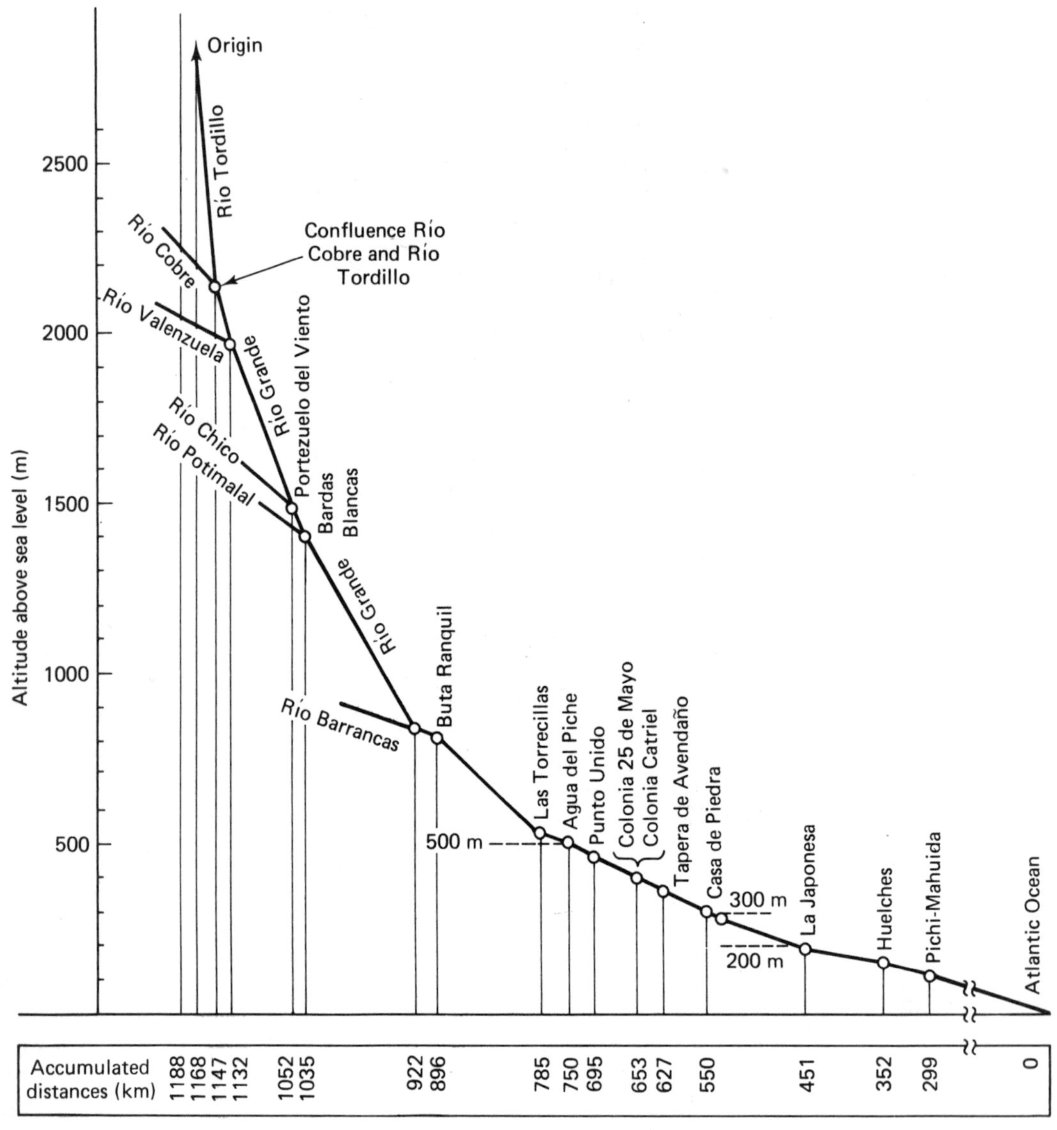

Figure 1-2
Profile of the Río Colorado.

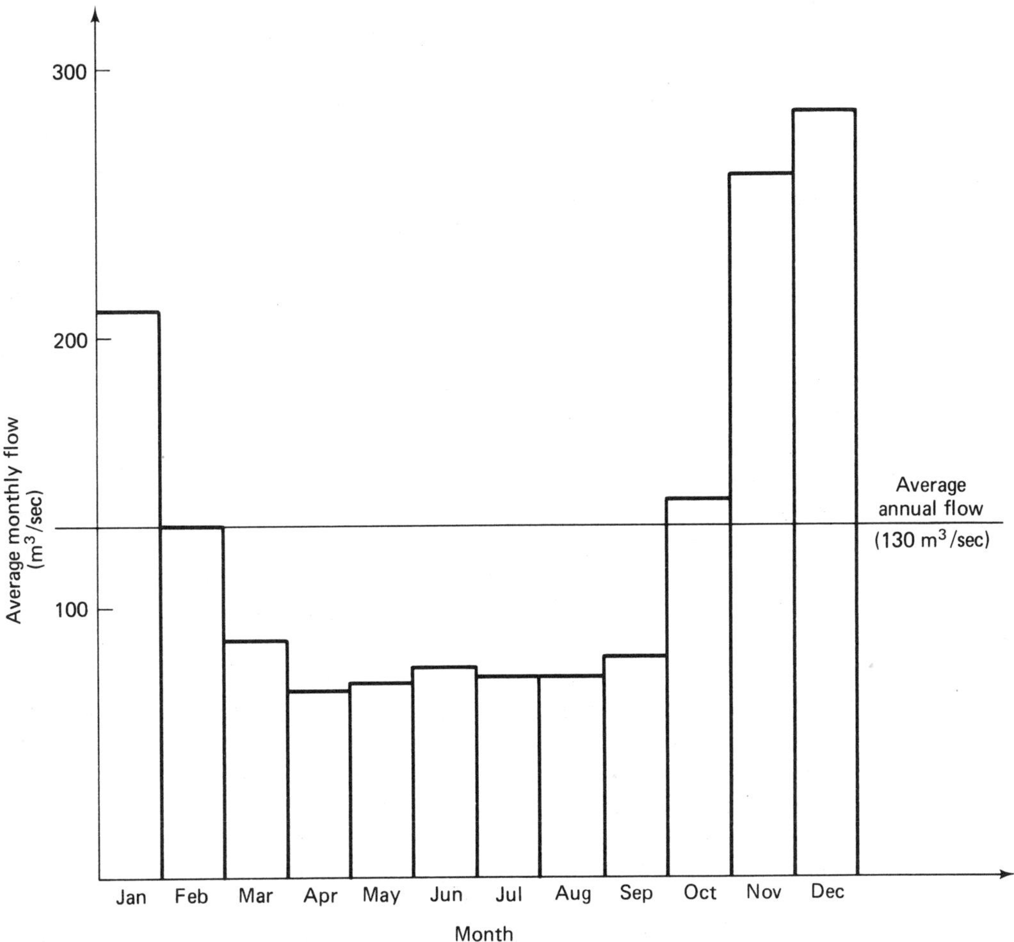

Figure 1-3
Flow pattern of the Río Colorado at Pichi Mahuida.

ments agreed to contract with the Geographic Institute of Argentina to make aerial photographs of the river and the surrounding area. At the third meeting, in 1960, the provinces recommended that a contract be made with Italconsult–Sofrelec, an international consulting group, to draw up a preliminary technical, economic, and financial report on the development of the river. Their report was submitted in 1961 (ITALCONSULT, 1961). Through 1969, each of the five provinces engaged in field work and carried out localized studies of potential projects. At the fifth meeting, in 1969 (a fourth meeting had been held earlier), an agreement was reached on general criteria for allocating water in the basin (Acta #4, 1969). In cases when all demands could not be met, allocation of water for consumptive use was to follow an established order of priorities: municipal water supply and supply for domestic consumption first, followed by agricultural uses, mining and industrial uses, and then other uses. The agreement also states that "the risk of variations in flow of the river should be apportioned to each province in proportion to the amounts of flow allocated to each," a provision upon which the shortage allocation procedure in the basic simulation model (Chapter 6) is based. The provinces also asked the Secretary of State for Water Resources to carry out a study to produce a development plan for the river. The Secretary accepted this commission from the provincial conference, and as a result the Río Colorado was chosen as the case study for the MIT contract with the Secretariat.

THE UPPER BASIN

In this and the following two sections we describe the upper, middle, and lower basins of the Río Colorado. The area defined in this study as the upper basin of the Río Colorado extends from the Chilean border to the confluence of the Río Barrancas and Río Grande. This includes the rugged mountains and sharply sloped valleys of the western Andes and the lower mountains and broader valleys further east. The province of Mendoza lies to the north and Neuquén to the south, as shown in Figure 1-4.

Earning a living is difficult throughout most of the upper basin, primarily because the terrain and the climate offer so few possibilities. The high mountains, covered with snow during most of the year, have no trees. Only a few shrubs and some grass-like herbs survive in sheltered ravines. To the east, at altitudes below 1,500 meters, the land is more habitable, although population growth has been negligible. Sheep and goat breeding are the most common occupations in the area (ITALCONSULT, 1961, p. 40). Small-scale mining is done as well. Only a few hectares in this region are suitable for irrigation. Mendoza Zone I, as defined in our study, is composed of several small areas along the Río Grande and Río Barrancas in Mendoza. No part of these areas is known to be currently irrigated. These areas contain soils inappropriate for most farming, and in our analysis only 60 ha in this zone are considered suitable for irrigation.

On the Río Grande, there are three potential sites for reservoirs (see Figure 1-4). The most important is the one at Portezuelo del Viento, with a possible storage capacity of over 3,000 MCM obtained with a dam somewhat higher than 150 m. A hydroelectric power plant could be built at its base with an installed capacity of over 150 MW. The other two potential sites for reservoirs are at La Estrechura and Bardas Blancas.

Several diversions from the upper basin to the Atuel basin in Mendoza have been considered. Two such alternatives are analyzed in our study (see Figure 1-4). The first is a diversion from the backwaters of the proposed small

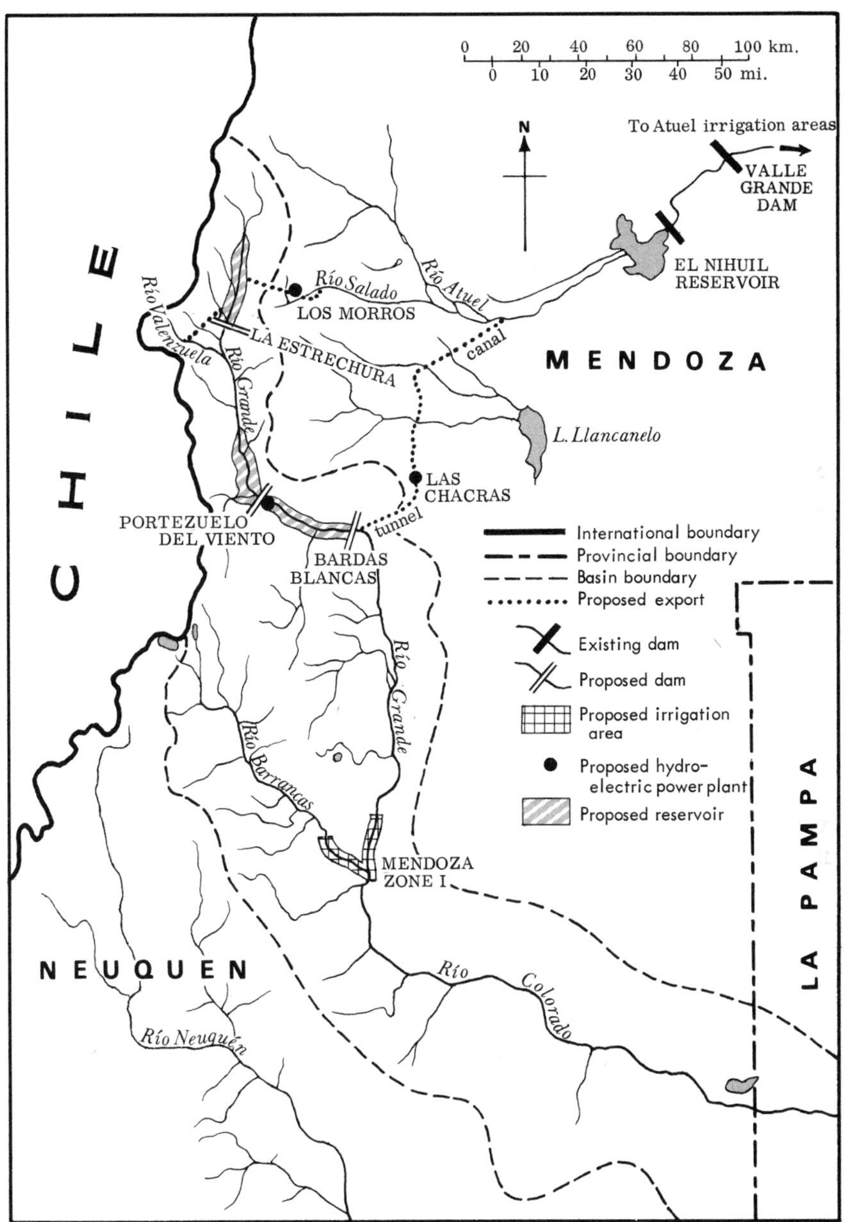

Figure 1-4
The upper basin of the Río Colorado.

reservoir at La Estrechura. To augment the flow here, a further diversion would be constructed from the river Valenzuela to the dam at La Estrechura. A power plant could be constructed at Los Morros on the diversion to the Atuel basin.

The second alternative, with a greater potential diversion capacity, would take water from the proposed reservoir at Bardas Blancas, downstream of Portezuelo del Viento. Along the diversion, a hydroelectric power plant could be constructed at Las Chacras.

THE MIDDLE BASIN

The milder, drier climate of the central tablelands, which can be said to extend from the confluence of the Río Barrancas and Río Grande to the proposed Casa de Piedra reservoir (Figure 1-5) presents a pasture landscape. This region blends on its eastern border into the scrub area, which has low, thorny shrubs and sparse grass in its drier sections and increasing vegetation cover in the damper zones. The tablelands slope down to the river valley in a series of terraces, broken at various points by several low hills and depressions. The interface of river bed with the sloping tablelands levels out into areas of land suitable for irrigation. There are also sections where the river is closely bound by its banks, for example at Agua del Piche. Considerable erosion occurs in the steep sections of the middle basin, not only increasing the solid load in the water but also increasing the chance of landslides, which at times block the river and cause the formation of lakes.

Many irrigation areas in the central basin could be developed. Furthest upstream, Mendoza Zone II, located immediately downstream of the confluence of the rivers Grande and Barrancas is composed of many small areas with soils suitable for development. Further downstream there are 500 ha currently irrigated at Buta Ranquil and an additional 500 ha that could also be irrigated. Downstream of Buta Ranquil is a sector of potentially irrigable land at Rincón de los Sauces. Currently, there are no irrigation works at Rincón de los Sauces. The total irrigable area, estimated at close to 2,500 ha, is located directly on the river. (If a dam downstream at Las Torrecillas were built, this entire area would be flooded.) The dam site at Las Torrecillas contains the greatest potential storage capacity in the basin, and at its base a hydropower plant of more than 200 MW installed capacity could be constructed. The Rincón Colorado area downstream of the dam is estimated to contain 500 ha of suitable farming land, none of which is currently irrigated. Immediately downstream is the proposed dam site at Agua del Piche, where the river goes through a gorge well suited for dam construction. A hydropower plant could be constructed here.

Peñas Blancas and Valle Verde in the province of Río Negro contain 6,400 ha currently being irrigated out of a potential irrigable area of about

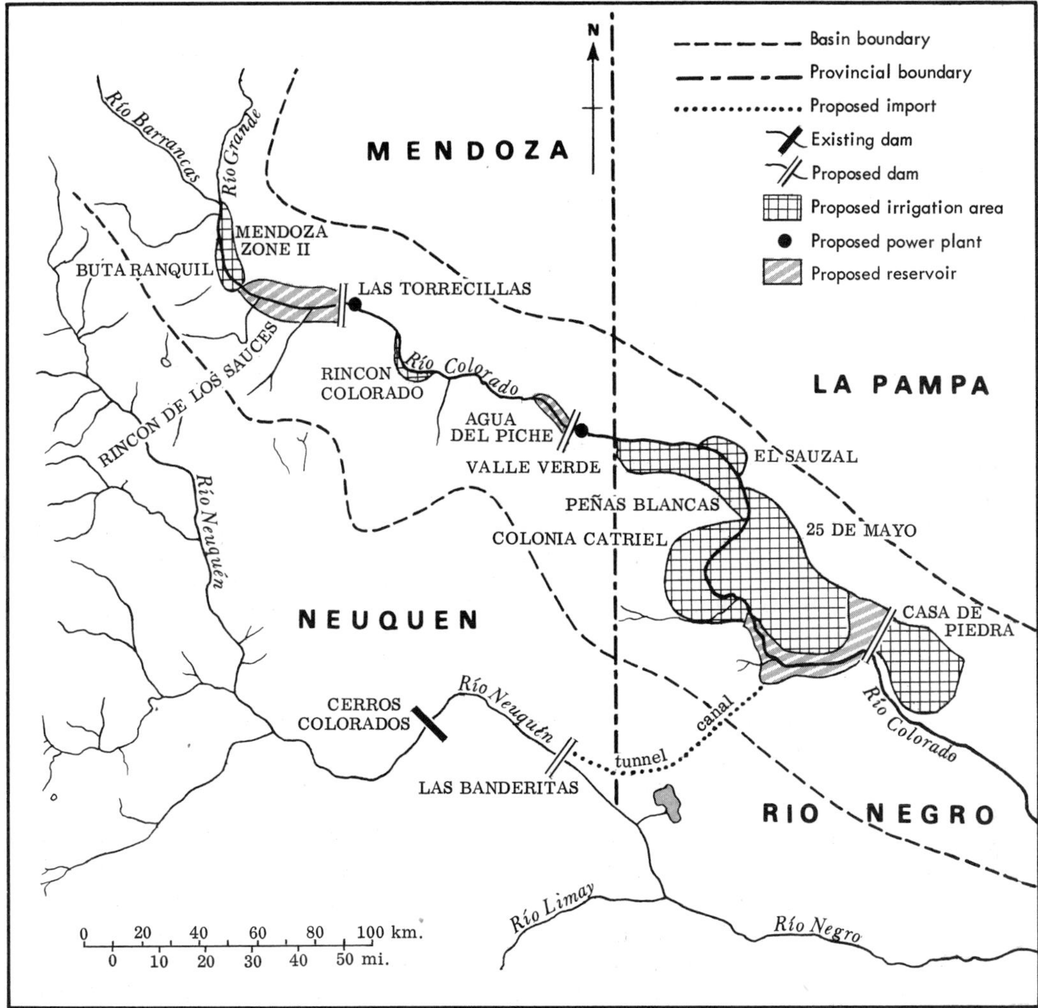

Figure 1-5
The middle basin of the Río Colorado.

20,000 ha. Across the river, at El Sauzal in La Pampa, there are 2,600 ha of potentially irrigable land.

The proposed irrigation area of 25 de Mayo is composed of five sections (see Figure 1-6). Parts of the main delivery canals have already been constructed at this site. Power plants at Los Divisaderos, Tapera de Avendaño, and Loma Redonda have also been proposed as part of the large development scheme in the 25 de Mayo area.

The irrigation area at Colonia Catriel is located in the province of Río Negro across from Colonia 25 de Mayo. There are currently 1,400 ha irri-

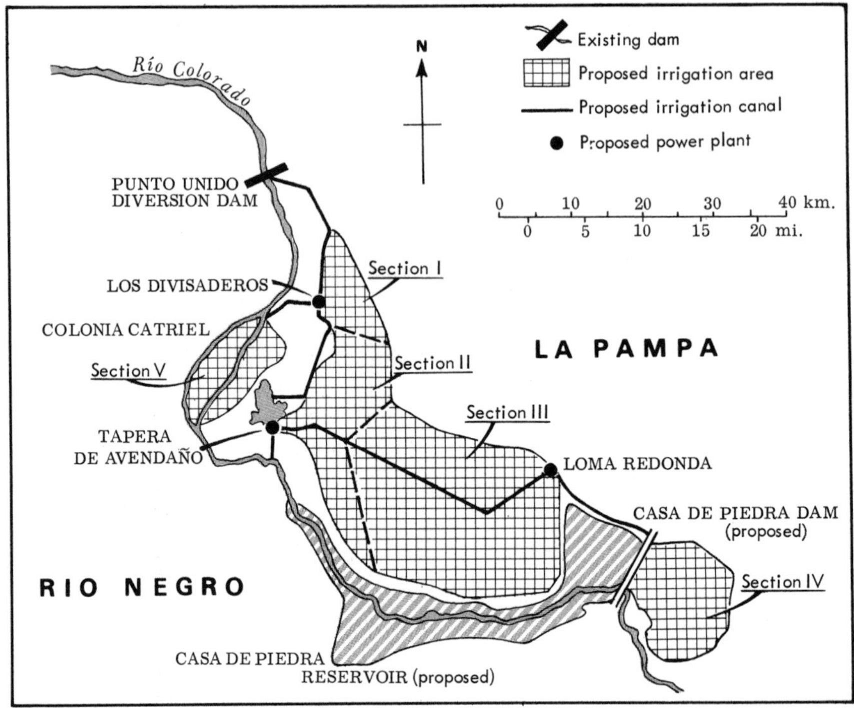

Figure 1-6
Map of 25 de Mayo.

gated with a potential irrigable area of 25,400 ha. The currently irrigated area takes its water from the Río Colorado by free intake. In order to expand the irrigation area, a siphon connecting Catriel with a principal canal of 25 de Mayo could be built.

One of the two potential alternatives for importing water from the Río Negro basin, developed by the Comisión del Río Colorado de la Provincia de La Pampa, consists of a diversion from the Río Neuquén at Las Banderitas to the backwaters of the proposed Casa de Piedra dam; this diversion would be over 110 km long.

THE LOWER BASIN

Delta conditions—alluvial deposits, mild climate, and full vegetation cover—prevail throughout the eastern plains, which occupy the remaining portion of the Río Colorado between the proposed Casa de Piedra dam and the sea (Figure 1-7). Consequently, more people and more irrigated agriculture line the banks of the Río Colorado, particularly in the province of Buenos Aires, in its last leg to the sea than anywhere else in the river basin. As the river

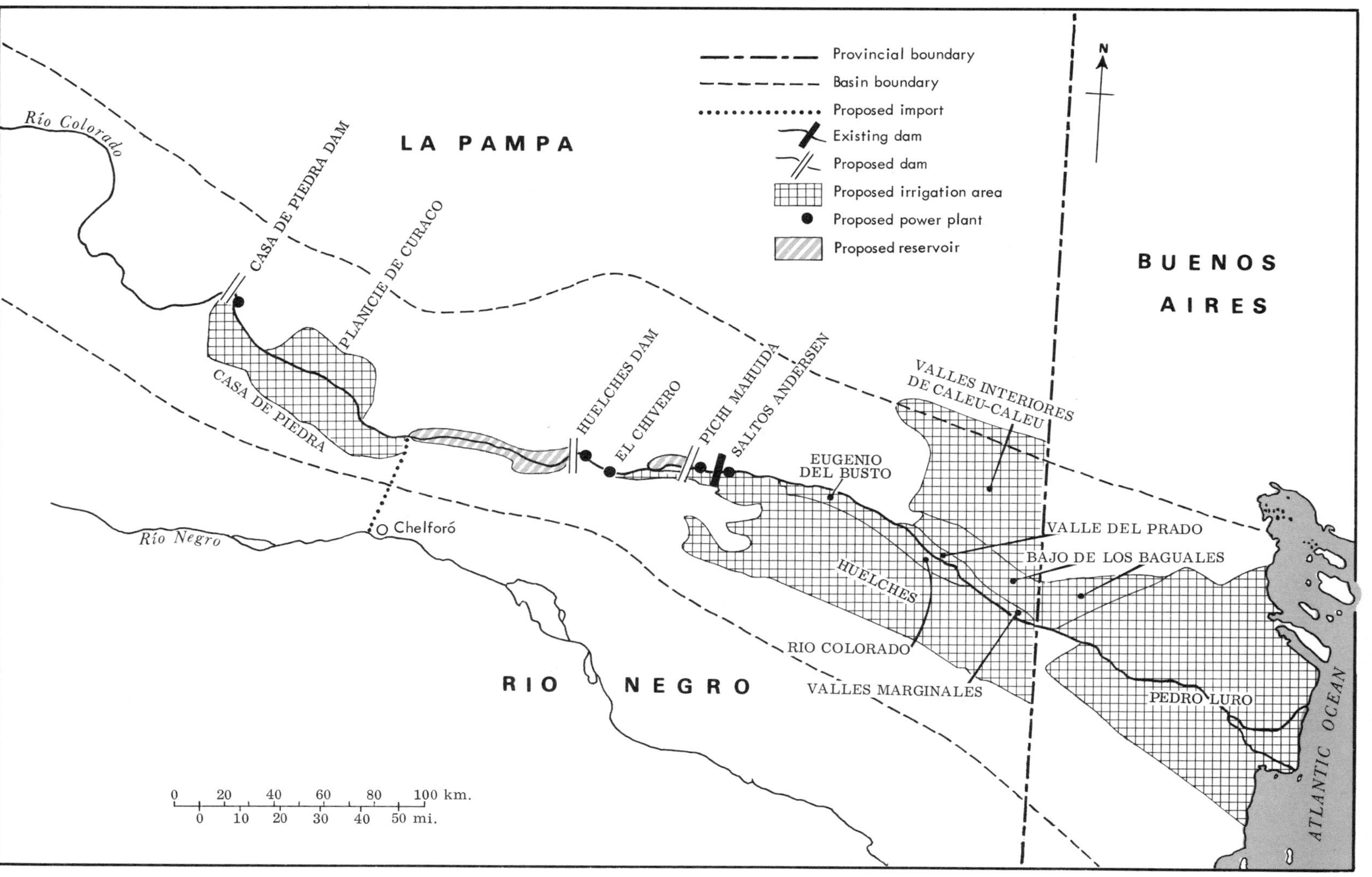
Provincial boundary
Basin boundary
Proposed import
Existing dam
Proposed dam
Proposed irrigation area
Proposed power plant
Proposed reservoir
N
LA PAMPA
BUENOS AIRES
RIO NEGRO
ATLANTIC OCEAN
Río Colorado
Río Negro
Chelforó
CASA DE PIEDRA DAM
PLANICIE DE CURACO
CASA DE PIEDRA
HUELCHES DAM
EL CHIVERO
PICHI MAHUIDA
SALTOS ANDERSEN
EUGENIO DEL BUSTO
VALLES INTERIORES DE CALEU-CALEU
VALLE DEL PRADO
BAJO DE LOS BAGUALES
HUELCHES
RIO COLORADO
VALLES MARGINALES
PEDRO LURO
0 20 40 60 80 100 km.
0 10 20 30 40 50 mi.

Figure 1-7
The lower basin of the Río Colorado.

flows over the plains, it creates its own banks from the alluvial material deposited and may even change its bed during times of high floods.

Experience has shown the soils in the eastern region to be well suited to irrigation, although excessive irrigation without proper drainage has led to increased salinity in some places. In sections where there has been no irrigation, in the "pampas" or grass-covered flat plains, the soils are sandy or sandy-loam becoming a layer of sand with fine silt and calcareous cement, soils that can support agriculture (ITALCONSULT, 1961, p. 38).

Many large projects have been proposed for this region. The proposed irrigation area at Casa de Piedra is situated in the province of Río Negro. The gross area is 115,000 ha, and the net irrigable area is estimated to be 78,000 ha. Across the river is the proposed irrigation area of Planicie de Curacó, whose estimated size is 25,600 ha. Both areas require at least a diversion dam at Casa de Piedra to provide adequate diversion head.

A reservoir at Huelches has been extensively studied by the Argentine power and water agency, Agua y Energía Eléctrica. A proposed diversion from the Río Negro downstream of El Chocón-Cerros Colorados at Chelforó would enter the Río Colorado at the upstream end of the Huelches reservoir. Downstream of the Huelches dam, an estimated 150,000 ha could be irrigated at the Huelches irrigation area.

Power plants have also been proposed as part of the Huelches development: at the foot of the dam, at El Chivero, and downstream at Pichi Mahuida, which has been identified as a possible site for the construction of a balancing reservoir of relatively small storage capacity. Further along, a power plant at the existing Saltos Andersen diversion dam has been suggested.

The Río Colorado community is a center of population in this area of the eastern plains. Apples and grapes are grown in the area, and several processing industries operate in the town. The Río Colorado area consists of several adjacent sites in Río Negro province: Eugenio del Busto, Juan de Garay, Río Colorado, and Colonia Julia y Echarren which we call collectively Río Colorado y Eugenio del Busto. The irrigable area is estimated at approximately 17,000 ha net with 4,500 ha currently irrigated. These 4,500 ha receive water from the Río Colorado at the existing diversion dam of Saltos Andersen; much of the main canal system is already constructed.

Across the river from the Río Colorado area, Valle del Prado consists of a potentially irrigable area of just over 1,000 ha, of which none is currently irrigated. An intake structure would include six pumps, and drainage would be provided by secondary drainage canals directly to the river. The net area of adjacent Valles Marginales is approximately 3,000 ha. No part is currently irrigated.

To the north, Valles Interiores de Caleu-Caleu is a large proposed irrigation site several kilometers from the river in the province of La Pampa. The gross area is 246,000 ha, of which approximately 110,000 ha are irrigable. Bajo de los Baguales contains an irrigable area of 19,600 ha in La Pampa and 20,400 ha in the province of Buenos Aires. A diversion dam is necessary to provide the head for irrigating most of this area.

Pedro Luro is the town associated with a large irrigation site administered by CORFO (Corporación de Fomento del Valle Bonaerense del Río Colorado) near the mouth of the Río Colorado in Buenos Aires province. There are currently 92,000 ha that can be irrigated when water is available. However, in terms of projected future crop mixes and agricultural methods the present canal system capacity and population are appropriate for only 60,000 ha of this irrigated area, a figure used in the present study as the existing area. Based on soil studies, the total irrigable area is estimated to be 218,000 ha. Because the present intake system is inadequate to provide dependable flow for even the existing area, several alternative diversion dams have been proposed.

SUMMARY OF DEVELOPMENT SITES

The information given in this chapter with respect to development sites is summarized here. The two main purposes of development on the river are irrigation and power. (Flood control and municipal water supply requirements can be taken care of by any reasonable development/storage plan.) There are over 20 irrigation sites in the basin that have been studied, with a total irrigable area of almost 800,000 hectares. Thirteen power sites have been studied, with a total potential installed capacity that could be as high as 1,500 MW. Exports to the Río Atuel system are possible from the Río Grande and two import systems from the Río Negro and the Río Neuquén are possible. The development sites described in this chapter are entered into the models described in later chapters according to the schematization shown in Chapter 4.

For readers interested in more detail on the Río Colorado, a good general reference on Argentina is Weil, Black, Blutstein, Hoyer, Johnston and McMorris (1974). A geographical review of the dry Andean and Pampa regions within which the basin lies is in De Aparicio (n.d., pp. 381ff. and 418ff.), and a description of the river basin is found in a general geography of Argentina by Daus (1957, pp. 265–267). Descriptions of earlier development plans for the basin are in CEPAL (1972) and ITALCONSULT (1961), the latter of which summarizes the economic, social, and geological characteristics of the Río Colorado area. Hellman (1972) contains information on migration patterns among the riverine provinces and other provinces in Argentina. A common problem in river basin planning—that census information is not collected in areas that correspond neatly to basin boundaries—holds true in the case of the Río Colorado. The most recent censuses of interest are República Argentina, Censo Nacional de Población, Familias, y Viviendas, 1970;

Censo Nacional Agropecuario, 1969, and the Censo Nacional Económico, 1964. A study of a region in Argentina that overlaps with the region of our study in the upper reaches of the Río Colorado is Frederick (1975).

REFERENCES

Acta #4 de la Comisión creada por Resolución del Ministerio del Interior No. 162/69 para el estudio y proposición de bases para la distribución de las aguas del Río Colorado. Buenos Aires, 1969.

Chow, Leslie J., Roberto L. Lenton, and David C. Major. "Sources of Information for Project Locations, The Río Colorado, Argentina." Staff Paper. Department of Civil Engineering, MIT, Cambridge, Mass., September, 1977.

CEPAL (Comisión Económica para América Latina). *Los Recursos Hidráulicos de América Latina: Argentina.* New York: United Nations, 1972.

Daus, Federico A. *Geografía de la República Argentina,* Vol. I: Parte Física. Buenos Aires, Argentina: Angel Estrada, 1957.

De Aparicio, Francisco, Ed. *La Argentina, Suma de Geografía,* Tomo I. Buenos Aires: Ediciones Peuser, n.d.

Frederick, Kenneth D. *Water Management and Agricultural Development: A Case Study of the Cuyo Region of Argentina.* Baltimore, Md.: Johns Hopkins, 1975.

Grayman, Walter M. "Río Colorado Data Report." Ralph M. Parsons Laboratory for Water Resources and Hydrodynamics, MIT, Cambridge, Mass., November, 1972.

Hellman, Jay John. "Migration in a Developing Country: A Systems Study: The Stimulation and Retention of Agricultural Migrants." Ph.D. thesis. Department of Civil Engineering, MIT, Cambridge, Mass., September, 1972.

ITALCONSULT. "Río Colorado: Development of Water Resources, Preliminary Report" (prepared for the Comisión Técnica Interprovincial del Río Colorado). Rome, 1961.

República Argentina. *Censo Nacional Agropecuario, 1969.*

República Argentina. *Censo Nacional Económico, 1964.*

República Argentina. *Censo Nacional de Población, Familias, y Viviendas, 1970.*

República Argentina. *Censo Nacional de Población, Familias, y Viviendas, 1970: Localidades con 1,000 y Más Habitantes* (Resultados Provisionales).

Velasco, Aquilino. "Estudio de la cuenca del Río Colorado: Síntesis Histórica." Subsecretaría de Estado de Recursos Hídricos, Buenos Aires, n.d.

Weil, Thomas E., Jan Knippers Black, Howard I. Blutstein, Hans J. Hoyer, Kathryn T. Johnston, David S. McMorris, *Area Handbook for Argentina,* 2nd ed. DA Pam 550-73. Washington, D.C., 1974.

CHAPTER TWO PLANNING THEORY: MULTIOBJECTIVES

DAVID C. MAJOR

This chapter provides an introduction to the use of multiple social, economic, and regional objectives in water resources planning (rather than the single objective of maximizing "economic" benefits as in traditional benefit–cost analysis). This is the first of the two principal conceptual bases of the study. The second basis, our approach to the use of mathematical modeling methods and, in particular, to the combined use of several types of models to generate alternative development configurations for a river, is described in Chapter 3.

These two conceptual bases can be related to each other and to the overall process of water resources planning by considering the four steps in system design suggested in *Design of Water-Resource Systems* (Maass et al., 1962, pp. 2–7). The four steps are:

1. Identifying the objectives of system design. This step involves selection of objectives in the political process.

2. Translating objectives into design criteria. This step includes the development of detailed criteria (for example, benefit and cost accounting schemes) for reflecting objectives in system design.

3. Developing system designs, using the design criteria, that reflect the objectives.

4. Reviewing the results of the design process.

Multiobjective theory underlies the entire set of steps, providing the conceptual basis for moving from objectives to design. Our approach to mathematical modeling, on the other hand, is the basis for our work in designing alternative development plans for the Río Colorado, step 3 of the four steps.

We first provide an introduction to multiobjective theory and then provide a brief overview of applications of multiobjective water resources planning. The chapter provides the basis for the discussion, in Chapter 4 and other chapters, of our procedures for applying multiobjective planning and related investment criteria to the Río Colorado.

A useful reference for multiobjective planning in general is Major (1977); more detailed expositions are in Maass et al., (1962) and UNIDO (1972). See also Major (1969), Marglin (1967), and the U.S. Water Resources Council (1973, 1976).

In general, multiobjective theory provides the basis for moving from the objectives of society to system design in an iterative fashion, using the four steps of water resources planning. Thus, the theory is concerned with the choice of objectives, the development of alternative feasible plans responsive to objectives, and the final choice of a plan. The theory is explained here in terms of these concerns.[1]

The choice of the objectives for planning is fundamental. The extent to which the objectives chosen are the right ones determines to a significant degree the success of a planning effort. Because for many planning operations in water resources a very large range of objectives is relevant, even if only in small degree, and because planning resources are generally limited, some criterion is required for the selection of objectives to be studied. The criterion proposed by Major (1977) is that those objectives should be included in analysis that are both important to society and are those on which the range of measures under consideration is likely to have some significant effect.

The application of this criterion requires judgment both on the part of the planner and on the part of the decision-maker. An iterative process should be at work. The initial set of objectives chosen for analysis on this criterion might not be the set of objectives that is really of importance. There should be checkpoints in the planning process to allow for expansion or contraction of the objective set as planning proceeds.

Suppose now that for a particular problem objectives have been selected in an appropriate way. (In the case of international rivers such as the Senegal or the River Plate, the objectives will represent the interests of several nations and their subdivisions—and perhaps groupings of nations. In the Río Colorado, the objectives represent national and provincial concerns.) For our example, we choose national income and income to a specified region such as a province.

As illustrated in Figure 2-1, a set of coordinates can be drawn with net discounted national income benefits measured on the vertical axis and net discounted regional income benefits measured on the horizontal axis. The

[1]The next several pages follow portions of Major (1977, chap. 2), which should be consulted for a more complete treatment.

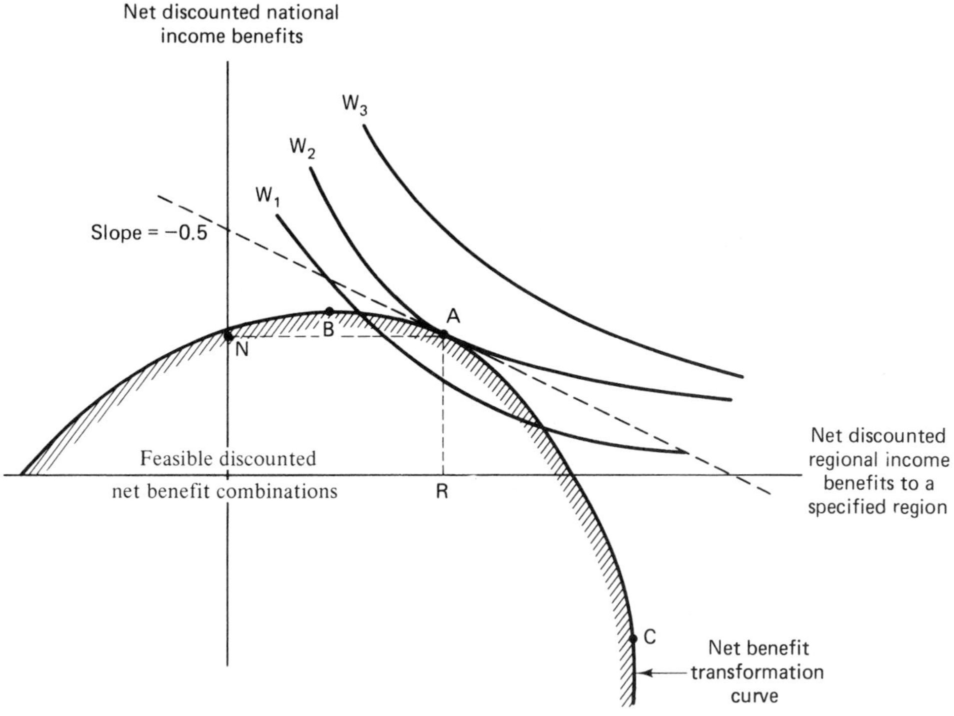

Figure 2-1
Multiobjective theory.

benefits are net because we are concerned with the net incremental effects of our management and development alternatives on benefits; they are discounted because we wish to be able to compare a variety of streams of benefits and costs toward objectives over time. The use of net benefits means that information such as gross costs cannot be read directly from the graph, but this information will be available from the planning documents used to generate the graphical analysis. Benefits and costs to both of these objectives happen to be measured in monetary units—for example, Argentine pesos. Benefits and costs for other objectives (for example, an environmental objective) will often be measured in other terms (e.g. in physical units).

The rules for counting national and regional benefits differ, however. Regional benefit and cost accounting requires that transfer payments in and out of a region be counted, whereas national income accounting does not (Major, 1977, chap. 3). Thus, pesos of income to a specified region do not represent a simple subset of pesos of national income. Also, the rates of interest used to discount benefits for these two objectives need not be the same and need not reflect directly market interest rates (Marglin, 1967). We also assume for convenience that there are no budget constraints on expenditure for development and management measures in our example. The way in which such constraints affect the analysis is described in Major (1977, pp. 43–47) [for a more detailed exposition, see Maass et al. (1962)]; our use of budget limits in the Río Colorado study is described in Chapters 4 and 9.

We now consider the sectoral planning possibilities that the planner in this example must take into account. These are the management and development measures that are available to him. For example, in the Río Colorado, a feasible technical combination might be two dams, one power station, and two irrigation areas; another might be a diversion to Mendoza, three dams, and four irrigation areas, and so on for a very large number of feasible alternatives. Each of these alternatives will have gross benefits and costs, in a given time stream, toward each of the objectives, and these we can discount and net out to estimate a point in the net benefit space. This point represents the net discounted contribution toward the objectives of a technically feasible management and development combination. The location of this point will reflect, of course, not only the engineering and hydraulic aspects of management and development schemes but also the economic, demographic, social, and environmental conditions that, in combination with the engineering and hydraulic aspects, give rise to net benefits.

Evidently there will be many such points of net benefit combinations for a given sectoral planning problem, and they can in principle all be plotted on the graph shown in Figure 2-1. For convenience in exposition, we assume a smooth boundary to the set of feasible points; this boundary is known as the *net benefit transformation curve.*

Before considering the shape of this curve, we should note that there is nothing in the exposition to this point that indicates that our net benefit combinations are confined to the northeast quadrant. There can be net benefit combinations in each of the quadrants. A point in the southwest quadrant, for example, indicates a feasible management and development measure that has negative net benefits toward both objectives. In terms of traditional national income benefit–cost analysis, a point in either the southwest or the southeast quadrant represents a project or program with a benefit–cost ratio of less than 1 (that is, negative net national income benefits).

If we assume that more net benefits toward both of our objectives are better than fewer net benefits, our attention becomes restricted to only a portion of the net benefit transformation curve, and we lose interest in the other parts of the curve and all of the interior points. This is because, if more is better than less (it need not always be, as in some religions) we can move from any interior point and from any point on that part of the boundary that does not slope from northwest to southeast to a point that is unambiguously better. We simply move in a northeasterly direction. On the part of the boundary of the feasible set that slopes from northwest to southeast, however, there are no such easy choices, because on this portion of the boundary, a movement in one direction implies a loss of benefits in another direction, and the simple criterion that more is better than less provides no guidance in this situation.

In Figure 2-1, all of the points of the transformation curve are included, as is appropriate in a theoretical presentation. In planning practice, of course, limited planning resources must be devoted to the estimation of relatively few points on the curve—those that are of most interest to decision-makers. [For the guidance given to U.S. water agencies in this regard, see U.S. Water Resources Council (1973)].

We now proceed to the role of preferences in multiobjective theory. We suppose that we can order social choices between combinations of net benefits in a satisfactory manner in the political process. From this ordering of each combination of net benefits we can draw curves (W_1, W_2, . . . , in Figure 2-1) that represent the loci of points of equal social utility. [See Arrow (1963) for the fundamental theoretical difficulties of generating such curves.] Curves lying to the northeast are superior to those lying to the southwest, in keeping with the mild assumption that more is better than less for our objectives. We do not need to know numerical values for the social welfare curves, but only the orderings that yield them. We show social preference curves for large numbers of combinations of net benefits; in practice it will not be necessary to derive information on preferences in such detail, because limited information about preferences usually will be sufficient to illuminate decision-making substantially.

OPTIMAL PROGRAM DESIGN

Given the net benefit transformation surface and the set of social welfare curves shown in Figure 2-1, we can determine by inspection that the highest attainable social utility from the set of feasible alternatives in our sectoral water resources planning problem is represented by the point *A*. This is the socially optimal combination of net benefits to the two objectives of the planning problem, increasing the national income and increasing the regional income of the specified region. It can be seen that this optimal point represents neither the maximization of national income (*B*) nor the maximization of regional income (*C*) but, rather, a mix of these two objectives. Although this result depends on the way in which we have drawn the curves in Figure 2-1, the reader will see immediately that it would only be by chance that the optimal point in general would represent the maximization of one or another of our planning objectives. This, in a nutshell, is the reason why optimal planning should not take place on the basis of limited-objective planning rules.

The characteristics of the optimal point *A* are of interest. The negative of the slope of the tangent line at *A* gives the weight that society places on an additional dollar of net regional income benefit to the specified region in terms of an additional dollar of net income to the nation. Thus, a slope of −0.5 means that the value placed by society on an additional dollar of regional income is 0.5. With this weight on regional benefits, society would be willing to give up at the margin \$1 of national income to obtain \$2 of regional income. [If we take the weight on national income to be one by convention, (1)\$1 = (0.5)\$2.0.] The weights on objectives are of great importance in practical planning operations with mathematical programming models. If the weights on objectives are specified in advance or if it is desired to experiment with solutions based on various weights, these can be specified and the solution obtained. In Figure 2-1, specifying a weight of 0.5 on regional income benefits is equivalent to moving a line with a slope of −0.5 continuously northeastward until it is tangent to the net benefit transformation surface.

The optimal point *A* in Figure 2-1 can be reached by two methods other than setting the weight. In the first method, a minimum level of net national income benefits can be set as a constraint, and the planner can be instructed to maximize regional income benefits subject to this constraint. If the constraint is set at *N*, the point that the planner will reach will be *A*. Similarly, a minimum level of regional income benefits can be set as a constraint, and the planner can be instructed to maximize national income benefits subject to this constraint. If the constraint is placed at *R*, the point of maximization will also be *A*. The transformation curve can be generated by successive applications of either the weighting or the constraint methods. [See Cohon and Marks (1973)]. These are equivalent mathematically and show that, in principle, objectives can be incorporated into planning as constraints or can be explicitly weighted. However, the methods will not, in general, be equivalent in effectiveness in applications; which methods will be the most appropriate will depend on the planning problem and the types of techniques available to the planners. In this study, we used both the weight method and the constraint method. (See Chapters 5 and 11.)

The representation in Figure 2-1 can be generalized to many dimensions. Beyond three dimensions the presentation must be in numerical terms, and this gives rise to the still largely unexplored problem of how best to present results for multidimensional problems to decision-makers. In the Río Colorado study, a few results were presented in graphical terms, but, generally, we used tabular versions of model results in which each alternative plan was described in terms of its multiple effects on objectives in tabular form (see Chapter 11). This was done in large part because, explicitly or implicitly, many of the model runs were relevant to more than three objectives and thus did not lend themselves to geometrical presentation in terms of transformation curves. (Note that such presentations can be made by holding all but two or three dimensions constant.)

APPLICATIONS OF MULTIOBJECTIVE PLANNING

It can be argued that water resources planning has always been multiobjective and that the multiobjective nature of planning has been artificially restricted by the utilization, as a criterion for evaluation, of the national income benefit–cost analysis developed after World War II in the United States. This point is made in Maass (1966, 1970) and, with reference to international as well as United States planning criteria, in Major (1977, chap. 1). The recognition of this problem has led to the development of multiobjective theory and the recommendation that it be utilized for Federal water resources planning in the United States (U.S. Water Resources Council, 1969, 1970a, 1970b, 1970c, 1970d, 1971, 1973, 1976; Major, 1977). There have been some controversies about multiobjective planning, but these have dealt in large part with the ability of agencies to carry out applied multiobjective analysis rather than with the theory itself. Many partial multiobjective assessments have been made in the United States in the form of "impact studies," which assess multiobjective effects of projects designed for, for example, only the national income criterion. There also have been some recent explicitly multiobjective studies that have utilized the theory throughout the course of the planning process. Perhaps the most interesting of these is the North Atlantic Regional Water Resources Study, which utilized both multiobjective theory and large-scale mathematical planning models at the regional planning level (rather than at the project level, as in the Río Colorado study). This study is reported in four articles in *Water Resources Research* (Schwarz, 1972; Schaake and Major, 1972; de Lucia and Rogers, 1972; Major, 1972). The planning documents are published by the U.S. North Atlantic Regional Water Resources Study Coordinating Committee (1972). The Appalachian water resources study was also multiobjective (U.S. Army Corps of Engineers, 1969) (for national income and regional income). Other studies are reported by the U.S. Water Resources Council (1970d). Examples of multiobjective accounting techniques applied to developing countries are to be found in the case studies in UNIDO (1972). An approach to multiobjectives for village water supply is given in World Bank (1976). Multiobjective principles have been approved for Federal water resources planning in the United States (U.S. Water Resources Council, 1973), although there remains substantial debate on the range of appropriate objectives (Major, 1977, chap. 2).

REFERENCES

ARROW, KENNETH J. *Social Choice and Individual Values*, 2nd ed. New York: John Wiley, 1963.

COHON, JARED L., and DAVID H. MARKS. "Multiobjective Screening Models and Water Resources Investment." *Water Resources Research*, **9**(4), 1973, pp. 826–836.

DELUCIA, RUSSELL J., and PETER ROGERS. "North Atlantic Regional Supply Model." *Water Resources Research*, **8** (3), June 1972.

MAASS, ARTHUR, MAYNARD M. HUFSCHMIDT, ROBERT DORFMAN, HAROLD A. THOMAS, JR, STEPHEN A. MARGLIN and GORDON MASKEW FAIR. *Design of Water-Resource Systems*. Cambridge, Mass.: Harvard University Press, 1962.

MAASS, ARTHUR. "Benefit–Cost Analysis: Its Relevance to Public Expenditure Decisions." *Quarterly Journal of Economics* LXXX, 1966, pp. 208–226.

MAASS, ARTHUR. "Public Investment Planning in the United States: Analysis and Critique." *Public Policy*, **18** (2), 1970, pp. 211–243.

MAJOR, DAVID C. "Benefit–Cost Ratios for Projects in Multiple Objective Investment Programs." *Water Resources Research*, **5** (5), 1969, pp. 1174–1178.

MAJOR, DAVID C. "Impact of Systems Techniques on the Planning Process." *Water Resources Research*, **8** (3), 1972, pp. 766–768.

MAJOR, DAVID C. *Multiobjective Water Resource Planning.* Washington, D.C.: American Geophysical Union, Water Resources Monograph 4. 1977.

MARGLIN, STEPHEN A. *Public Investment Criteria.* Cambridge, Mass.: MIT Press, 1967.

SCHAAKE, JOHN C., JR., and DAVID C. MAJOR. "Model for Estimating Regional Water Needs." *Water Resources Research*, **8** (3), 1972, pp. 755–759.

SCHWARZ, HARRY E. "The NAR Study: A Case Study in Systems Analysis." *Water Resources Research*, **8** (3), 1972, pp. 751–754.

UNIDO (United Nations Industrial Development Organization). *Guidelines for Project Evaluation.* New York: United Nations, 1972.

United States Army Corps of Engineers, Office of Appalachian Studies. *Development of Water Resources in Appalachia.* Cincinnati, Ohio, 1969.

United States North Atlantic Regional Water Resources Study Coordinating Committee. *North Atlantic Regional Water Resources Study, Report, Annexes, and Appendices.* United States Army Corps of Engineers, North Atlantic Division, New York, 1972.

United States Water Resources Council. *Report to the Water Resources Council by the Special Task Force: Procedures for Evaluation of Water and Related Land Resource Projects.* Washington, D.C., 1969.

United States Water Resources Council. *Report to the Water Resources Council by the Special Task Force: Principles for Planning Water and Land Resources.* Washington, D.C., 1970a.

United States Water Resources Council. *Report to the Water Resources Council by the Special Task Force: Standards for Planning Water and Land Resources.* Washington, D.C., 1970b.

United States Water Resources Council. *Report to the Water Resources Council by the Special Task Force: Findings and Recommendations.* Washington, D.C., 1970c.

United States Water Resources Council. *A Summary Analysis of Nineteen Tests of Proposed Evaluation Procedures on Selected Water and Land Resource Projects.* Washington, D.C., 1970d.

United States Water Resources Council. "Proposed Principles and Standards for Planning Water and Related Land Resources." *Federal Register 36* (245), December 21, 1971, pp. 24144–24194.

United States Water Resources Council. "Water and Related Land Resources: Establishment of Principles and Standards for Planning." *Federal Register 38* (174), 1973, pp. 24778–24869.

United States Water Resources Council. *Planning and Cost Sharing Policy Options for Water and Related Land Programs* (pts. 1–8). Washington, D.C., 1976.

World Bank. *Village Water Supply.* Washington, D.C., 1976.

CHAPTER THREE
PLANNING THEORY: THE ROLE OF MATHEMATICAL MODELS IN WATER RESOURCES PLANNING

FRANK E. PERKINS

This chapter[1] provides an introduction to the second principal conceptual base for our study of the Río Colorado, our approach to the use of mathematical models in water resources planning. Certain characteristics of the water resource planning process are suggested in an attempt to define the role that we feel should be played by mathematical models in that process; that is, we seek to define what objectives are sought from modeling. Important characteristics of different types of models are then presented to permit assessment of their strengths and limitations.

One of the most significant characteristics of planning is that it is a dynamic process and therefore can be characterized in terms of a set of activities that take place over time and that interact through the transmission and feedback of information. It is the function of these activities to convert that information into forms from which a set of decisions (i.e., plans) can be produced. At all stages of this process, questions arise that, if properly posed and adequately answered, will lead to plans that in some sense are better than if the questions had not been posed or adequately answered. Our view of the modern planning process is that the concepts of multiobjective investment criteria will lead to the posing of better or more appropriate questions in the planning process and that the use of mathematical models will lead to better answers to these questions.

[1]The material in this chapter is based on chapter 3 of Perkins, Schaake, Marks, and Major (1973).

Thus, the role of models may be viewed as that of tools from which to derive answers to well-posed questions about the performance or behavior of the system that is being planned. However, because of the dynamics of the planning process, it may happen that the answers derived from the models will suggest that the original questions were not well conceived and need to be reformulated. Hence, the role of models is iterative. They are used to produce information that may be fed forward to aid in decision-making (i.e., plan formulation). With equal value, they may produce information that is fed back to aid in redefining the problem.

A further essential point concerning the role played by models in the planning process is that the information they provide must be quantitative and in sufficient detail and accuracy to provide real guidance to the decision-maker. There are three key words in this statement. The first of these is the word "quantitative." Model outputs can provide a basis for decision-making only when the results have some measure or rank associated with them. The second key word is "sufficient." There is a natural tendency to use models to produce answers that are as detailed and accurate as possible. However, as in all planning and design, a balance must be struck between the needs of the problem at hand and the resources available for its solution. Third, operation of the model should provide "guidance" to the decision-maker. The role of the model is not to do the planning or to replace the planner. Nor is the role of models to provide completely precise answers to the questions posed. Rather, the model should produce information that will validly guide the thinking of the planner concerning the decision that must be made.

As planners, we are called upon to suggest how complex systems should be operated and/or altered to achieve a desired set of objectives. For systems of even relatively low complexity, the number and nature of alternatives, interactions, and responses that are possible far exceed our capacity to enumerate and evaluate completely, and we are hesitant to base our decisions solely on intuition or past experience. We thus turn to models because of their potential for assisting us in decision-making.

The preceding discussion can be summarized in terms of three valuable functions that can be fulfilled by models. These are:

1. *Amplification*—When properly used, models can amplify our available knowledge of the behavior of complex systems. Models do not produce new information; however, they permit the extraction of greater amounts of information from our existing data base. In this sense they increase our understanding of the problem under study and of the options for dealing with it. (This was a principal function of the system dynamics model of farmer migration discussed in Appendix A.)

2. *Organization*—Among the biggest problems encountered in planning are representing and displaying in simple terms the numerous characteristics of complex systems and proposed plans. Models can perform these functions as well as provide effective frameworks for organizing data (see Chapters 9 and 10).

3. *Evaluation*—Models can and should be designed to incorporate measures of performance of the system under study and may therefore be designed to produce comparative evaluations of performance. Optimization models (such as ours described in Chapters 5 and 8 for example) serve this function by comparing the performance of various alternatives and identifying that which is best in some sense.

Viewed in these terms, models essentially are tools for supplementing the planner's judgment, intuition, and past experience. Models provide only approximations to certain aspects of reality. Two fundamental questions then arise: (1) Which aspects of reality must, in fact, be modeled if the model's objectives are to be achieved? (2) How good must the approximations be in order to provide insights that are useful and correct relative to our planning decisions? These questions are fundamental to modeling and in this book, we have attempted to make these questions explicit.

It has been our observation that at least two erroneous beliefs are prevalent among many planners and decision-makers in their approach to the use of models. These modeling myths can create difficulties for those trying to use models where they are not currently employed and for those trying to present the results of models to decision-makers.

The first of these modeling myths is that there exists a single model that will completely solve the planning problem. It is doubtful that only one model is required in many real-world problems. Our experience, as presented in the subsequent chapters, suggests that a family of models is likely to be of greatest value in the planning process. And even then, no set of models will completely solve the problem; rather, as noted earlier, the models can only provide guidance as integral components of the planning process.

A second myth is that models somehow require more data than other procedures or more data than can possibly be made available. This myth arises from the fact that some particular new model may in fact require more data than a previously existing procedure or more data than is currently available in a particular planning exercise. However, these deficiencies are not inherent characteristics of models but only of the particular application. When properly conceived, models are designed to operate on the existing data base (for the base for our study, see Chapters 1, 9, and 10) to produce the greatest possible amount of information from the data. When a particular model demonstrates that the data are inadequate to make an intelligent decision, the deficiency lies not with the model but with the data. (However, it is also true that the better the data and the deeper the understanding of the physical and social realities that the models are to represent, the better the study will be, other things being equal.)

It is useful to organize and categorize the available mathematical models according to their primary functions or mathematical techniques. This categorization is best thought of not as one that absolutely distinguishes various models but rather as a mechanism for better illustrating the relative characteristics of various types of models and demonstrating how these models can best be used together. The screening-simulation-sequencing model process described in Chapters 5 through 8 is illustrative of the complementary role of models of different types.

All mathematical models may be said to be constructed from three fundamental components:

1. *Parameters*—These are (typically) numerical values that describe fixed and assumed-to-be-known properties of the system to be modeled. Familiar examples in water resources planning are the economic value of a kilowatt-hour of energy or the resistance coefficient of an open channel. Parameters are generally specified independently of the model by the user of the model and typically do not change during one "run" of the model, although, of course, parameter values are frequently subjected to sensitivity analysis via multiple runs.

2. *Variables*—These serve to define the behavior and the performance of the system being modeled. In the formulation of the model they are symbolic representations of quantities of interest to the modeler, and they assume numerical values only during the operation of the model. Typical water resources examples are the size of a proposed reservoir or the maximum stage reached during a particular flood event.

3. *Constraints*—These are the relations that describe the system's operation on the parameters and variables. They are typically mathematical statements in the form of algebraic equalities and inequalities or integral or differential equations. Familiar examples are relationships governing hydroelectric power generation or the balance of inflow and outflow at a stream junction.

These three components are generally present in all mathematical models. A primary subdivision of model types can be made on the basis of the role played by the variables. In one class of models, the variables merely take on particular numerical values as an indication of the behavior of the system being represented. Thus, these variables describe the state of the system in response to various stimuli but give no direct measure of what decisions should be taken to improve the performance of the system. Such models are sometimes referred to as *descriptive* or *cause-and-effect models*. We shall adopt the more common classification of *simulation models*.

In contrast to the simulation models are those that produce numerical values for one or more of the variables such that some specified objective is optimized. These define the category of models that are referred to as *prescriptive*, or, more commonly, *optimization models*, and that are embodied in the general theory of mathematical programming. The optimization models are characterized by a mathematical statement of the objective function and a formal search procedure for finding values of those decision variables that optimize the objective function.

Within each of these major categories one may identify different subcategories of models. We describe first a categorization scheme for optimization models and then one for simulation models.

OPTIMIZATION TECHNIQUES

For our purposes, optimization procedures can be conveniently arranged into four groups based on the mathematical characteristics of the models:

1. *Linear Programming*—If the objective function and all of the constraint equations can be expressed in linear, algebraic form (equalities and inequalities) with known, constant coefficients, then the problem is of the linear programming type. Although the linearity restrictions are frequently severe, linear programming is often employed because generally applicable, reliable computer programs are available for its solution. Linear programming has been widely treated in many different texts, among them Dantzig (1963), Hadley (1962), Wagner (1969), and Simmons (1972). For applications of linear programming to water resource planning, the reader may refer to Maass *et al.*, (1962), Hall and Dracup (1970), Buras (1972), Meta Systems (1975), and Biswas (1976) among many others.

2. *Integer Programming*—Integer programming is directly related to linear programming, because all of the constraint equations and the objective function must be linear; however, the decision variables are allowed to take on only integer values. (In mixed integer programming, only some of the decision variables are integers). As will be seen by its application in this book, the use of integer variables increases the ability of mathematical programming to express various planning conditions and interrelationships. As in the case of linear programming, generally applicable computer programs exist for the solution of integer programming problems, making these two techniques the most frequently used optimization techniques. Treatments of integer programming may be found in Wagner (1969) and Hu (1969). Applications of integer programming to agriculture and energy resource planning are described in Goreux and Manne (1973).

3. *Nonlinear Programming*—Nonlinear programming problems differ from the linear programming problem in that the objective function and/or one or more of the constraint equations involve nonlinear terms. General solution procedures for this category of problems do not exist; however, special-purpose solution techniques are available that are applicable to limited subsets of the general problem. These include procedures such as quadratic programming, geometric programming, and a variety of controlled search techniques. Nonlinear programming is treated in depth by Zangwill (1969), Hadley (1964), and Simmons (1975). A description of many of the available special-purpose solution algorithms can be found in Himmelblau (1972).

4. *Dynamic Programming*—This is a solution procedure that can be used in linear or nonlinear problems in which the decision variables possess an appropriate sequential character. Situations of this type arise when the problem can be represented as a sequence of stages, where one or more decisions is required at each stage, and where the decision at one stage directly affects only the next adjacent stage. There is no standard dynamic programming algorithm as in linear programming; the algorithm must be tailored to the individual problem. Where the sequential nature of the system can be established and where the number of state and decision variables is not too large, the computational procedures are simple and practical.

Dynamic programming was first developed by Bellman (1957). It has been extensively treated in many general texts, including Wagner (1969) and Hillier and Lieberman (1967). Many applications of dynamic programming to water resource problems, particularly reservoir operation, are described in Buras (1972) and Hall and Dracup (1970).

SIMULATION TECHNIQUES

Simulation is a problem-solving technique in which an understanding of the behavior and response of a system is obtained by:

1. Development of a model of the system;
2. Operation of the model (i.e., generation of outputs resulting from the application of inputs);
3. Observation and interpretation of the resulting outputs.

Hence, the essence of simulation is modeling and experimentation. Simulation requires both a model and the conducting of experiments with that model to produce useful results. (These steps are also characteristic of the other class of models used in our study—optimization models—with the difference that the way in which the steps are carried out for simulation models as opposed to optimization models is not constrained by the particular formulation characteristics required of the latter.)

It is important to note that simulation does not, in general, directly produce "the answer" to a given problem. Rather, simulation provides information about the likely behavior of a system under study when the system and/or its inputs are varied. This information generated by simulation is then utilized along with information from other sources to effect a solution to the original problem. The importance of simulation in this problem-solving process depends, of course, on the relative importance of those parts of the problem that are and are not simulated.

Simulation encompasses a wide variety of procedures. In order to choose among and use these effectively, the potential user must know something about how they operate, how they can be expected to perform, and how this performance relates to the problem under investigation.

For the purpose of categorization, we could classify simulation models either according to the class of mathematical techniques with which they are formulated (such as ordinary differential equations, partial differential equations, Markov processes, etc.) or according to the numerical procedures used to convert them to a form suitable for the digital computer. However, such an approach is likely to mask the essential nature of simulation models.

Rather, we have chosen to focus attention on the components that are likely to be present in any simulation model and whose method of representation characterizes the particular simulation model. One possible classification of these components is as follows:

1. *Inputs*—Simulation models accept a set of inputs and transform these into outputs according to a set of relationships that approximate the behavior of the modeled system. Hence, the inputs are those quantities that "drive" the model and are generally considered to be determined independently of the model itself. In many water resources models, a principal input is the set of streamflow time histories obtained either from the physical record or generated synthetically. Other typical inputs include rainfall sequences, pollution loads, and water and power demands. (Note that almost all computer simulation programs require many other "data inputs"; however, these are simply parameters to be used in other components of the model. Data input to the program should not be confused with the input that drives the model.)

2. *Physical Relationships*—This refers to the mathematical expression of the relationships that exist among the physical variables of the system being modeled. These are likely to include both equality and inequality relations and may be expressed in the form of algebraic equations or in a tabular form. Whatever their form, they are ultimately expressions of physical laws (continuity, energy conservation, etc.), empirical observations, or externally imposed constraints. Examples of these relations as found in typical water resources problems include algebraic relations between reservoir volume and pool elevation, reservoir outflow relations, finite-difference forms of the routing equation, and flow-frequency equations.

3. *Nonphysical Relationships*—This component has been defined separately from classification 2 to emphasize that many of the relations that must be satisfied may involve nonphysical variables. The most obvious are those that define economic variables such as the costs of physical facilities. In addition, however, simulation can extend to many other nonphysical factors such as political conflict, public awareness, and community behavior, for which suitable relationships (and definitions) are required.

4. *Operating Rules*—In any system in which there are opportunities to exercise a degree of operational control, the rules that govern this control must be defined and incorporated into the model. Where the control is well defined, such as by existing automatic equipment or legislated controls, the statement of the rules in the model may be a straightforward task. In other situations, such as those where poorly defined manual operation is to be represented, this may be quite difficult. In many instances, the development of operating rules that are "best" in some sense is a prime objective of the simulation experiments.

5. *Outputs*—In a typical simulation, a set of inputs are operated on by the physical and nonphysical relations in accordance with prescribed operating rules. The final product of these operations is a set of outputs that are measures of the modeled systems' responses to the stated conditions. The outputs may take many different forms, depending on how the computer programs are organized, and may range from a simple indication of the likely physical responses to a detailed indication of potential economic consequences expressed in terms of an objective function.

In addition, the outputs may be various statistical measures of the actual model responses. The important point here is that one can choose many different measures of response as outputs from a simulation model; the choice depends on the utility of the outputs to the decisions that are to be made.

Applications of simulation to water problems include the Stanford Watershed Model (Crawford and Linsley, 1966), the Delaware River basin model (Hufschmidt and Fiering, 1966) and the widely used simulation models of the U.S. Army Corps of Engineers Hydrologic Research Center, for example U.S. Army Corps of Engineers (1975). The two simulation models used in the Río Colorado study are described in Chapters 6 and 7 of this book.

CHOICE OF MODELS

The need to make a conscious choice among the many types of models that are available is often overlooked, yet the decisions made at this stage may greatly influence the remaining steps of the process. At the very least, the analyst should constantly be prepared to question the appropriateness of the particular model that has been adopted and be prepared to alter the model whenever there appears to be good reason to do so (see Appendix A). One should never be misled into thinking that the presence of working models guarantees that all of the relevant characteristics of the modeled system have been adequately accounted for (or that the models are completely consistent with one another in their assumptions, something difficult to achieve because of the differences in characteristics of different types of models). One hopes that the models reproduce in a reasonable way those properties that are essential to the particular problem under study, but the necessity to abstract from the real world always leaves unresolved questions about the completeness and validity of the results that they provide.

There are difficult decisions that must be made in determining the appropriateness of various modeling techniques for a given situation. Many factors enter into this evaluation of models, but in summary it may be considered to be a trade-off between the fidelity of the model and its computability. Fidelity is a measure of how valid the answers produced by the model are relative to the decisions that must be made. It depends on the time and space resolution built into the model, the accuracy of the parameters and input data provided, and the correctness of the mathematical relations assumed. A less acknowledged but equally important fact is that the fidelity of a model depends on the questions it is asked by the analyst and the ability of the modeler to interpret the model's results.

More readily evaluated is the computability of a given model. Generally speaking, as the complexity, scope, number of variables, and level of detail increase, the time and cost of using a model will increase. The time and cost include not only the actual computer operation but also, and often more important, the time and cost of associated data preparation and output interpretation. As anyone who has worked with computer models will appreciate, these are not negligible considerations. (The influence of computability on our choice of models for the Río Colorado study is described in Appendix A.)

The essential point is that trade-offs are involved in designing and selecting models for particular planning problems, as trade-offs are involved among the social, economic, and other objectives of planning. Discussions of both types of trade-off are encountered in later chapters.

REFERENCES

BELLMAN, RICHARD E. *Dynamic Programming.* Princeton, N.J.: Princeton University Press, 1957.

BISWAS, ASIT K., ed. *Systems Approach to Water Management.* New York: McGraw-Hill, 1976.

BURAS, NATHAN. *Scientific Allocation of Water Resources.* New York: American General Service Publishing Company, Inc., 1972.

CRAWFORD, H. H., and RAY K. LINSLEY. "Digital Simulation in Hydrology: Stanford Watershed Model IV." Technical Report 39. Department of Civil Engineering, Stanford University, Stanford, Calif., 1966.

DANTZIG, GEORGE. *Linear Programming and Extensions.* Princeton, N.J.: Princeton University Press, 1963.

GOREUX, LOUIS M., and ALAN S. MANNE, eds. *Multi-level Planning: Case Studies in Mexico.* Amsterdam and New York: North-Holland and American Elsevier, 1973.

HADLEY, G. *Linear Programming.* Reading, Mass.: Addison-Wesley, 1962.

HADLEY, G. *Non-linear and Dynamic Programming.* Reading, Mass.: Addison-Wesley, 1964.

HALL, WARREN A., and JOHN A. DRACUP. *Water Resources Systems Analysis.* New York: McGraw-Hill, 1970.

HILLIER, FREDERICK S., and GERALD J. LIEBERMAN. *Introduction to Operations Research.* San Francisco: Holden-Day, 1967.

HIMMELBLAU, DAVID M. *Applied Non-linear Programming.* New York: McGraw-Hill, 1972.

HU, T. C. *Integer Programming and Network Flows.* Reading, Mass.: Addison-Wesley, 1969.

HUFSCHMIDT, MAYNARD M., and MYRON B FIERING. *Simulation Techniques for Design of Water Resource Systems.* Cambridge, Mass.: Harvard University Press, 1966.

MAASS, ARTHUR, MAYNARD M. HUFSCHMIDT, ROBERT DORFMAN, HAROLD A. THOMAS, JR., STEPHEN A. MARGLIN, GORDON MASKEW FAIR. *Design of Water-Resource Systems.* Cambridge, Mass.: Harvard University Press, 1962.

Meta Systems, Inc. *Systems Analysis in Water Resources Planning.* Port Washington, N.Y.: Water Information Center, Inc., 1975.

PERKINS, FRANK E., JOHN C. SCHAAKE, JR., DAVID H. MARKS, and DAVID C. MAJOR. "Notes and Readings for the MIT Short Course Case Studies in Water Resources Planning." Department of Civil Engineering, MIT, Cambridge, Mass., 1973.

SIMMONS, DONALD M. *Linear Programming for Operations Research.* San Francisco: Holden-Day, 1972.

SIMMONS, DONALD M. *Non-linear Programming for Operations Research.* Englewood Cliffs, N.J.: Prentice-Hall, Inc., 1975.

United States Army Corps of Engineers, Hydrologic Engineering Center. "HEC-5: Simulation of Flood Control Systems, Users' Manual." Davis, California, July, 1975.

WAGNER, HARVEY M. *Principles of Operations Research.* Englewood Cliffs, N.J.: Prentice-Hall, Inc., 1969.

ZANGWILL, W. I. *Non-linear Programming: A Unified Approach.* Englewood Cliffs, N.J.: Prentice-Hall, Inc., 1969.

CHAPTER FOUR
PLANNING FOR THE RIO COLORADO: AN OVERVIEW

This chapter provides the reader with an overview of the methodology applied to the Río Colorado. With this overview in mind, the reader can proceed to the succeeding chapters that treat the principal aspects of the methodology in detail.

The principal elements in the application of the methodology to the Río Colorado are: (1) a series of models used to generate alternative plans for the river; and (2) the multiobjective investment criteria that were embodied in the models. In this chapter, both the system of models used to generate plans and the multiobjective investment criteria are described. Also described is the representation of the river basin and its potential development sites as used in the models. The series of models and the multiobjective investment criteria used in the study were, of course, developed together during the study. The series of models is described first in this chapter for ease of exposition, because it is within the models that the investment criteria are embodied.

THE SYSTEM OF MODELS

The system of models was based broadly on the proposition that no one model could represent adequately all the features of interest in the allocation problem for the Río Colorado (see Chapter 3). It was thought that the best way to represent the problem would be through a series of models, each designed to elucidate some of the principal issues involved. Many models were built or considered for the project; a description of the considerations that influenced the selection of models at different stages of the study is provided in Appendix A. A system of three models was ultimately settled upon. These are: a "screening model," to choose initial configurations of plan elements; a "simulation model," to examine the effects of streamflow variability on the initial configurations and to change these when warranted; and a "sequencing model," designed to sequence projects optimally over the planning horizon. These models are described in detail in, respectively, Chapters 5, 6, and 8 of this volume.

The Screening Model. The screening model is formulated for two purposes —irrigation water supply and power production—and its decision variables are the sizes of the several dozen potential dams, irrigation areas, power stations, and import and export sites on the river. A deterministic hydrology is assumed—the mean flow historically for each of three seasons in a year is assumed always to prevail in that season. The number of seasons chosen was based upon the characteristics of irrigation and power demands. Most of the nonlinear functions in the model are approximated by piecewise linear functions. Some of the benefit and cost functions have curvatures such that global optima are not guaranteed. The model was used for production runs as a mixed-integer programming model with about 900 decision variables, including eight 0–1 integer variables (variables that can take a value of either 0 or 1, but no other value) representing initial costs for dams, and about 600 constraints. A large number of runs was made with this model in one or another of its forms during the course of the project.

Objectives were incorporated either into the objective function or as constraints on the system. One objective function formulation was to maximize net discounted national income benefits plus weighted net discounted regional income benefits for each of the five provinces. An example of a constraint formulation of objectives was that in which power production was constrained out of some model solutions to reflect the provincial objective of emphasizing irrigation.

The Simulation Model. The most promising configurations from the screening model, consisting of optimally sized works for power, irrigation, and imports and exports, were run on the basic simulation model of the Río Colorado. This permitted these configurations to be evaluated in terms of net benefits and of hydrologic reliability. The model also included operating policies to fulfill such tasks as allocating flows in years of shortage. As a result of runs by the simulation model, the configurations from the screening model could be altered to improve their hydrologic reliability, and the benefits and costs toward objectives of the new configurations could be estimated. The simulation model was operated with 50 years of seasonal (4-month) flows.

The Sequencing Model. After the hydrologic reliability of configurations was evaluated on the simulation model and any warranted changes in project scale and location were made, the results were run in a "sequencing model," the third and last of the three models used to generate program alternatives for the case study.

The purpose of this model was to take a configuration of projects that had been run on the simulation model and to schedule it optimally in four future time periods taking into account benefits over time, budget constraints, constraints on the number of farmers available to work new irrigation areas, and project interrelationships such as the necessity to ensure that an irrigation area is not built before the construction of a dam to supply it. The sequencing model had about 60 continuous variables, 120 integer variables, and 110 constraints depending on the exact configuration that was being modeled.

THE RIVER BASIN AS REPRESENTED IN THE MODELS

The models used, like all models, are abstractions from reality. One important way in which they are abstractions is in the fact that the river basin as seen in the models is simplified as compared to the actual physical basin and its development sites. Simplifications are made both because the detail of the real basin need not, for planning purposes, necessarily be represented in full in the models, and also because many real relationships cannot be satisfactorily represented in modeling terms. In the Río Colorado study, partly because of the simplicity of the river in hydrologic terms and partly because we were not engaged in detailed project design, the simplifications made in the representation of the river and its development sites used in the models were, we believe, primarily of the former type.

The river as seen by the models, then, was represented in schematic form, and this is shown in Figure 4-1. The principal simplifications embodied in this schematic are the aggregation, for modeling purposes, of some of the smaller irrigation sites into larger units, and the assumption that the return flows from each irrigation area reenter the river at a single specified location. Thus, when the results discussed in Chapter 11 refer to size of a particular irrigation area what is really meant in some cases is a series of smaller areas in that neighborhood. In addition to the aggregation of areas already referred to in Chapter 1, the following irrigation areas are aggregated in the schematic: Buta Ranquil and Rincón de los Sauces; Mendoza Zone I and II; Peñas Blancas and Valle Verde; Río Colorado and Eugenio del Busto; and Valles Marginales and Valle del Prado. The second, third, and fourth sections (II, III, and IV) of 25 de Mayo are aggregated into one project

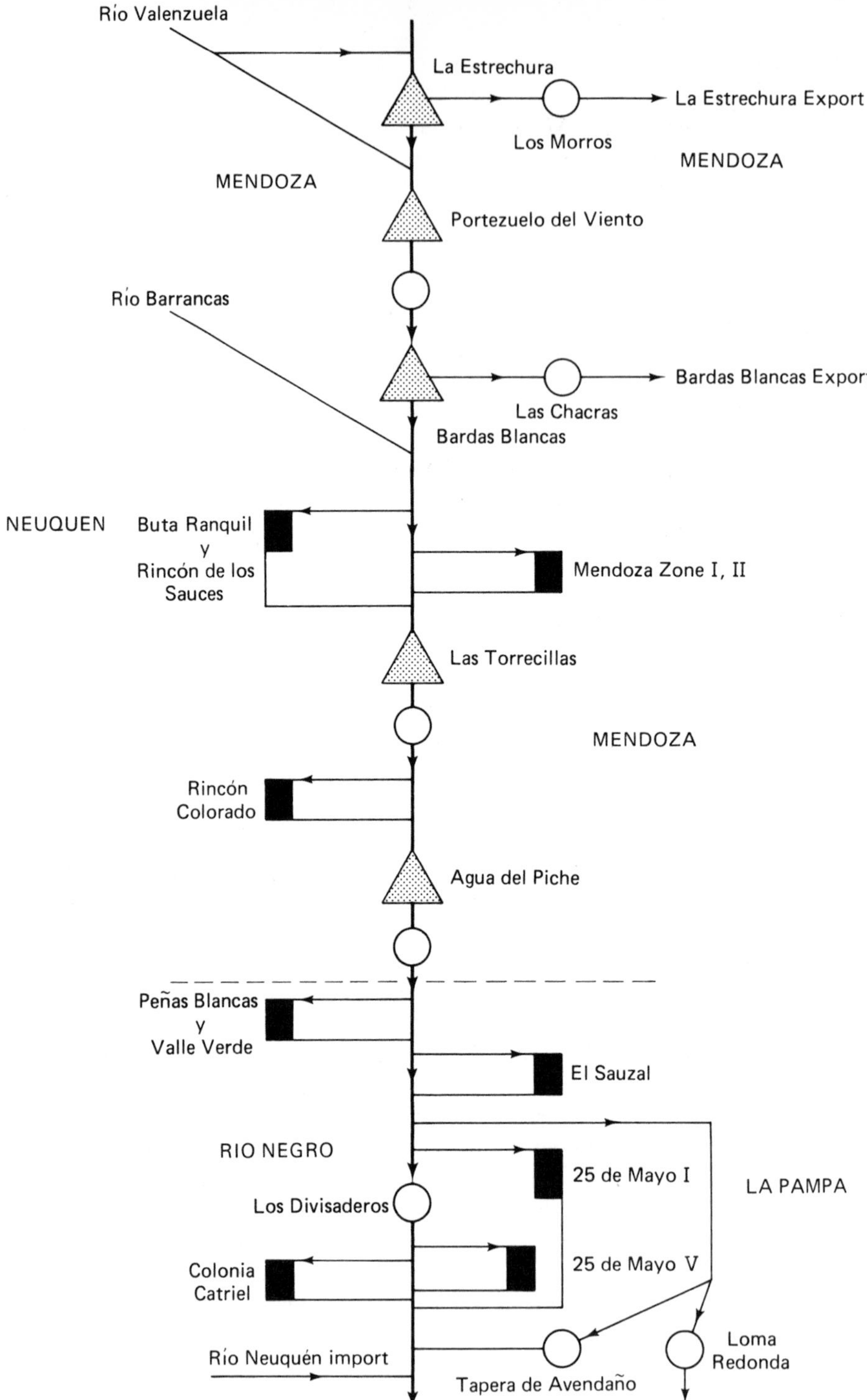

Figure 4-1
Schematic of the Río Colorado basin.

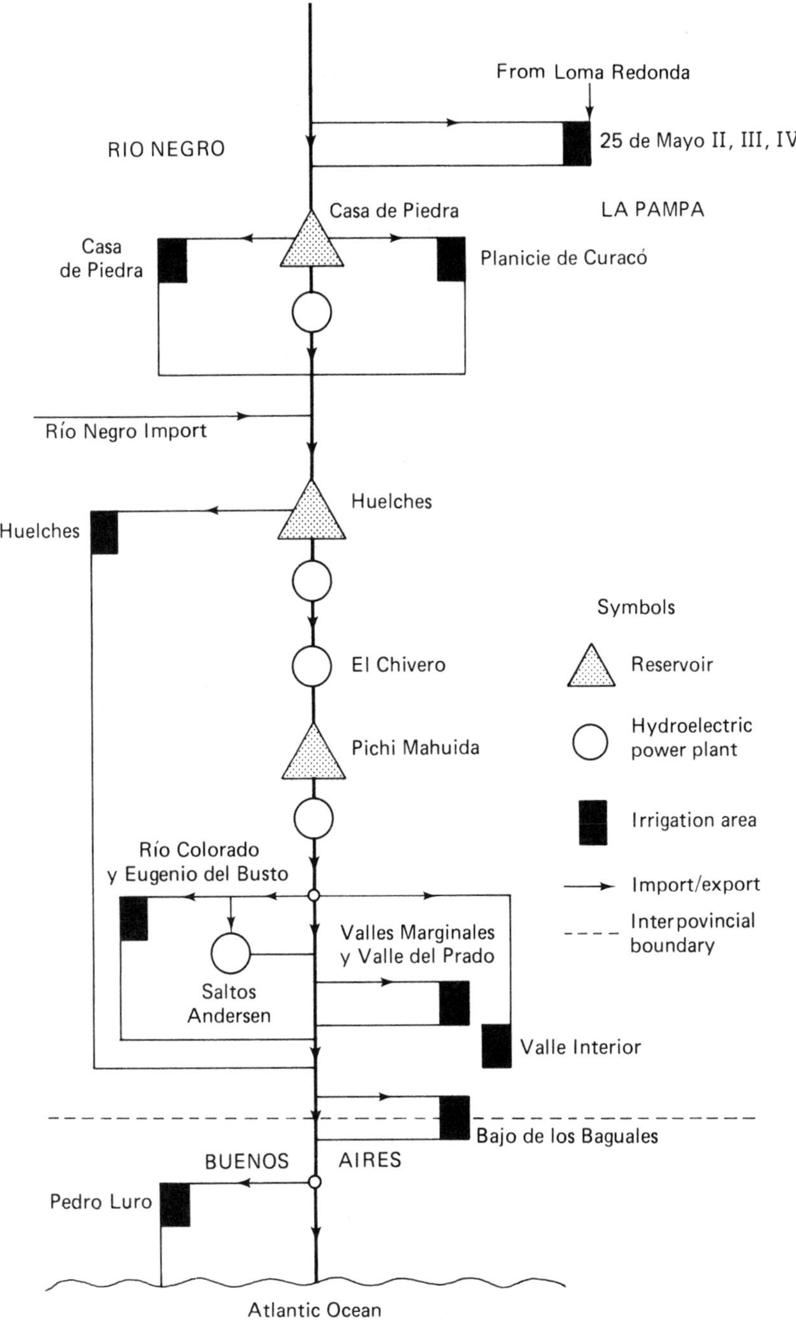

Figure 4-1
(continued)

denoted 25 de Mayo II, III, IV, and the first and last sections (I and V) of this project are entered separately in the schematic. The potential dams, power stations, and exports and imports are all represented individually in the schematic.

The schematic shown in Figure 4-1 is used in essentially the same form for each of the three models used in developing plans for the Río Colorado, except that in the sequencing model the larger irrigation areas are disaggregated in order to permit them to be built in stages, and some of the smaller areas are aggregated to increase the computational simplicity of the model, as described in Chapter 8.

The time dimension is also represented in the models in simplified form. In the screening and simulation models, each year is divided into three 4-month seasons. This is done because irrigation demands can be aggregated in the Río Colorado basin into 4-month seasons—one season with negligible water requirements and two seasons with high demands. Two high-demand seasons are required, rather than only one, because the flow characteristics of the river differ during the two seasons. The three seasons are Season I, May to August, comprising the southern hemisphere winter months; Season II, September to December, comprising the first growing months, when the flow in the river is highest; and Season III, January to April, comprising the later growing months when the flow in the river is lower. The sequencing model represents the time dimension in ways described in Chapter 8.

In addition to the simplifications of the river system embodied in the schematic, there are, of course, the numerous simplifications of hydrologic processes, operating policies, etc., that are embodied in the models themselves. These are discussed in the chapters to follow.

Process of Model Use. The procedure used in implementing the techniques summarized above was to make a fairly large number of runs with the screening model, to choose the most interesting runs from that model for examination in the simulation model, and then to choose the runs of most interest from that model to run in the sequencing model. Altogether, leaving aside development and test runs, more than 20 runs for production purposes were made with the screening model, based on a wide variety of assumptions concerning objectives and parameter values. Five of these were selected for examination in the simulation model, and each of these was subjected to a number of runs in that model to examine the effects of various changes in decision variables on reliability and net benefits. Of these five input runs, modified versions of three were run in the sequencing model. In general, the criteria used to narrow down the number of runs in each successive model were based on the judgment of the analysts as to the relevance and importance of each run to decision-making in Argentina—that is to say, to Argentine objectives. The system of models is summarized in Figure 4-2.

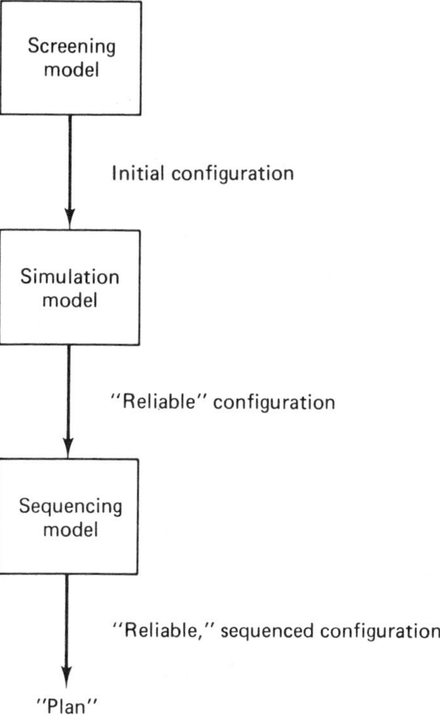

Figure 4-2
Process of model use.

OBJECTIVES FOR THE RIO COLORADO

The objectives used in the planning process were developed from discussions with planners and participants in the political process and from studies of Argentine Federal and provincial documents. Members of the planning team at MIT, both Argentine and American, made numerous trips to Buenos Aires and the provinces, and Argentine officials visited MIT.

A range of objectives was considered. Among these were: increasing Argentine national income; increasing income to each of the five riverine provinces; emphasizing irrigation rather than power production (a provincial objective stemming from long Argentine involvement with irrigation); achieving an equitable allocation of water among the riverine provinces; controlling interbasin transfers; and achieving "territorial integration," an Argentine goal involving the development of underpopulated areas of the nation. The ways in which each of these objectives were incorporated into the planning methodology are discussed in later chapters.

OTHER INVESTMENT CRITERIA

The multiobjective approach should be utilized together with a set of optimal investment criteria. Such criteria have been in large part elaborated for multiobjective planning and may be found in convenient form in Maass, et al. (1962), Marglin (1967), UNIDO (1972), and Major (1977). Here we simply list the criteria and make brief reference to their application described in detail in later chapters in our study.

Benefit and Cost Accounting Rules. These are required to provide ways and means of measuring positive and negative contributions to the objectives of planning. The most elaborate application of such rules in this study was for irrigation benefit measures [Chapter 9, this volume, and Pascuchi (1972)], but applications also were made for other purposes and objectives (see Chapter 9).

Interest Rates. The question of the interest rate in multiobjective planning is elaborated in Marglin (1967). In this study, we used an interest rate of 8% for national income and regional income benefits and costs that we felt to be appropriate given the nature of the Argentine economy, but we also performed sensitivity runs for higher and lower interest rates (16%, 4%) (see Chapter 11). Other interest rates recommended or used for various water resources planning studies have ranged from less than 4% up to 20% and higher. The interest rate is, of course, a crucial parameter in project evaluation because of the substantial effects that changing the value of the rate can have on project design. In multiobjective planning, the interest rate can vary among objectives, although we did not explore this variation in this study.

Budget Constraints. Optimal project design should include the effects of present and projected budget constraints (Maass and Major, 1972). In the Río Colorado study, on the basis of available information, the projected expenditures estimated by the models appeared to be within the reasonable constraints on water resources development expenditures in the Río Colorado, and so the results of the models were not constrained by budgetary considerations (see Chapter 9). This might change under certain cost allocation schemes. Provision for examining the effects of budget constraints is built into the sequencing model.

Risk and Uncertainty. Risk can be dealt with by analysis of underlying probability distributions; this is reflected in our work on the Río Colorado in the use of simulation models. Uncertainty cannot be dealt with in an unambiguous way; principal uncertainties in the Río Colorado problem may be said to be the availability of farmers for new lands and the availability of markets for produce. Our approach was to use sensitivity analysis on key parameters to ask whether investment plans changed substantially in response to changing parameter values.

Pricing and Cost Allocation for Multiobjectives. Optimal multiobjective design depends on pricing and cost allocation policies; and, in turn, optimal pricing and cost allocation policies are functions of the objectives of design. In the Río Colorado study, relatively little information was available about cost allocation policies; we estimated these for use in sensitivity runs for the regional income objective.

Scheduling. In principle one should study not only the optimal size of projects and programs but also the optimal dates of implementation of each. We have attempted to deal with some of the problems involved by means of the sequencing model, described in Chapter 8.

Relationship of Sectoral Planning to National Parameters. In practice, water resources planning tends to be sectoral planning. In sectoral planning, one must attempt to estimate the relevant national planning parameters and to apply investment criteria in accordance with them. This can take many forms. One example used in the Río Colorado study was the development of an estimated shadow price for foreign exchange, treating the Argentine economy as a disequilibrium economy (see Chapter 9). This parameter is a national parameter and estimates the value of foreign exchange at the margin. It has to be estimated with respect to national values, yet it must be used in sectoral planning if sectoral planning is to have meaning. The same is true for national weights on objectives in certain cases, for national market studies, and the like. A description of this problem is found in UNIDO (1972), where the analysis is carried out in terms of sectoral planning in relation to national parameters.

REFERENCES

MAASS, ARTHUR, MAYNARD M. HUFSCHMIDT, ROBERT DORFMAN, HAROLD A. THOMAS, JR., STEPHEN A. MARGLIN, and GORDON MASKEW FAIR. *Design of Water-Resource Systems.* Cambridge, Mass.: Harvard University Press, 1962.

MAASS, ARTHUR, and DAVID C. MAJOR. "Budget Constraints and Multiobjective Planning." *Engineering Issues, Proceedings American Society of Civil Engineers,* **98** (*PP3*), 1972, pp. 359–362.

MAJOR, DAVID C. *Multiobjective Water Resource Planning.* Washington, D.C.: American Geophysical Union, Water Resources Monograph 4, 1977.

MARGLIN, STEPHEN A. *Public Investment Criteria.* Cambridge, Mass.: MIT Press, 1967.

PASCUCHI, JAVIER. "Métodos para la Estimación de los Beneficios del Riego." Ralph M. Parsons Laboratory for Water Resources and Hydrodynamics, MIT, Cambridge, Mass., September, 1972.

UNIDO (United Nations Industrial Development Organization). *Guidelines for Project Evaluation.* New York: United Nations, 1972.

Part II Description of Principal Mathematical Models

CHAPTER FIVE THE MATHEMATICAL PROGRAMMING SCREENING MODEL

JARED COHON
TOMAS FACET
DAVID MARKS

This chapter describes the mathematical programming screening model used in the study to choose initial configurations of plan elements. The most promising of these configurations, responsive to alternative objective functions, constraints, and parameter values, were subject to further analysis by simulation, as described in Chapter 4.

The screening model described in this chapter, the initial version of which (Appendix A) follows Loucks (1969), has among its principal characteristics the use of deterministic, mean hydrologic inputs. It is a steady-state model. All of the projects selected in a given run are assumed to be implemented in the first year of a 50-year planning period, each year of which is taken to be the same hydrologically. Each year is composed of three 4-month seasons. The formulation utilizes integer variables to represent dam capital costs, and for certain other purposes, and is solved with a mixed-integer programming algorithm.

The model can be conveniently disaggregated into eight sections: continuity constraints, reservoir constraints, irrigation constraints, hydroelectric energy constraints, import/export constraints, conditionality constraints, policy constraints, and the objective function. Each of these aspects of the model is discussed in this chapter. A summary of the formulation and a list of variables and parameters used in the model are presented in Appendixes 5A and 5B. Descriptions of alternative forms of the model not used in production runs are given in Appendix A. Among the pioneering studies of screening models and their use in water resources planning upon which we have drawn are those of Dorfman (1965), Hufschmidt (1965), and Maass et al. (1962).

CONTINUITY CONSTRAINTS

Continuity constraints are those constraints that are included in the screening model to ensure conservation of mass. In terms of a river system, this means that the water that enters a point on the stream must leave that point on the stream if it has not been stored in a reservoir or diverted out of the stream. This basic continuity principle applies throughout the entire reach of the stream. (The way in which the continuity equations and constraints are actually incorporated in the model depends on modeling considerations.) A sample site is shown in Figure 5-1. The basic continuity relationship can be written, referring to Figure 5-1, as

$$S_{s,t+1} = S_{st} + Q_{st} + I_{st} - E_{st} - D_{st} \tag{5.1}$$

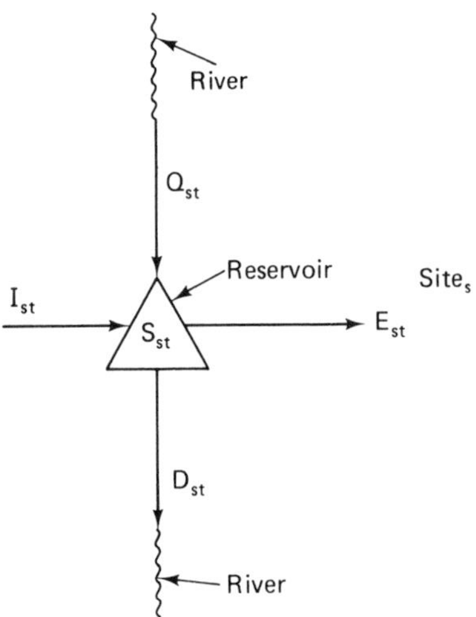

Figure 5-1
The continuity relationship at a reservoir.

which says that the storage in the reservoir at the beginning of the following season ($S_{s,t+1}$) must equal the storage at the beginning of the present season (S_{st}) plus any additions during the present season (the inflow, Q_{st}, and any imports, I_{st}) minus any deductions during the present season (the reservoir release, D_{st}, and any diversions, E_{st}), where the subscript s denotes site number and t the season. All of the inflow and outflow terms in Eq. (5.1) represent average flow volumes (MCM/season) throughout the season.

In Eq. (5.1), all of the variables except Q_{st} represent decisions that are made at site s. On the other hand, Q_{st}, the upstream inflow, depends on natural streamflow and on the decisions made immediately upstream, at site

$s - 1$. Figure 5-2 illustrates this relationship. Applying the same conservation of mass principle that was invoked to derive Eq. (5.1), we get, from Figure 5-2,

$$Q_{st} = D_{s-1,t} + \Delta F_{st} \tag{5.2}$$

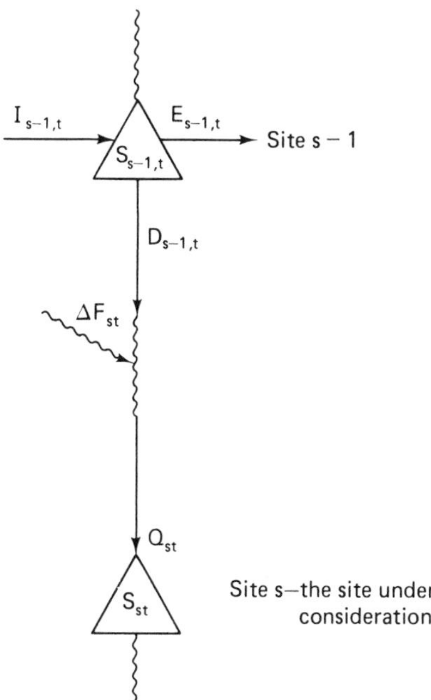

Figure 5-2
The continuity relationship with an upstream reservoir.

where all variables are defined as before and ΔF_{st} represents the increment to natural streamflow between sites $s - 1$ and s. In Eq. (5.2), imports and diversions occurring at the reservoir at site $s - 1$ are not included explicitly; instead, these two terms are implicitly accounted for by the reservoir release, $D_{s-1,t}$. This situation occurs, for example, in the exports to the Atuel basin in Mendoza, which lead out of two of the potential upstream reservoirs. However, imports and diversions occurring downstream of $s - 1$ but upstream of s are included in Eq. (5.2) because their immediate impact is on Q_{st}. The case where $s - 1$ is an irrigation site is shown in Figure 5-3; in this case, the irrigation return flow, $RI_{s-1,t}$, is included in the expression for Q_{st} at site s because it is not accounted for by $D_{s-1,t}$. This point illustrates the nature of continuity relationships: At any site on the stream, it is only necessary to account for the effects of the site immediately upstream, because all effects of those above it are accounted for in the upstream continuity equations. The situation in which there are two or more immediately upstream sites (e.g., where there are important tributaries with development sites) can be handled easily. It is only necessary to sum up all of these upstream sites in Eq. (5.2). In general, Q_{st}

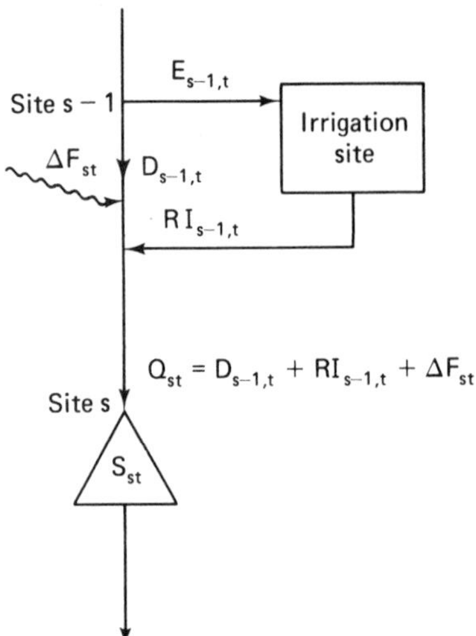

Figure 5-3
The continuity relationship with an upstream irrigation site.

in Eq. (5.1) can be replaced by $\sum_{r \in K_s} Q_{rt}$ where K_s is the set of all sites immediately upstream of site s.

The expression for Q_{st} in the case of a reservoir at site $s - 1$, Eq. (5.2), may now be substituted into Eq. (5.1). After terms are rearranged, the result is

$$S_{s,t+1} - S_{st} + D_{st} + E_{st} - I_{st} - D_{s-1,t} = \Delta F_{st} \tag{5.3}$$

in which all terms appearing on the left-hand side are decision variables, whereas ΔF_{st} on the right-hand side is input to the model. The value of ΔF_{st} in Eq. (5.3) represents the major hydrologic choice in the model, because ΔF_{st} is the only representation of natural streamflow in the constraint set.

The model is deterministic, because ΔF_{st} represents mean seasonal streamflows that are taken to occur with certainty. The value of ΔF_{st} is taken as the difference between the mean seasonal streamflows at sites $s - 1$ and s and represents the flow into the stream from the drainage area between $s - 1$ and s, as shown in Figure 5-4. Notice that ΔF_{st} is not the total streamflow at site s because $D_{s-1,t}$, which appears in Eq. (5.3), is the flow in the stream at $s - 1$ after development of the basin. Thus, ΔF_{st} represents the increment (or decrement) to $D_{s-1,t}$ due to snowmelt, tributary flow, infiltration or exfiltration, evaporation, and any previously existing development effects. However, none of these hydrologic processes are treated in the model; rather, ΔF_{st} is taken simply as the difference between measured mean seasonal streamflows at sites $s - 1$ and s:

$$\Delta F_{st} = F_{st} - F_{s-t,t} \tag{5.4}$$

The values of F_{st} and $F_{s-1,t}$, the mean seasonal streamflows, are obtained from streamflow records available at gaging stations on the river. Because

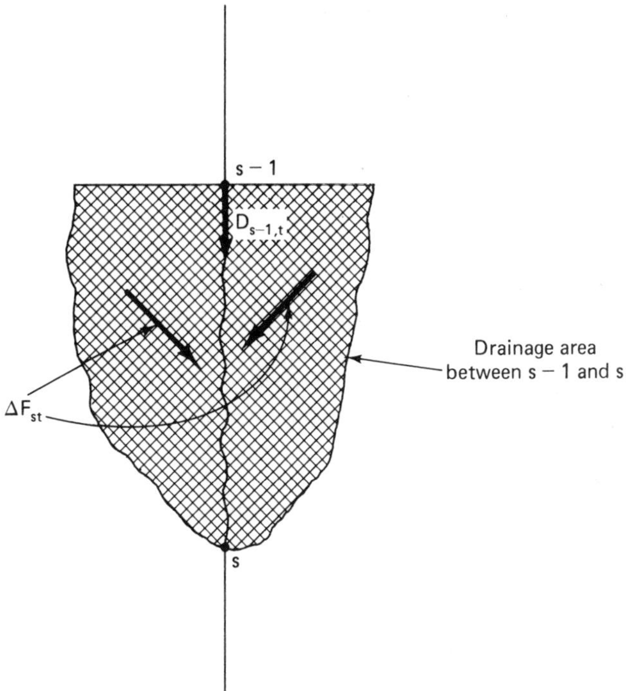

Figure 5-4
Representation of natural inflow into site s.

gaging stations are frequently not located at proposed sites, however, it becomes necessary to estimate F_{st} for those sites s that do not coincide with existing gages (Chapter 10).

Given estimates of streamflows, the substitution of Eq. (5.4) into Eq. (5.3) results in the stream continuity equation,

$$S_{s,t+1} - S_{st} + D_{st} + E_{st} - I_{st} - D_{s-1,t} = F_{st} - F_{s-1,t} \qquad (5.5)$$

The units of all terms in Eq. (5.5) are volumetric in MCM. However, it is desirable to express the flow terms, i.e. all the terms other than $S_{s,t+1}$ and S_{st}, in m^3/sec. When flow terms are expressed in m^3/sec, dimensional consistency is maintained by multiplying the storage terms by 10^6 and dividing by k_t, the number of seconds in season t, to obtain

$$\frac{10^6}{k_t} S_{s,t+1} - \frac{10^6}{k_t} S_{st} + D_{st} + E_{st} - I_{st} - D_{s-1,t} = F_{st} - F_{s-1,t} \qquad (5.6)$$

Equation (5.6) represents the form of the continuity constraints included in early forms of the screening model. To include the effect of evaporation from reservoirs, a parameter, EVAP_{st}, was introduced into Eq. (5.6). EVAP_{st}, the average evaporation loss expressed as a fraction of storage from the reservoir at site s during season t, was applied to the storage at the beginning of the present season in Eq. (5.6), to give

$$\frac{10^6}{k_t}S_{s,t+1} - \frac{10^6}{k_t}(1 - \text{EVAP}_{st})S_{st} + D_{st} + E_{st} - I_{st} - D_{s-1,t} = F_{st} - F_{s-1,t} \qquad \forall_{st} \qquad (5.7)^{*1}$$

A further change to the continuity constraint [Eq. (5.6)] occurred later in the study when it was determined that in the inactive central and lower regions of the basin (where no runoff contributes to the river flow) substantial streamflow losses occur. As described in Chapter 1, most of the potential development sites are in fact contained within the inactive central and lower basins. It was felt that the representation of natural effects by F_{st} in Eq. (5.7) was adequate only in the active basin, where the projects were closely spaced and large natural inflows were in evidence. In the central and lower basins, something else was needed to reflect the gradual natural loss of water, primarily due to seepage losses, observed from Buta Ranquil to the Atlantic Ocean. Furthermore, the losses were observed to be a function of seasonal differences in streamflow, so that the development alternatives selected in the screening model were expected to have an effect on river losses. The model's representation of losses in the central and lower basins used a linear relationship between losses and the difference in streamflow at the site immediately upstream, $s - 1$, in the previous season, $t - 1$, and the current season, t,

$$\text{LOSS}_{st} = a_s + b_s(D_{s-1,t} - D_{s-1,t-1}) \qquad (5.8)$$

in which LOSS_{st} is the loss between site s and $s - 1$ in season t and a_s and b_s are coefficients found by a regression analysis using historical data.

The consideration of losses in the central and lower basins yielded a different representation for Q_{st}. Referring to Figure 5.5, this representation is

$$Q_{st} = D_{s-1,t} - \text{LOSS}_{st} \qquad (5.9)$$

By substituting Eqs. (5.8) and (5.9) and rearranging,

$$Q_{st} = -a_s + (1 - b_s)D_{s-1,t} + b_s D_{s-1,t-1} \qquad (5.10)$$

Equation (5.10) says simply that there is always some loss between sites s and $s - 1$ represented by a_s. Furthermore, due to groundwater effects, a higher flow in the previous season than in the current season at site $s - 1$ tends to decrease losses in the current season. Conversely, lower flows last

[1]An asterisk (*) represents a constraint that is included in the final model.

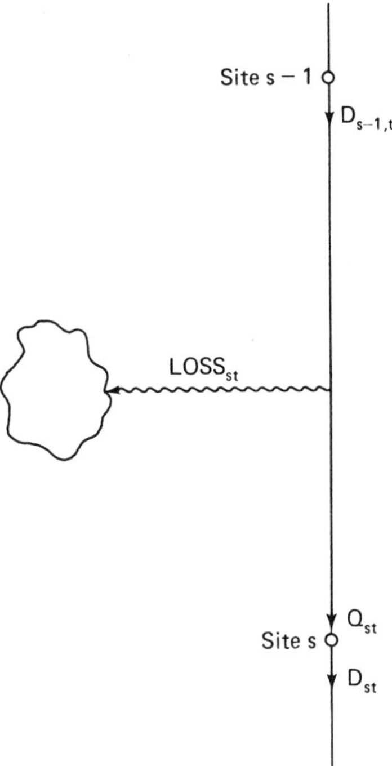

Figure 5-5
Representation of streamflow losses in the lower (inactive) basin.

season tend to increase losses this season. This is thus a representation of the groundwater system acting as a natural reservoir. By substituting the expression for Q_{st} in Eq. (5.10) into Eq. (5.1), rearranging, and adding the evaporation-loss coefficient and the unit conversion factor,

$$\frac{10^6}{k_t}S_{s,t+1} - \frac{10^6}{k_t}(1 - \text{EVAP}_{st})S_{st} + D_{st} + E_{st} - I_{st} - (1 - b_s)D_{s-1,t} - b_s D_{s-1,t-1} = -a_s \qquad \forall_{st} \tag{5.11*}$$

In summary, both Eqs. (5.7) and (5.11) appear as constraints in the model. Equation (5.7) is written for sites in the active basin. Both Eqs. (5.7) and (5.11) are intended to be general continuity constraints. When the constraints are written for a specific site, other terms may appear, as indicated in Figure 5-3 for an irrigation site. I_{st} and E_{st} are surrogate quantities for any inflows or outflows (other than upstream inflow and release). In an actual application, these two terms may represent interbasin imports or exports, or diversions for irrigation; the forms of Eqs. (5.7) and (5.11) can differ for each type of development site.

The assumption of determinism in the basin's hydrology appears in the right-hand sides of Eqs. (5.7) and (5.11). As previously stated, seasonal streamflows F_{st} and the parameters a_s and b_s were taken as mean values. This was done in large part to limit the computational burden of solution. The implications for system design of assuming mean values are tested in subsequent analyses using the simulation models, as described in the next two chapters.

Another major assumption appears in the general continuity constraints. The model was run for one typical year, implying that all years in the project's life are the same. In a continuous model, the assumption implies that what happened at the beginning of the first season of a given year is equal to what happens at the beginning of the first season of the next year. For T seasons in a year, this means mathematically that

$$S_{s,T+1} = S_{s,1} \tag{5.12}$$

The one-year assumption, along with the use of average hydrologic inputs, is limiting because the model cannot consider overyear storage; the consideration of overyear storage was accomplished by use of the simulation models.

RESERVOIR CONSTRAINTS

We require that the storage in a reservoir cannot exceed the storage capacity during any season t or at any site s,

$$S_{st} - V_s \leq 0 \qquad \forall_{st} \qquad (5.13)^*$$

in which V_s is the storage capacity of the reservoir at site s. Allowing V_s to be a decision variable in the model, constraint Eq. (5.13) permits the optimal storage capacity of the reservoir to be found. An upper bound that represents the largest practical dam size is placed on V_s. An upper bound on the capacity of a dam becomes necessary to maintain bounded solutions when reservoir cost functions are linear.

In the final formulation of the model, a 0–1 integer variable was included for each reservoir alternative in the river basin. This allows an appropriate representation of reservoir cost curves and also permits certain of the project interrelationships present in the basin to be captured. The use of integer variables for these purposes is explained in later sections. However, it is noted here because in the final form of the model, the following additional constraint replaced the upper bound on storage capacity in Eq. (5.13),

$$S_{st} - \text{CAPD}_s y_s \leq 0 \qquad \forall_{st} \qquad (5.14)^*$$

where CAPD_s is the storage capacity of the largest physically feasible dam that can be built and y_s is a 0–1 integer variable.

Another constraint is the storage-head relationship needed for reasons explained in the section on constraints for hydroelectric production. The constraint says that the storage, S_{st}, is related to the depth of water behind the dam, A_{st}, by

$$S_{st} - \sigma_s(A_{st}) = 0 \tag{5.15}^*$$

In early forms of the model, the function $\sigma_s(A_{st})$ was taken to be linear. This is, of course, a very unrealistic assumption. In later forms of the model, the storage-head function, σ_s, was assumed to be nonlinear and was approximated by a piece-wise linear function. Solutions were obtained using separable programming. As shown in Figure 5-6, a dummy variable related to A_{st} is

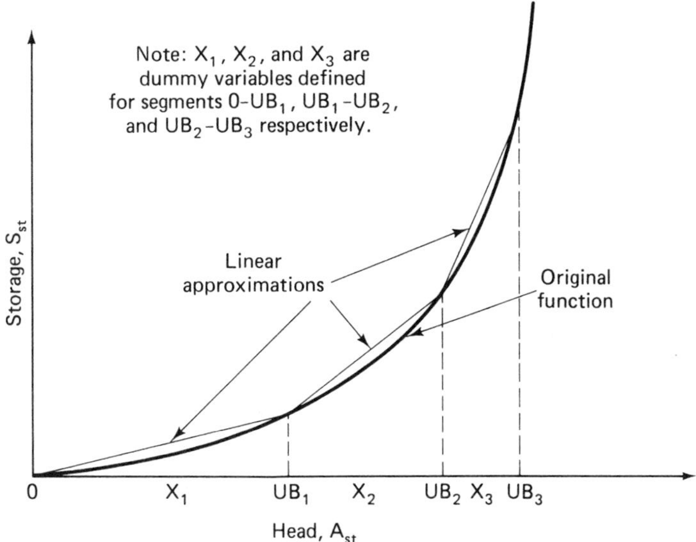

Figure 5-6
Linear approximation of a nonlinear storage-head relationship for separable programming.

defined for each segment of the piece-wise approximation. Although this representation was significantly more realistic than the purely linear assumption first used, it also resulted in local optima, a serious difficulty that is discussed in Appendix A.

IRRIGATION CONSTRAINTS

These constraints shape the relationships between water and the production of crops. The irrigation process is difficult to model, because of the great number of variables that affect agricultural production. Crop production depends on irrigation water volumes, temporal distribution of irrigation water volumes, water quality, solar radiation, precipitation, and a host of soil properties. Furthermore, the significance of each of these variables varies from crop to crop.

A number of simplifications were made in order to model irrigation. It was assumed (1) that the unit amount of water that produced the maximum yield per hectare would be applied to each crop, and (2) that this amount τ_s [illustrated in Figure 5-7(a)] could be estimated from empirical data (see Chapter 10).

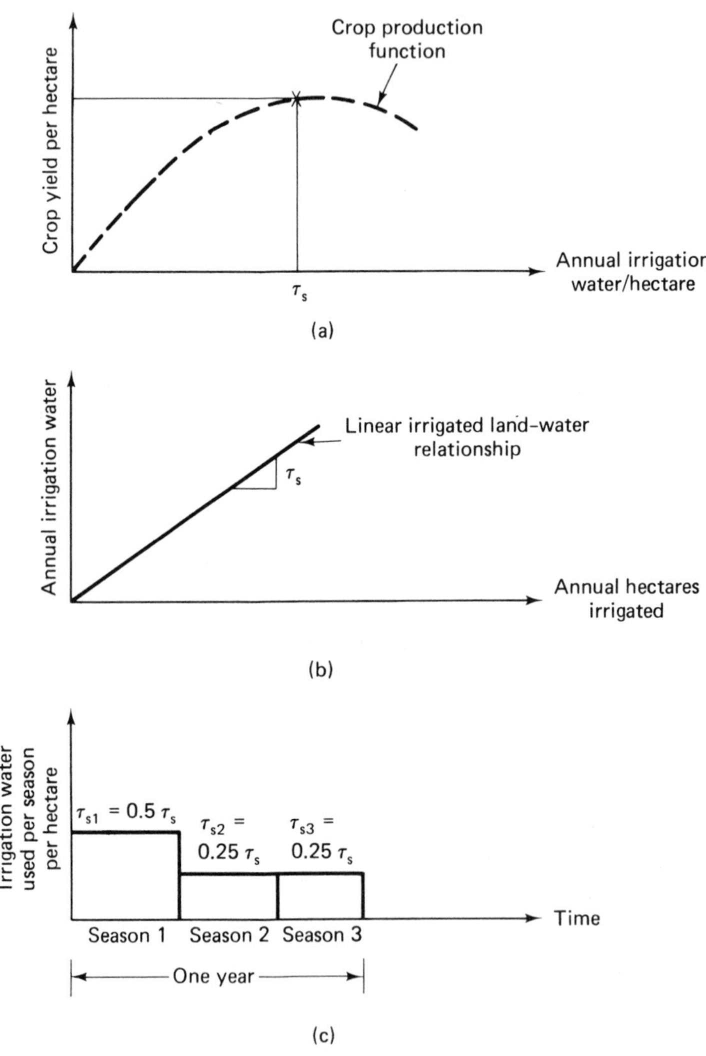

Figure 5-7
(a) Agricultural production function. (b) Assumed land-water relationship. (c) An example of the temporal distribution of irrigation water requirements. Note: $\sum \tau_{st} = \tau_{s1} + \tau_{s2} + \tau_{s3} = .5\tau_s + .25\tau_s + .25\tau_s = \tau_s$.

It was further assumed that the annual amount of irrigation water per hectare (τ_s) was a constant for each site, giving a constant yield per hectare. This annual land-to-water relationship is linear with slope τ_s, as shown in Figure 5-7(b).

The time distribution of crop water requirements was accounted for by distributing the annual water-use coefficient [Figure 5-7(c)]. The annual water-use coefficient then becomes a set of seasonal irrigation water-use coefficients (τ_{st}), which can be estimated from existing data (see Chapter 10).

The linear function relating irrigated land (L_{st}) to the volume of water supplied for irrigation (IR_{st}) is the main irrigation constraint:

$$IR_{st} - \frac{\tau_{st}}{10^6} L_{st} = 0 \qquad \forall_{st} \tag{5.16}^*$$

where the subscripts s and t refer to site number and time, respectively, and the units of τ_{st} are m^3/ha.

It should be stressed that the model does not solve for a cropping pattern (i.e., a spatial distribution of crops), but, rather, a cropping pattern is assumed for each site and this implies a value for τ_{st}.

Another constraint is required to reflect the assumption that benefits and costs are related to land cultivated for the whole growing period rather than for a single growing season alone. This constraint is written:

$$L_{sm} - L_{st} \leq 0 \qquad \forall_{st} \tag{5.17}^*$$

where L_{st} is the land planted during a season t and L_{sm} is the amount of land planted in all seasons.

The remaining irrigation constraints are simple statements of continuity. One constraint relates water supplied for irrigation (IR_{st}) to water diverted for irrigation (E_{st}):

$$IR_{st} - \frac{k_t}{10^6}(1 - \epsilon_{st})E_{st} = 0 \qquad \forall_{st} \tag{5.18}^*$$

where k_t is the number of seconds in season t and converts E_{st} from m^3/sec to MCM, and ϵ_{st} is a coefficient that represents the fraction of water lost in transport from the stream to the irrigation site.

Another continuity constraint relates water diverted for irrigation (E_{st}) to water returned to the stream from the irrigation site (RI_{st}).

$$RI_{st} - (1 - \mu_{st})E_{st} = 0 \tag{5.19}$$

where μ_{st} is the total loss coefficient for irrigation. It represents a combination of the losses due to transport (ϵ_{st}) and consumptive use requirements (ρ_{st}). It can be seen from Figure 5-8 that $\mu_{st} = \rho_{st}(1 - \epsilon_{st})$ when all transport losses are assumed to return to the stream.

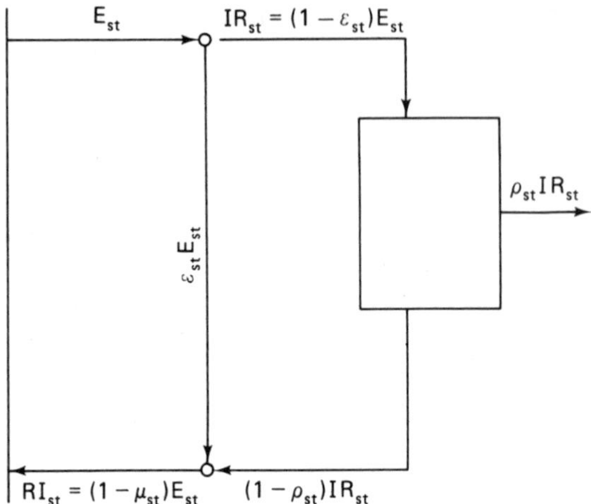

Figure 5-8
Representation of return flow from an irrigation site.

There is an additional assumption in Eq. (5.19) that the canal losses return to the stream within the same season in which they were lost. This assumption was relaxed in later formulations of the model. Weights were introduced into Eq. (5.19) to account for the lag times observed in the groundwater system. Different weights were applied to seepage losses from intake canals and to seepage losses from drainage canals. The aggregate coefficient, μ_{st}, in Eq. (5.19) was disaggregated to reflect these two distinct processes.

$$RI_{st} = (1 - \mu_{st})E_{st} = \epsilon_{st}E_{st} + (1 - \rho_{st})(1 - \epsilon_{st})E_{st} \qquad (5.20)$$

The first term on the right-hand side of Eq. (5.20) represents seepage losses from intake canals, and the second term reflects seepage losses from drainage canals. Rearranging Eq. (5.20), and applying the appropriate weights to the return flows, gives

$$RI_{st} - \sum_{i=1}^{3} [\omega_{sti}\epsilon_{si} + \chi_{sti}(1 - \rho_{si})(1 - \epsilon_{si})]E_{si} = 0 \qquad \forall_{st} \quad (5.21)^*$$

where ω_{sti} is the portion of the intake canal losses at site s in season i that returns to the stream in season t; a similar definition applies to the weighting coefficient χ_{sti} for drainage canals. It was assumed that all seepage losses return to the stream in the same year, so that

$$\sum_{i=1}^{3} \omega_{sti} = \sum_{i=1}^{3} \chi_{sti} = 1 \qquad (5.22)$$

A final constraint established an upper bound on the size of each irrigation area. This constraint is written as

$$L_{sm} \leq \text{CAPL}_s \qquad \forall_s \tag{5.23}^*$$

where CAPL_s is the maximum irrigable area at site s.

HYDROELECTRIC ENERGY CONSTRAINTS

The production of hydroelectric energy is a relatively well defined technical process. There are only three decision variables that affect energy production substantially enough to warrant incorporation in our model: (1) the flow through the turbines of the power plant, (2) the head associated with this flow, and (3) the installed capacity of the power plant. The energy constraints in the screening model reflect the relationships of these variables to hydroelectric energy production.

The first constraint arises from the production function for hydroelectric energy,

$$P_{st} - (2.73 \times 10^{-6})(e_s)(k_t)D_{st}A_{st} \leq 0 \tag{5.24}$$

where P_{st} is the energy produced at site s during season t in MWh, D_{st} is the average release from reservoir s during season t in m^3/sec, A_{st} is the head of water in reservoir s at the beginning of season t in m, e_s is the power plant efficiency, k_t is the number of seconds in season t, and (2.73×10^{-6}) is a unit conversion factor.

There are two assumptions made in writing Eq. (5.24). First, in order to use D_{st}, the release from the reservoir, as a representation of the flow through the power plant turbines, it must be assumed that all releases for use downstream are routed through the power plant (this does not include uses at the reservoir). Second, in using the head at the beginning of the season in Eq. (5.24), it is assumed that the head does not vary appreciably over the season. If this assumption proves to be invalid after analysis of the solution, then A_{st} can be replaced by an average head, $(A_{st} + A_{s,t+1})/2$.

In Eq. (5.24), the decision variables are P_{st}, D_{st}, and A_{st}. Because D_{st} is multiplied by A_{st}, Eq. (5.24) is nonlinear, and it must be linearized to be included in the screening model. The linearization method adopted consisted of the inclusion of two constraints, one with an assumed value of the discharge, D^*_{st}, and another with an assumed value of the head, A^*_{st}. The two constraints are

$$P_{st} - (2.73 \times 10^{-6})(e_s)(k_t)(D^*_{st})A_{st} \leq 0 \qquad \forall_{st} \tag{5.25}^*$$

$$P_{st} - (2.73 \times 10^{-6})(e_s)(k_t)(A^*_{st})D_{st} \leq 0 \qquad \forall_{st} \tag{5.26}^*$$

The advantage of this approach is that both release and head are explicitly considered by the model in the design of power plants. However, care must be taken when choosing the assumed values D^*_{st} and A^*_{st}. Beginning the iterative process with low assumed values may result in an artificially constrained solution. The iterations should begin with assumed values that are at the upper bound of physical feasibility. Subsequent runs should use successively lower assumed values until satisfactory agreement is reached.

The only other variable to be accounted for in the process of energy production is the power plant capacity, which represents an upper bound on energy production,

$$P_{st} - h_t H_s \leq 0 \qquad (5.27)$$

in which h_t is the number of hours in season t, and H_s is the capacity of the power plant in MW. Equation (5.27) will yield results in which the power plant is designed to produce at capacity all of the time. Therefore a factor Y_{st}, defined as the ratio of the average daily production to the daily peak production, is introduced into Eq. (5.27) to represent the daily variation in production patterns. However, because P_{st} is the seasonal energy production, it must be assumed that the production pattern does not vary appreciably from day to day. After the incorporation of the parameter Y_{st}, Eq. (5.27) becomes

$$P_{st} - Y_{st} h_t H_s \leq 0 \qquad \forall_{st} \qquad (5.28)^*$$

National income benefit coefficients in the objective function must take into account the value assumed for Y_{st}.

Solutions of the model frequently displayed wide seasonal variation in reservoir heads during the year, in some cases ranging from 1 meter to 100 meters. Such pronounced head variation results in very inefficient energy production. The following three constraints were added to limit the magnitude of head variation:

$$\text{AMIN}_s - A_{st} \leq 0 \qquad \forall_{st} \qquad (5.29)^*$$

$$\text{AMAX}_s - A_{st} \geq 0 \qquad \forall_{st} \qquad (5.30)^*$$

$$\text{AMAX}_s - 2\text{AMIN}_s \leq 0 \qquad \forall_{st} \qquad (5.31)^*$$

AMIN_s and AMAX_s are the minimum and maximum heads at site s, respectively. Equation (5.31) requires that the maximum head not be greater than twice the minimum head.

IMPORT/EXPORT CONSTRAINTS

Imports to the Río Colorado from the Río Negro to the south, and exports from the Río Colorado to the Río Atuel system in Mendoza to the north, represent major decision alternatives in the Río Colorado, reflecting not only national income but regional income and other regional considerations. To represent these possibilities in the screening model, two types of constraints are required: (1) continuity constraints at the points of possible import and export, and (2) constraints on the maximum size of each possible export or import.

For imports, these latter constraints are

$$I_{st} - I_{sm} \leq 0 \qquad \forall_{st} \tag{5.32)*$$

where I_{st} is the average water imported from another river basin at site s during season t in m^3/sec and I_{sm} is the capacity of the import in m^3/sec.

Similarly, for exports,

$$EX_{st} - EX_{sm} \leq 0 \qquad \forall_{st} \qquad (5.33)^*$$

where EX_{st} is the average export to another river basin during the season t at site s in m^3/sec and EX_{sm} is the capacity of the export in m^3/sec.

CONDITIONALITY CONSTRAINTS

Conditionality constraints are constraints that are written in the screening model to depict the situation when one project cannot or should not be constructed without another being constructed also. An example of such a situation is when an export must be built in conjunction with a dam of at least a certain height (so that flow can be by gravity). The constraints discussed thus far would not in themselves prevent the model from selecting the export without the dam (because of the way benefit functions are attributed to individual projects). The conditionality constraints take care of this problem.

In the screening model for the Río Colorado, these constraints were written for the case just cited, and also for the case in which diversions to irrigation areas were made from the backwater of reservoirs. Conditionality constraints are so-called "integer" constraints of the type explained in the discussion of integer programming in Chapter 3; the necessity for these is one of the reasons that "mixed-integer" programming was used for the screening model rather than simple linear programming.

Two integer constraints are required to model the conditional export of water to another basin. The first is

$$EX_{sm} - (\text{CAPEX}_s)y_s \leq 0 \qquad \forall_s \qquad (5.34)^*$$

where EX_{sm} is the capacity of the export in m^3/sec and CAPEX$_s$ is some upper bound on export. The decision variable y_s is required to be an integer and to take on the value of 0 or 1, but no other value. The second constraint is written to ensure that the dam is of a minimum height (or minimum storage MINS_s) when water is exported from the backwater of the reservoir.

$$S_{st} - (\text{MINS}_s)y_s \geq 0 \qquad \forall_{st} \tag{5.35*}$$

Because y_s is a 0–1 integer decision variable, the export of water requires y_s to take on a value of 1 by (5.34), which in turn requires at least MINS_s storage in each season from Eq. (5.35).

POLICY CONSTRAINTS

It was noted in Chapter 2 that, in principle, objectives can be represented directly in an objective function, or as constraints. In the Río Colorado screening model, it was often simpler to use the constraint representation for certain objectives than to put these into the objective function; such constraints are described here generically as "policy" constraints. These constraints were typically included for a few runs to represent particular cases of interest to decision makers. Constraints of this type are familiar in many planning studies, although their equivalence in the objective function is not always made clear.

The policy constraints used in the Río Colorado screening model are relatively simple in modeling terms. For example, one such constraint, intended to reflect in certain runs the basic regional objective that irrigation development should be given priority over power, was written as

$$L_{sm} = L_{sm}^* \qquad \forall_s \tag{5.36}$$

Here, L_{sm}^* was equal to the optimum area of land to be irrigated at site s when no power production in any part of the basin is permitted (determined from a prior model run). The inclusion of the foregoing constraint when power production was permitted ensured that those power plants that did appear in the solution did not interfere with irrigation development, thus reflecting the desired objective.

THE OBJECTIVE FUNCTION

The general form of the objective function is the maximization of the weighted sum of net benefits from each planning objective; for example,

$$\text{Max } Z = \lambda_{NI}(\text{NIB}) + \sum_{i=1}^{p} \lambda_i(\text{RIB}_i) \tag{5.37}$$

where λ_{NI} is the weight on discounted net national income benefits, λ_i is the weight on discounted net regional income benefits to the ith region (see

Chapter 9), NIB is discounted net national income benefits, and RIB_i is the discounted net regional income to region i.

For most runs of the screening model, the objective function included only one objective: the maximization of net discounted national income benefits. However, most of those runs that included only one objective in the objective function were actually multiobjective runs, with the influence of the other objectives represented by constraint formulations. Both the objective function and the policy constraints are thus mechanisms by which social preferences are made to shape the selection of development alternatives.

Net national income benefits are calculated as the difference between users' willingness to pay for project outputs, such as hydroelectric energy and irrigation production, and the costs of producing these outputs. Mathematically, the objective function is written as

$$\text{Max NIB} = B - C \tag{5.38a)*$$

where

$$B = \sum_s \{\beta_s^I(L_{sm}) + \sum_t [\beta_{st}^P(P_{st}) + \nu_{st}(EX_{st})]\} \qquad (5.38b)*$$

and

$$C = \sum_s [\alpha_s(V_s) + \delta_s(H_s) + \phi_s(L_{sm}) + \gamma_s^E(EX_{sm}) + \gamma_s^I(I_{sm})] \qquad (5.38c)*$$

In Eqs. (5.38) β_s^I, β_{st}^P, and ν_{st} are functions that represent discounted benefits for irrigation (net of farm level costs), energy production, and export, respectively. The function ϕ_s relates discounted total (capital, operation and maintenance) costs for irrigation (including social infrastructure but excluding farm level costs) to hectares of irrigated land, L_{sm}. The terms α_s, δ_s, γ_s^E, and γ_s^I are discounted total cost functions for reservoirs, power plants, export canals and tunnels, and import structures, written in terms of the reservoir storage capacity, power plant installed capacity, export diversion capacity, and import diversion capacity, respectively. (The dependence of power plant costs on head as well as installed capacity is taken into account by a priori judgments as to the operating head for each plant in the system; see Chapter 10.)

As will be described in Chapter 9, the assumptions used to estimate the benefits of project outputs permitted the use of linear benefit functions for the screening model. (In these cases, the symbols β_s^I, β_{st}^P and ν_{st} are used to denote the slopes of the linear functions rather than the linear functions themselves.)

The capital cost functions were typically nonlinear. Early formulations of the model employed linear approximations of the cost curves. As the model developed, more and more of the cost curves were modeled as separable nonlinear functions. The final form of the model includes piece-wise linear approximations for all the nonlinear cost functions, with the exception of reservoir cost curves.

Reservoir cost curves are a special case, because, as will be noted in Chapter 10, there is usually a large initial cost associated with the construction of reservoirs. The "fixed charge" nature of reservoir capital costs was included in the form of the model used for final project runs by employing 0–1 variables. The objective function entry for reservoirs was

$$\alpha_s(V_s) = (FC_s)y_s + (VC_s)V_s \qquad \forall_s \tag{5.39*}$$

where (FC_s) is the "fixed charge" for the reservoir at site s; (VC_s) is the variable cost; y_s is the 0–1 integer decision variable, which must equal 1 if the reservoir is built [as required by Eq. (5.14)]; and V_s is the reservoir capacity. This situation is illustrated in Figure 5-9.

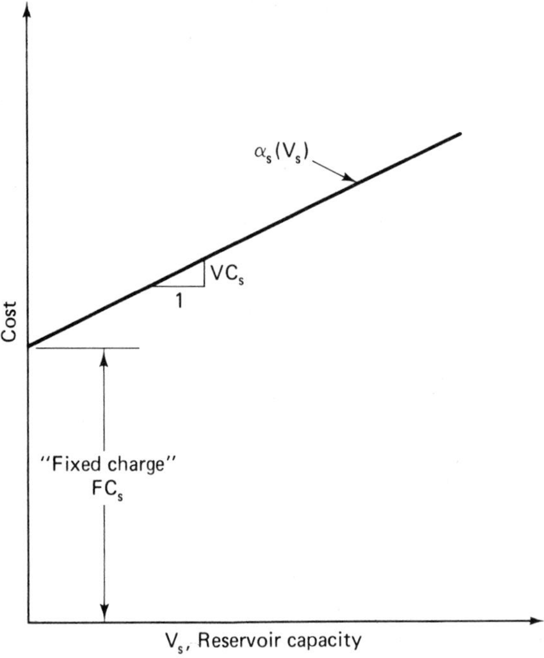

Figure 5-9
Cost curve for a reservoir with fixed charge.

An alternative form of the objective function, also reflecting both national income and regional considerations, was

$$\text{Min } Z_d = \sum_{i=1}^{5} |WR_i - WRA| \tag{5.40}$$

where Z_d = sum of the absolute deviations of provincial water use from average water use (m^3/sec),

$$WRA = \frac{1}{5}\sum_{i=1}^{5} WR_i \quad \text{(average provincial water use in m}^3\text{/sec)} \tag{5.41}$$

$$WR_i = \sum_{t=1}^{T} \sum_{s \in R_i} (E_{st} + EX_{st})$$

$$i = 1, \ldots, 5 \text{ (water used by province } i) \quad (5.42)$$

and R_i is the set of all sites in region i.

The expression in Eq. (5.40) is nonlinear and thus cannot be included directly in the linear programming model. A transformation that permits inclusion of Eq. (5.40) in the model is:

$$\text{Min } Z_d = \sum_{i=1}^{5} (G_i + T_i) \quad (5.43)$$

$$WR_i - WRA = G_i - T_i \qquad i = 1, \ldots, 5 \quad (5.44)$$

$$G_i, T_i, WR_i, WRA \geq 0 \qquad i = 1, \ldots, 5 \quad (5.45)$$

in which G_i and T_i are the deviations of WR_i from WRA, and only G_i or T_i (not both) can be nonzero for each of the constraints, as can be seen by inspection of the form of the constraints and the objective function. For a given deviation, $G_i - T_i$, the sum $G_i + T_i$ is minimized when G_i or $T_i = 0$.

In order to use this version of the objective function to define the transformation curve between the national income objective and the provincial water allocation objective by the constraint method (see Chapter 2), we require two additional constraints: First,

$$\text{NIB} \leq \text{UBNI} \quad (5.46)$$

where UBNI is a variable upper bound on national income NIB; and second, an equation defining NIB as in Eq. (5.38).

The formulation of the model with this objective function [Eq. (5.43)] then includes the constraints of Eqs. (5.41), (5.42), (5.44), (5.45), (5.46), and Appendix 5A, and the constraint defining NIB as in Eq. (5.38).

REFERENCES

LOUCKS, DANIEL P. "Stochastic Methods for Analyzing River Basin Systems." Technical Report No. 16. Cornell University Water Resources and Marine Sciences Center, Ithaca, N.Y., August 1969.

DORFMAN, ROBERT. "Formalization in the Design of Water Resource Systems." *Water Resources Research*, **1**, (*3*), 1965, pp. 329–336.

HUFSCHMIDT, MAYNARD M. "Field Level Planning of Water Resource Systems." *Water Resources Research*, **1**, (*2*), 1965, pp. 147–163.

MAASS, ARTHUR, MAYNARD M. HUFSCHMIDT, ROBERT DORFMAN, HAROLD A. THOMAS, JR., STEPHEN A. MARGLIN, and GORDON MASKEW FAIR. *Design of Water-Resource Systems*. Cambridge, Mass.: Harvard University Press, 1962.

APPENDIX 5A FORMULATION OF THE MIXED-INTEGER SCREENING MODEL

CONTINUITY CONSTRAINTS

Continuity for the active basin:

$$\frac{10^6}{k_t}S_{s,t+1} - \frac{10^6}{k_t}(1 - \text{EVAP}_{st})S_{st} + D_{st} + E_{st} - I_{st} - D_{s-1,t}$$
$$= F_{st} - F_{s-1,t} \qquad \forall_{st}$$

For the inactive basin:

$$\frac{10^6}{k_t}S_{s,t+1} - \frac{10^6}{k_t}(1 - \text{EVAP}_{st})S_{st} + D_{st} + E_{st} - I_{st}$$
$$- (1 - b_s)D_{s-1,t} - b_sD_{s-1,t-1} = -a_s \qquad \forall_{st}$$

RESERVOIR CONSTRAINTS

$$S_{st} - V_s \leq 0 \qquad \forall_{st}$$
$$S_{st} - \sigma_s(A_{st}) = 0 \qquad \forall_{st}$$
$$S_{st} - \text{CAPD}_s y_s \leq 0 \qquad \forall_{st}$$

IRRIGATION CONSTRAINTS

$$IR_{st} - \frac{\tau_{st}}{10^6} L_{st} = 0 \qquad \forall_{st}$$

$$L_{sm} - L_{st} \leq 0 \qquad \forall_{st}$$

$$IR_{st} - \frac{k_t}{10^6}(1 - \epsilon_{st})E_{st} = 0 \qquad \forall_{st}$$

$$RI_{st} - \sum_{i=1}^{3} [\omega_{sti}\epsilon_{si} + \chi_{sti}(1 - \rho_{si})(1 - \epsilon_{st})]E_{si} = 0 \qquad \forall_{st}$$

$$L_{sm} \leq \text{CAPL}_s \qquad \forall_s$$

HYDROELECTRIC ENERGY CONSTRAINTS

$$P_{st} - (2.73 \times 10^{-6})(e_s)(k_t)(D^*_{st})A_{st} \leq 0 \qquad \forall_{st}$$

$$P_{st} - (2.73 \times 10^{-6})(e_s)(k_t)(A^*_{st})D_{st} \leq 0 \qquad \forall_{st}$$

$$P_{st} - Y_{st}h_t H_s \leq 0 \qquad \forall_{st}$$

$$\text{AMIN}_s - A_{st} \leq 0 \qquad \forall_{st}$$

$$\text{AMAX}_s - A_{st} \geq 0 \qquad \forall_{st}$$

$$\text{AMAX}_s - 2\text{AMIN}_s \leq 0 \qquad \forall_s$$

IMPORT CONSTRAINTS

$$I_{st} - I_{sm} \leq 0 \qquad \forall_{st}$$

EXPORT CONSTRAINTS

$$EX_{st} - EX_{sm} \leq 0 \qquad \forall_{st}$$

CONDITIONALITY CONSTRAINTS

$$EX_{sm} - (\text{CAPEX}_s)y_s \leq 0 \qquad \forall_s$$

$$S_{st} - (\text{MINS}_s)y_s \geq 0 \qquad \forall_{st}$$

All variables are nonnegative, and $y_s = 0/1$, $\forall_s$.

OBJECTIVE FUNCTION (NET NATIONAL INCOME BENEFITS)

$$\text{Max } Z = \sum_s \{\beta^I_s(L_{sm}) + \sum_t [\beta^p_{st}(P_{st}) + \nu_{st}(EX_{st})]\}$$
$$- \sum_s [\alpha_s(V_s) + \delta_s(H_s) + \phi_s(L_{sm}) + \gamma^E_s(EX_{sm}) + \gamma^I_s(I_{sm})]$$

APPENDIX 5B LIST OF VARIABLES AND PARAMETERS USED IN THE SCREENING MODEL

List of Decision Variables

Variable	*Definition*	*Units*
A_{st}	Reservoir head at beginning of season t at site s	m
D_{st}	Average flow from site s during season t	m^3/sec
EX_{st}	Average interbasin export at site s during season t	m^3/sec
E_{st}	Average diversion for irrigation at site s during season t	m^3/sec
EX_{sm}	Maximum average export during year from site s	m^3/sec
H_s	Power plant capacity at site s	MW
I_{st}	Average interbasin import at site s during season t	m^3/sec
I_{sm}	Maximum average import at site s	m^3/sec
IR_{st}	Volume of water supplied for irrigation at site s during season t	MCM
L_{st}	Amount of land irrigated at site s during season t	ha
L_{sm}	Amount of land irrigated during the whole year at site s	ha
Q_{st}	Inflow into site s during season t	m^3/sec
P_{st}	Hydroelectric energy produced at site s during season t	MWh
RI_{st}	Average return flow from site s during season t	m^3/sec
S_{st}	Volume of water in storage at site s at the beginning of season t	MCM
V_s	Capacity of reservoir at site s	MCM
y_s	Integer variable that equals 1 if the reservoir at site s is built and 0 if it is not built	—

List of Parameters

Variable	Definition	Units
a_s, b_s	Coefficients found from analysis of streamflow and stream losses at site s in the inactive basin	—
CAPD_s	Physical upper bound on reservoir capacity at site s	MCM
CAPEX_s	Upper bound on export capacity at site s	m^3/sec
CAPL_s	Maximum irrigable area at site s	ha
EVAP_{st}	Evaporation loss coefficient at reservoir s during season t	—
e_s	Power plant efficiency at site s	—
F_{st}	Average streamflow at site s during season t	m^3/sec
h_t	Number of hours in season t	hr
k_t	Number of seconds in season t	sec
MINS_s	Minimum storage allowed at site s when water is diverted from reservoir backwater	MCM
ω_{sti}	Portion of intake canal losses at site s lost in season i that returns to the stream in season t	—
χ_{sti}	Portion of drainage canal losses at site s lost in season i that returns to the stream in season t	—
Y_{st}	Power factor at site s during season t	—
$\alpha_s(\cdot)$	Total cost function for reservoir s	$* vs. MCM
$\beta_s^I(\cdot)$	Gross benefit function for agricultural output at site s	$* vs. ha.
$\beta_{st}^P(\cdot)$	Gross benefit function for energy production at site s during season t	$* vs. MWh.
$\gamma_s^E(\cdot), \gamma_s^I(\cdot)$	Total cost functions for export and import structures, respectively, at site s	$* vs. $m^3\ sec^{-1}$
$\delta_s(\cdot)$	Total cost function for power plant at site s	$* vs. MW
ϵ_{st}	Water loss coefficient for flow through irrigation diversion canals at site s during t	—
μ_{st}	Total irrigation loss coefficient at site s during t	—
$\nu_{st}(\cdot)$	Gross benefit function derived from interbasin export of water from site s during t	$* vs. $m^3\ sec^{-1}$
ρ_{st}	Consumptive use coefficient for irrigation at site s during t	—
$\sigma_s(\cdot)$	Storage-head function for reservoir at site s	MCM vs. m
τ_{st}	Irrigation water use coefficient at site s during season t	m^3/ha
$\phi_s(\cdot)$	Total cost function for irrigation works at site s	$* vs. ha

*See Chapter 9 for the monetary unit used in model runs.

CHAPTER SIX SIMULATION ANALYSES: THE BASIC MODEL

EDWARD McBEAN
ROBERTO LENTON
JOHN C. SCHAAKE, JR.

The previous chapter described the mathematical programming screening model used to provide preliminary development configurations responsive to alternative objectives and constraints. As described in Chapter 4 these alternative configurations were then evaluated by means of simulation analyses in order to study improvements in the configurations. The purpose of this chapter is to describe the basic simulation model that was developed during the study to perform these analyses. The description of the basic simulation model contained in this chapter refers to the version of the model used for final production runs during the study. The model has been revised and improved since the runs described here were made; two later versions of the model are described in Schaake (1974) and Lenton and Strzepek (1977).

The basic model was not the only simulation model used in the Río Colorado study. A second model, called the detailed simulation model, was developed for physical simulation of specific components of the basin. The detailed simulation model is described in Chapter 7.

In this chapter the background, general nature, and overall structure of the basic simulation model are described first. These are the sections that will be of most interest to the nonspecialist reader. Then, the parts of the model representing irrigation, power, exports, water allocation rules, and the objective function are described. These descriptions relate the details of the various components of the basic simulation model to those of the screening model;

in each case, the differences are primarily due to the use of stochastic hydrology in the simulation model.

THE BASIC MODEL

The simulation model is a mathematical representation designed to estimate the contributions to objectives that would result if a proposed set of management and development measures were implemented. Such simulation models have been widely used since the publication of the pioneer text in this field, *Design of Water-Resource Systems* (Maass, et al., 1962). The basic model described here contains some of the features of the models described in Maass' text and later developed further by Hufschmidt and Fiering (1966). These features include the possibility of dealing with a large number of alternative configurations (project sizes and target outputs are input variables); the computation of system costs and benefits and the economic losses arising from water deficits; and the utilization of large time intervals (in this case, 4-month periods). An additional feature of these models is that they generally have been used in conjunction with synthetic streamflow models (Fiering, 1967) that provide many alternative sets of streamflow sequences.

GENERAL DESCRIPTION OF THE MODEL

The setup of the basic model is straightforward. In order to replicate the behavior of any given river basin configuration, it is first necessary to represent the different components of the basin and the proposed development plans. This is done in the basic model by defining a series of "nodes" defined as locations on the river where flow is modified by natural means or by man-made structures. Thus, the river system is pictured as a sequence of "start" nodes, "reservoir" nodes, "confluence" nodes, "irrigation" nodes, "continuation" nodes, "import/export" nodes, and "terminal" nodes, connected to each other by "reaches," or arcs.

Given this representation, the model performs the necessary algebraic operations to obtain an accounting of the flow in each node in the basin at each time step of the simulation interval. Once the flow at each node is known, the model calculates the benefits toward the different objectives derived by the use of that flow for irrigation, energy, and export purposes, and the short-term losses in benefits caused by water shortages if these occur.

The output information provided by the model is designed to help planners to analyze the consequences of implementing alternative plans. It provides estimates of the benefits and costs toward the different objectives that would accrue as a result of implementation of alternative plans. It also provides information on the reliability of the water supply at the different points of water use, the production of hydroelectric energy by each of the individual projects and by the system as a whole, and other types of project-specific engineering data.

The characteristics of the various types of nodes in the model are described in the next section.

THE RIVER SYSTEM AS A NETWORK OF NODES

In the model, a river basin is pictured as a network of nodes connected by reaches. Figure 6-1 illustrates a simple node arrangement.

A *start* node identifies an upstream end of the system. This type of node represents the location where an input flow time series is introduced into the system. No node is permitted upstream of a start node.

A *reservoir* node designates a dam or lake that can regulate streamflow. It can have a hydroelectric power plant associated with it.

A *confluence* node identifies a point on the stream at which a confluence or bifurcation occurs, either natural or man-made (as, for example, a diversion to an irrigation area).

An *irrigation* node represents an irrigation area.

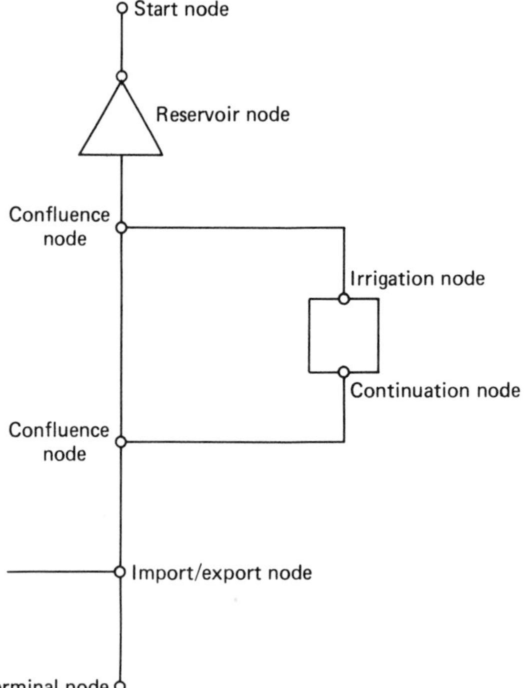

Figure 6-1
Example configuration.

A *continuation* node is a node used to connect two reaches. An example of its use is to indicate the end of an irrigation location.

An *import/export* node identifies a location at which water is added to or taken away from the river system, as the result of an interbasin transfer.

A *terminal* node indicates a downstream termination point of the system. No branch or node is permitted downstream of this type of node. The program allows more than one node in the basin to be defined this way; this is required, for example, in the case of a river that has more than one outlet to the sea.

Associated with those nodes that represent structural components are one or more "design variables"—that is, variables that define system configurations and that are chosen by the analyst as input to the simulation model. (In the screening model, these are decision variables, determined as a result of solving the model.) The design variables associated with each node are listed in Table 6-1.

Table 6-1 Input Design Variables

Node Type	*Design Variables*
Start node	—
Reservoir node	Reservoir storage capacity (MCM) Seasonal target reservoir releases (m^3/sec) Installed capacity (MW) of associated power plant, if applicable Seasonal energy production targets (MWh) of associated power plant, if applicable
Confluence node	—
Irrigation node	Size of irrigation area (ha)
Continuation node	—
Import/Export node	Import/Export diversion capacity (m^3/sec) Seasonal import flows or export target flows (m^3/sec)
Terminal node	—

The node structure of the model permits an important economy of operation in the basic simulation model. When the data deck for the model was constructed, provision was made on the computer cards for each of the nodes that could possibly be in the Río Colorado system, if all possible projects were implemented. However, the model is so constructed that each node remains potential until nonzero values are entered for it. Thus, for each run of the model, nodes are defined for all of the potential projects in the system, but only those projects for which nonzero values have been entered are taken into account in the flow and benefit–cost calculations for that run. This procedure allows the analyst to put projects in, to take them out, or to change their sizes in successive runs in an efficient way. The analyst needs only to make simple changes in the basic deck that activate projects, deactivate them, or change their sizes; he need not revise the basic node structure of the model for each successive run.

The accounting of streamflow movement is accomplished as follows. At each node the model reads, for each month, the input data giving the streamflow values for the "start" nodes. It then applies the equations governing flow between nodes (in most cases identical to those of the screening model) in order to determine flow along the river up to the terminal node. At reservoirs and diversions, flow is determined by use of the reservoir operating or water allocation rules, which are described later in this chapter. The calculations commencing at the "start" nodes are repeated for each time step. The sequence of operations for a given time step is illustrated in Figure 6-2.

SYNTHETIC STREAMFLOW

One important consequence of the model's accounting is that the flow records at each of the "start" nodes must be of the same length. In the Río Colorado (as often happens), the flow records available at the different gaging stations were not of the same length. When this occurs, the shorter records must be extended to the length of the longest records. This can be done by synthetic streamflow models, whose role can thus be twofold. They can be used to generate the extended segments of a streamflow series in order to create a homogeneous data set. In addition, the homogeneous data set can be used as a base for the synthetic streamflow model to generate many alternative sets of streamflow sequences of equal likelihood of future occurrence.

The synthetic streamflow input to the basic simulation model is generated by the detailed simulation model, which contains a module for streamflow synthesis (Chapter 7). In the Río Colorado study, this module was used to create a homogeneous data base of length equal to the longest record in the basin, which was 51 years.

RELATIONSHIP OF THE BASIC SIMULATION MODEL AND THE SCREENING MODEL

The flow relationships expressed in the basic simulation model are the same as those of the screening model. (To emphasize this similarity, the same notation has been used.) This is true of many of the other model relationships as well (such as hydroelectric energy production), because the role of the simulation model here is not to model the system to a greater level of detail than the screening model but, rather, to be able to evaluate the effect of streamflow stochasticity on the system's net benefits. The only significant simulation model equations that differ from their counterparts in the screening model are those related to streamflow variability, shortages, and their effects. In the screening model, the concept of shortages does not exist; a project is feasible

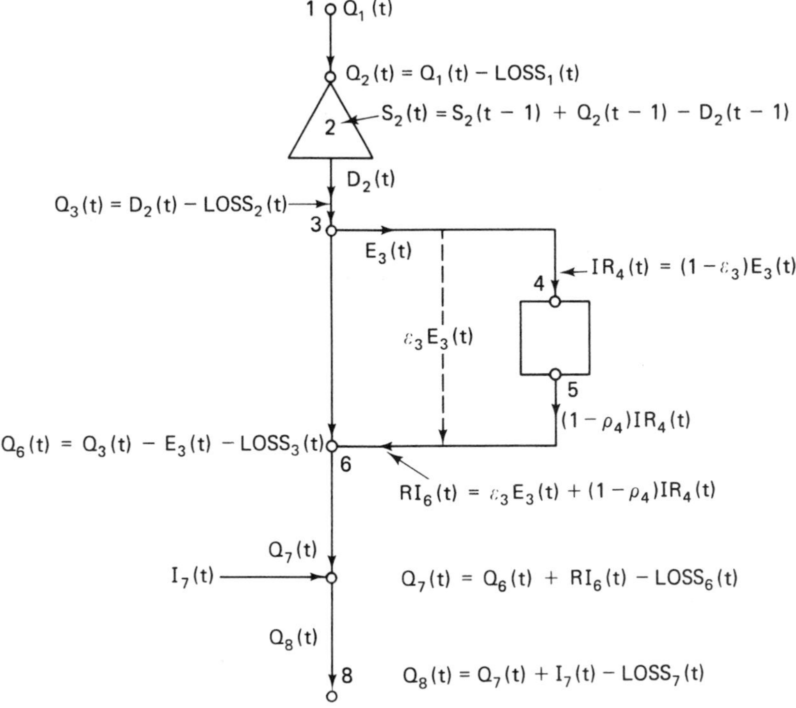

Figure 6-2
Basic simulation model flow calculations.

if its water requirements are totally satisfied (given the mean seasonal flows that are assumed), and infeasible if they are not. The concept of shortages is explicitly incorporated in the simulation model and is fundamental to it. Some other small differences between the models also exist—for example, the calculation of evaporation losses as a function of area rather than of storage, but these have negligible impact on model results.

The first important characteristic of the basic simulation model that is a consequence of its consideration of shortages is that a distinction must be made between "actual" reservoir and diversion releases and "target" releases. In the deterministic screening model, no distinction is necessary; however, the consideration of stochastic streamflow in the basic simulation model requires that the "target" releases be prespecified and that the "actual" releases be determined during the simulation run by means of an operating policy.

A second characteristic of the basic model, which is related to the fact that both models contain the same equations, is that if the basic model is used to simulate a given configuration obtained from the output of the screening model, and if the time series of streamflow is set to consist of the seasonal means repeating themselves year after year (so that no shortages occur), then the resultant value of the objective function determined from the simulation run will coincide with that of the screening model. When the streamflow series exhibits natural variability, the simulation objective function will be lower than that of the screening model, because water shortages cause short-term losses in benefits, and no gains are assumed to result from water excess.

Because the basic simulation model uses to a large extent the same equations as the screening model, only the additional components that are included in the simulation model to account for shortages are described here. These can be summarized as follows:

1. Effects of irrigation water shortages on crop yield and thus on benefits.
2. Effect of reservoir storage and release variability on energy generation and thus on energy benefits.
3. Effect of diversion release variability on export benefits.
4. Operating rules for apportioning water among projects during shortages.
5. Reservoir operating rules for apportioning water over time.

IRRIGATION

The effects of irrigation water shortages have commonly been described in terms of "short-term" losses [see, for example, Hufschmidt and Fiering (1966, pp. 54–56)]. This can be explained by means of Figure 6-3. In the figure, the ray from the origin represents the long-term benefits that occur for different levels of target irrigation flow. Once a target flow has been selected, short-term deviations from the target will cause short-term losses in benefits. Branch (a) denotes the decreased benefit levels encountered when the amount of water received by the irrigation area is less than the target irrigation flow. Similarly, branch (b) corresponds to the case when the water received exceeds the target flow, if it is assumed that benefits do not increase above the target level. Branches (a) and (b) do not coincide with the long-term benefit function, because farmers cannot adjust for unanticipated shortages and excesses.

The estimation of short-term losses is more complex than is implied by this formulation, because of a variety of physical, economic, and behavioral factors. In the basic simulation model, an attempt was made to capture one of these factors. This is the dependence of the short-term losses on the level of previous shortages.

The approach taken to model this dependence is based on two aspects of the relationship between crop yield, water supply, and water shortage. The first is that shortages early in the growing year tend to result in a reduction of demand for water in the remainder of the growing year, assuming that the shortages are severe enough to produce a reduction of the cultivated land area. The second is that water shortages at any time throughout the growing

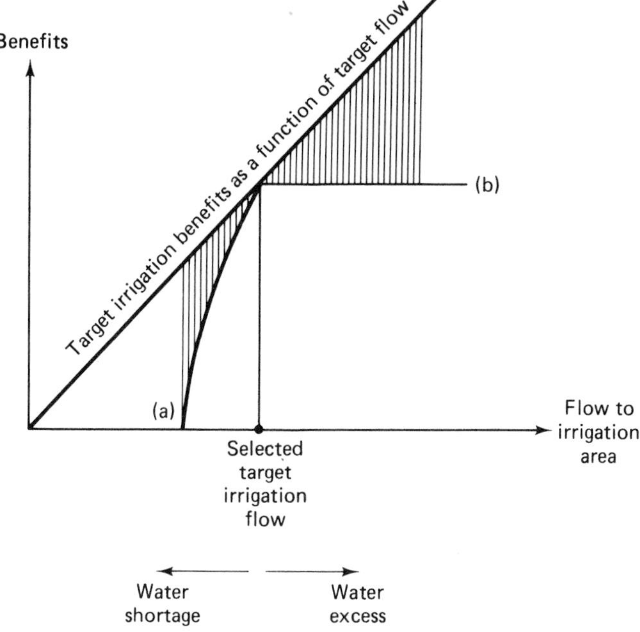

Figure 6-3
Long-term benefits and short-term losses for irrigation.

year will tend to result in salt build-up. This requires an increased amount of water in the following seasons to leach the salt.

The first aspect is modeled by allowing the target diversion to be a function of the amount of water diverted to the irrigation area in previous seasons. The second aspect is considered by defining a target diversion that includes leaching water requirements, which are themselves a function of irrigation water shortages in previous seasons. The net effect of both these considerations is that the magnitude of the reduction in crop yield benefits due to water shortage is modeled as a function not only of the magnitude of these shortages but of their time history as well.

HYDROELECTRIC ENERGY

At a hydroelectric power plant at site s, total energy generation during a given season t is calculated by [see Eq. (5.24)][1]

$$P_s(t) = (2.73 \times 10^{-6})(e_s)k(t)D_s(t)A_s^*(t) \tag{6.1}$$

[1]Notation in this chapter is as in the screening model (Appendix 5B) except that time t is given in parentheses rather than as a subscript.

where

$$k(t) = \text{number of seconds in season } t$$
$$e_s = \text{power plant efficiency at site } s$$
$$D_s(t) = \text{average turbine release at site } s \text{ during season } t \text{ (m}^3\text{/sec)}$$
$$A_s^*(t) = \text{average turbine head at site } s \text{ during season } t(m)$$
$$P_s(t) = \text{total energy generation (MWh) at site } s \text{ in season } t$$

The value of $A_s^*(t)$ is calculated within the run by

$$A_s^*(t) = \frac{A_s(t) + A_s(t+1)}{2} \tag{6.2}$$

where

$$A_s(t) = \text{head at the start of season } t$$
$$A_s(t+1) = \text{head at the start of season } t+1$$

Energy production as given by Eq. (6.1) is constrained by the installed capacity H_s of the power plant [see screening model Eq. (5.27)].

The effect of storage and release variability is considered in the following way. Storage fluctuations caused by net differences between inflow and release produce variations in the average turbine head $A_s^*(t)$, which enter Eq.(6.1). The release $D_s(t)$ is determined by the reservoir operating rule to satisfy current and future demand where possible, but in time of shortage, $D_s(t)$ might be reduced below that required to meet a given energy target. [In the screening model, $A_s^*(t)$ and $D_s^*(t)$ are decision variables, and the "target" energy production is an output value determined by the optimal values taken on by these decision variables. In the simulation model, the energy target is an input design variable (see Table 6-1).] For this reason, the model divides total energy production into that which does not exceed the energy target and that above the target. In the Río Colorado study, benefits were only attributed to that part of the total power production that did not exceed the energy target. Energy generation above the target was not credited with benefits, although in some planning studies it would be appropriate to do so.

EXPORTS

Export flows are determined on the basis of water allocation and reservoir operating rules (see following sections). Benefits are assigned as a linear function of annual diversion; a linear reduction in gross benefits is thus assumed whenever export flow is less than the export target.

WATER ALLOCATION RULES

A first important aspect in designing rules for water allocation is that there must be close correspondence between the performance of a water resource system at the design stage and that attainable after the system is built (Maass et al., 1962, pp. 444–45); it must be ensured that the assumed water allocation rules are consistent with feasible management of the future real-world system. Second, water allocation rules should be closely associated with the objectives for the development of the water resources of the basin.

In the Río Colorado, an interprovincial organization existed with potential authority for regulating water distribution among users. Furthermore, an agreement was made among the provinces that established, among other things, that water supply deficits in times of shortage must be shared proportionately among the river's users in times of drought (Chapter 1).

This situation led to the assumption, in the basic simulation model, of an operating rule that established that when the flow in the river is insufficient to cover the total demand, the deficit in the supply of water would be shared by all the system units in proportion to their respective demands. If the net total demand at and downstream of a diversion at site s is denoted as $N_s(t)$, the flow in the river at the diversion point as $Q_s(t)$, and the target diversion as $T_s(t)$, then the amount of water diverted in season t, $E_s(t)$, is

$$E_s(t) = \begin{cases} T_s(t) & \text{if} \quad Q_s(t) \geq N_s(t) \\ \dfrac{Q_s(t)T_s(t)}{N_s(t)} & \text{if} \quad Q_s(t) < N_s(t) \end{cases} \tag{6.3}$$

This rule is illustrated in Figure 6-4. (The dashed line in Figure 6-4 represents the water that would be diverted if there were no consideration of downstream demands in the allocation of water to diversion areas—in other words, if upstream users received priority in times of shortage.)

It should be noted that although this rule is conceptually simple, it is somewhat difficult to implement in practice because of the difficulty of estimating the net downsteam demands (both in the model and in actual implementation). This estimation must account for all available downstream water

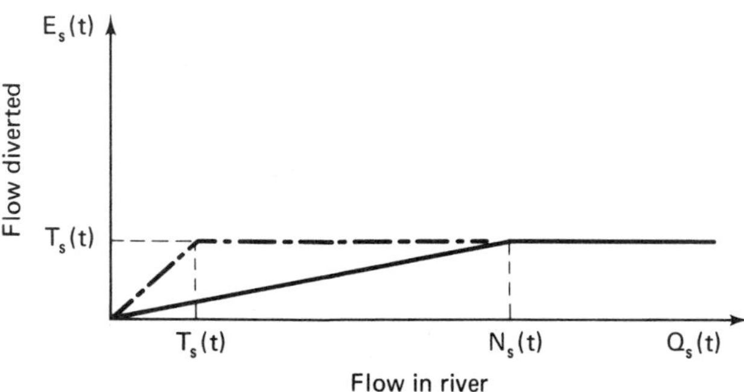

Figure 6-4
Water allocation rule.

in storage and from irrigation return flow, as well as for the downstream demands themselves.

RESERVOIR OPERATING RULES

Reservoir releases are determined by the operating rule, which must be specified for each reservoir. The basic dilemma of operation is whether to release in times of shortage all the available water in order to best meet current downstream demand, or to keep part of it in storage in order to reduce future potential shortages.

The principal operating rule used in the model is the "standard" operating rule (Fiering, 1967). The standard operating rule can be described as follows. For every season it is required to determine the release $D_s(t)$ as a function both of target releases $T_s(t)$ and of water availability, defined as the sum of the inflow $Q_s(t)$ plus the storage at the beginning of the season $S_s(t)$. Three cases can be identified (see Figure 6-5):

- I Water availability is insufficient to meet the target requirements; the rule assumes that the reservoir will be emptied in order to try to meet the demand.
- II There is enough water to meet the demand. Water not required downstream is kept in storage.
- III The available water minus the demand exceeds storage capacity. All water that cannot be kept in storage must be spilled.

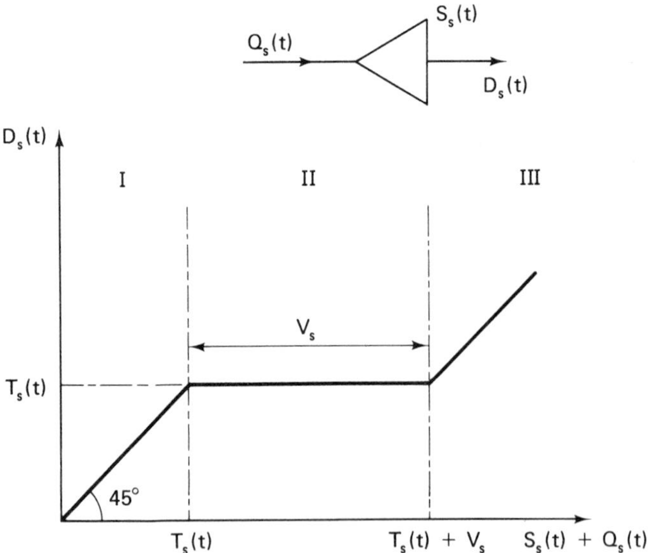

Figure 6-5
Standard reservoir operating rule.

These considerations lead to the following equations for $D_s(t)$:

$$D_s(t) = \begin{cases} S_s(t) + Q_s(t); & S_s(t) + Q_s(t) \leq T_s(t) \\ T_s(t); & T_s(t) < S_s(t) + Q_s(t) \leq T_s(t) + V_s \\ S_s(t) + Q_s(t) - V_s; & S_s(t) + Q_s(t) > T_s(t) + V_s \end{cases} \tag{6.4}$$

Storage, $S_s(t + 1)$, at the beginning of the following season can then be represented by

$$S_s(t + 1) = \begin{cases} 0; & S_s(t) + Q_s(t) \leq T_s(t) \\ S_s(t) + Q_s(t) - T_s(t); & T_s(t) < S_s(t) + Q_s(t) \leq T_s(t) + V_s \\ V_s; & S_s(t) + Q_s(t) > T_s(t) + V_s \end{cases} \tag{6.5}$$

This rule does not consider, for Case I, the possibility of hedging against future shortages. A further significant simplification is that it assumes that each reservoir will operate independently.

Within the standard operating rule, two alternatives are represented in the basic model. The first is to give priority to irrigation. In this case, the seasonal targets $T_s(t)$ are associated with seasonal irrigation needs; in the nongrowing seasons, there is no release for energy production unless the available water exceeds storage capacity. The second is to give priority to energy generation. In this case, the target releases $T_s(t)$ are calculated each month on the basis of a seasonal energy target (in MWh), given the initial storage and the characteristics of the power plant.

A second rule, called the "final storage rule," was also implemented as an alternative to the "standard" rule. This rule establishes that reservoir releases are determined in such a way that final storage at the end of a period is as close as possible to a predetermined target level. This rule reflects a desire to hedge against shortages caused by seasonal streamflow variations.

THE OBJECTIVE FUNCTION

As does the screening model, the simulation model contains an objective function whose general form is a weighted sum of net benefits. However, in production runs of the basic simulation model, only one objective was included explicitly—net discounted national income benefits. Regional aspects were included in operating policies and through choice of configuration changes when required. The explicit objective function was thus

$$Z = B - C$$

where C is the present value of the sum of the national income costs of all the projects in the basin, and B is the present value of the sum of the national income benefits of all the projects in the basin. Mathematically, the expression for the national income costs, C, is formally the same as that of the screening model [Eq. (5.38c)]. However, the expression for national income benefits, B, is different, because these benefits vary from year to year due to the effects of shortage. If we denote the following,

$BI_s(t)$ = gross benefits from irrigation at site s in year t
$BP_s(t)$ = gross benefits from energy generated at site s in year t
$BX_s(t)$ = gross export benefits at site s in year t

then the discounted gross benefits are estimated by

$$B = \frac{1}{f} \sum_s \left[\frac{1}{N} \sum_{t=1}^{N} BI_s(t) + BP_s(t) + BX_s(t) \right] \tag{6.6}$$

where N is the length of the simulation period, and f is the capital recovery factor corresponding to the appropriate discount rate and planning horizon.

REFERENCES

FIERING, MYRON B. *Streamflow Synthesis.* Cambridge, Mass.: Harvard University Press, 1967.

HUFSCHMIDT, MAYNARD M., and MYRON B FIERING. *Simulation Techniques for Design of Water Resource Systems.* Cambridge, Mass.: Harvard University Press, 1966.

LENTON, ROBERTO L., and KENNETH M. STRZEPEK. "Theoretical and Practical Characteristics of the MIT River Basin Simulation Model." Technical Report No. 225. Ralph M. Parsons Laboratory for Water Resources and Hydrodynamics, MIT, Cambridge, Mass., August 1977.

MAASS, ARTHUR, MAYNARD M. HUFSCHMIDT, ROBERT DORFMAN, HAROLD A. THOMAS, JR., STEPHEN A. MARGLIN, and GORDON MASKEW FAIR. *Design of Water-Resource Systems.* Cambridge, Mass.: Harvard University Press, 1962.

SCHAAKE, JOHN C., JR., ed. "Systematic Approach to Water Resources Plan Formulation." Technical Report No. 187. Ralph M. Parsons Laboratory for Water Resources and Hydrodynamics, MIT, Cambridge, Mass., July, 1974.

CHAPTER SEVEN

SIMULATION ANALYSES: THE DETAILED MODEL

JUAN VALDES
BRENDAN HARLEY
JOHN C. SCHAAKE, JR.

The evaluation of the overall performance of alternative development configurations for the Río Colorado by means of simulation analyses was carried out using the basic simulation model already described. The objective of this chapter is to describe the detailed simulation model, which was used for the important supporting tasks of parameter estimation, streamflow generation, and verification.

The nature and use of the detailed simulation model can be best described in overview by contrasting it with the basic model. The basic model operates in this way: Using the nodal structure already described, a set of projects is incorporated into the model in the appropriate nodes, and then a time series of streamflow is run through the system year by year (with three seasons per year). The benefits and costs in each successive year resulting from the particular configuration incorporated in the model are then recorded. The basic model is a unified model with relatively simple physical representations, the main task of which is to perform analyses of complete river basin alternatives in terms of their benefits and costs.

The detailed simulation model is organized in a different way. The detailed simulation model has three types of components or modules. The first are the modules representing the hydrologic cycle as it represents the Río Colorado: snowmelt runoff, channel routing, overland flow, infiltration and evapotranspiration, groundwater flow, and salt balance. Thus, unlike the basic model, the detailed model includes explicit representations of hydrologic processes. The second type of modules are those that represent the types of development projects in the Río Colorado: dams, irrigation areas, hydroelectric plants, and diversions, imports, and exports. The third type of module is that for generating synthetic streamflow series, providing what, for project purposes, was a superior alternative to the generation of flow from the snowmelt runoff model.

These different components are employed in simulation analyses in a different way than in the basic simulation model. In the basic model, streamflow series are run through the entire system year by year, whereas in the detailed model, the entire set of streamflows is run through the module that is furthest upstream; then, the executive program of the model calls the next module downstream, and the entire series of flow is run through that, and so on until the flow exits at the downstream end of the system. The analysis in each module can be performed in terms of very small time steps (hourly, daily, or weekly); the length of the time step used for each module can be varied depending on the degree of detail required for any particular aspect of the system. The flow of information between modules is accomplished by a series of file manipulation programs acting upon the data bank system that is built into the model (see Figure 7-1). The advantage of the sequential operation of the model is that particular parts of the river system and development schemes can be studied in detail. A disadvantage is that there is no way of incorporating directly into the model the effects of downstream operations on upstream operations, as can be done in the basic model—for example, in implementing shortage allocation rules.

This approach to the detailed simulation model reflects the original objective of the model (see Appendix A), which was to provide analyses of the configurations taken from the screening model—the role, in fact, that was ultimately played by the basic simulation model. The detailed model, however, proved to be too large and expensive to be used for routine simulation of entire configurations, and it came to be seen that the appropriate use of the detailed model was for parameter estimation for the other models (for example, the irrigation area return flow weights—see Chapters 5 and 10), for the generation of the augmented streamflow series used in the basic model, and for verification of components of the other models.

Reference should be made to the nature of the detailed simulation model in terms of previous models of a similar type. Although some of the modules were designed on the basis of new research, most of them were based on procedures that had been tested before. The most important contribution in developing this model was the linking of all these procedures into a total model capable of accessing all or some of the procedures for a given application. In these terms, the model is unusual, although one can mention the Stanford Watershed Model (Crawford and Linsley, 1966) and the MIT Catchment Model (Harley, Perkins, and Eagleson, 1970) as being the forerunners in the field of modeling the physical processes of a river basin.

The individual modules of the detailed simulation model are explained in the pages that follow. Figures 7-2 and 7-3 illustrate how the various modules

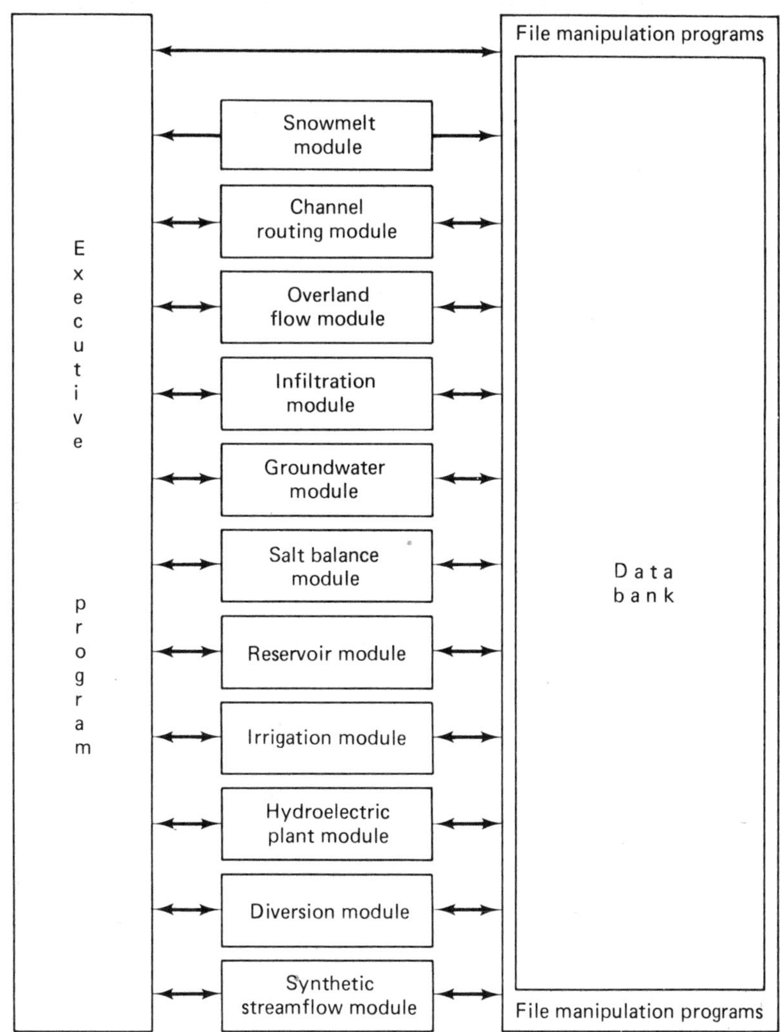

Figure 7-1
Flow of information in the detailed simulation model.

are linked. Figure 7-2 shows an example segment of the Río Colorado, and Figure 7-3 shows how the various modules of the detailed simulation model interact to simulate this particular segment of the river.

SIMULATION MODULES FOR HYDROLOGIC PROCESSES

A variety of simulation modules was developed, capable of simulating each of the different hydrologic processes relevant to the Río Colorado. The goal was to base each module on the dynamics of the physical systems rather than on a "black box" approach; thus each module incorporates the applicable governing differential equations, yielding procedures that simulate the dyna-

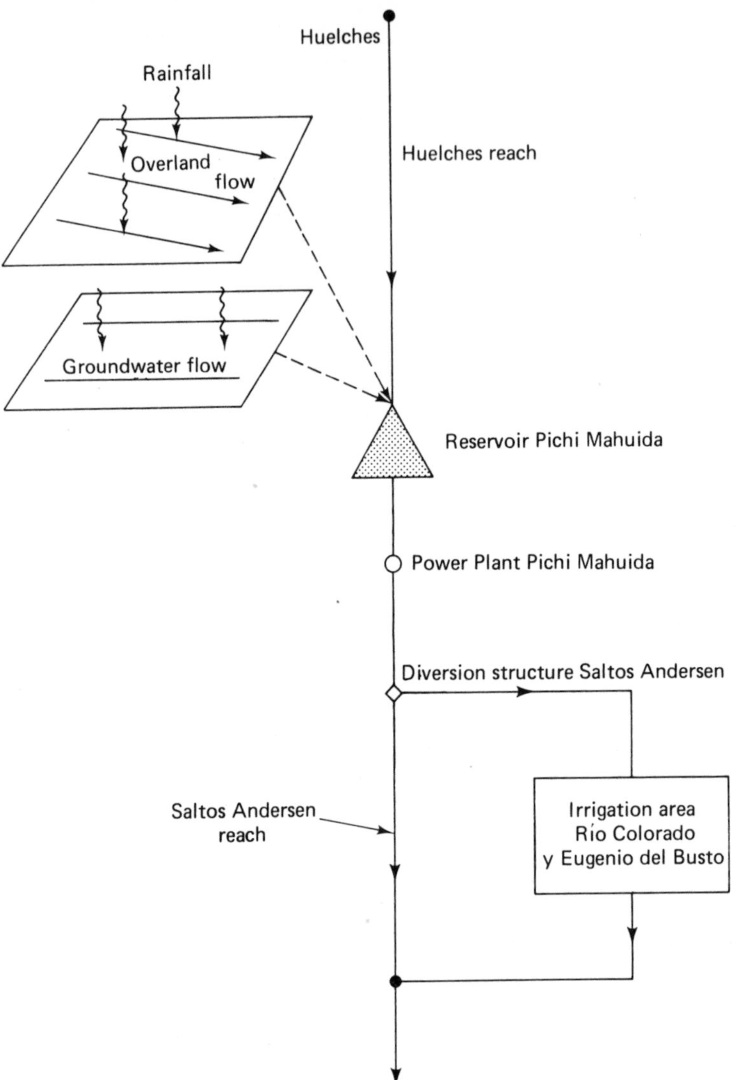

Figure 7-2
Segment of the Río Colorado as represented in the detailed simulation model.

mic behavior of the system. In some cases, the same hydrologic process was modeled at different levels of detail, allowing the user to apply the representation most suitable in any given situation.

SNOWMELT

The module for snowmelt (Laramie and Schaake, 1972) simulates the accumulation of snow and the process of melting as a function of air temperature, wind velocity, relative humidity, precipitation, and other meteorological data.

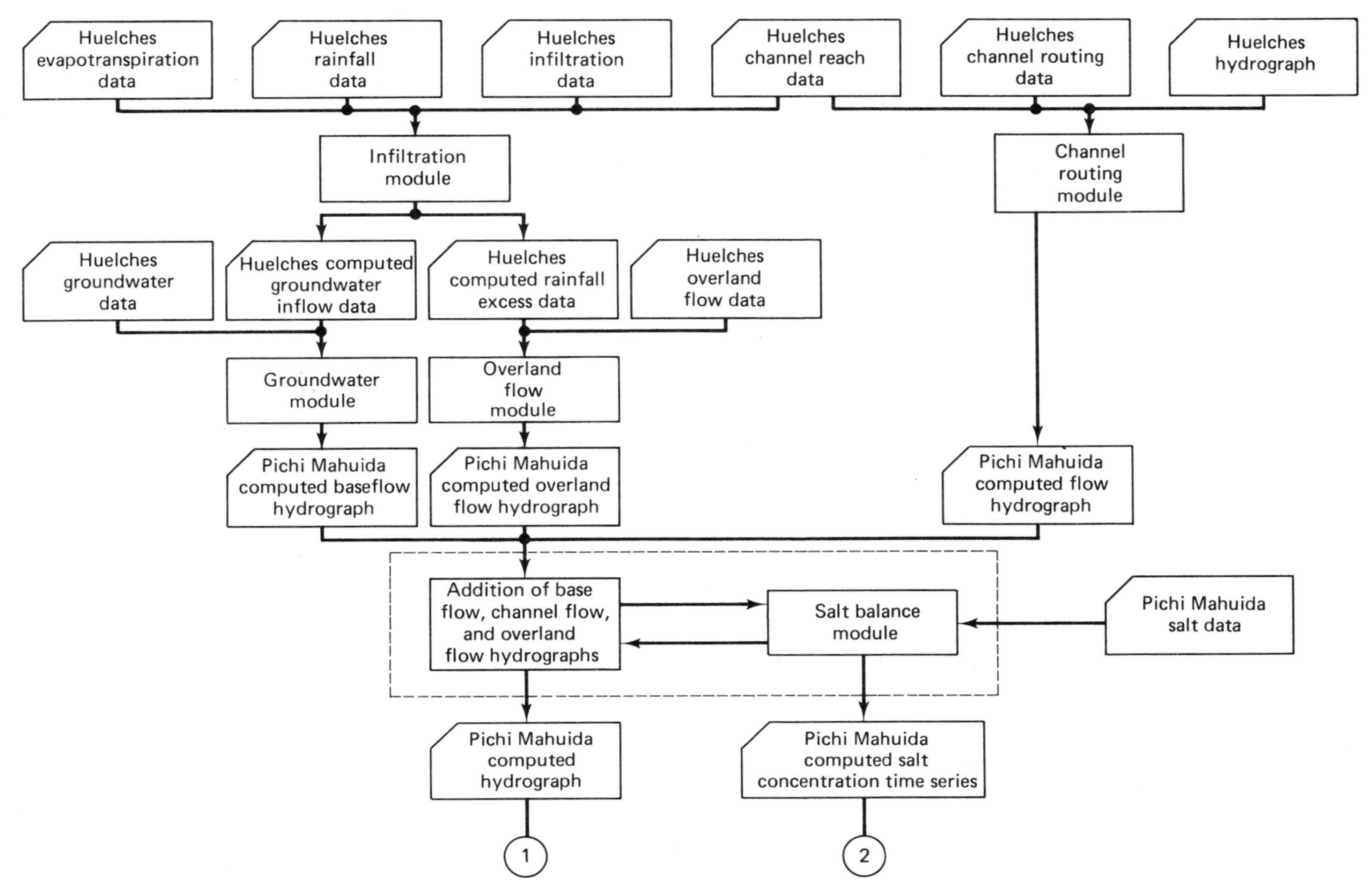

Figure 7-3
Illustration of detailed model use.

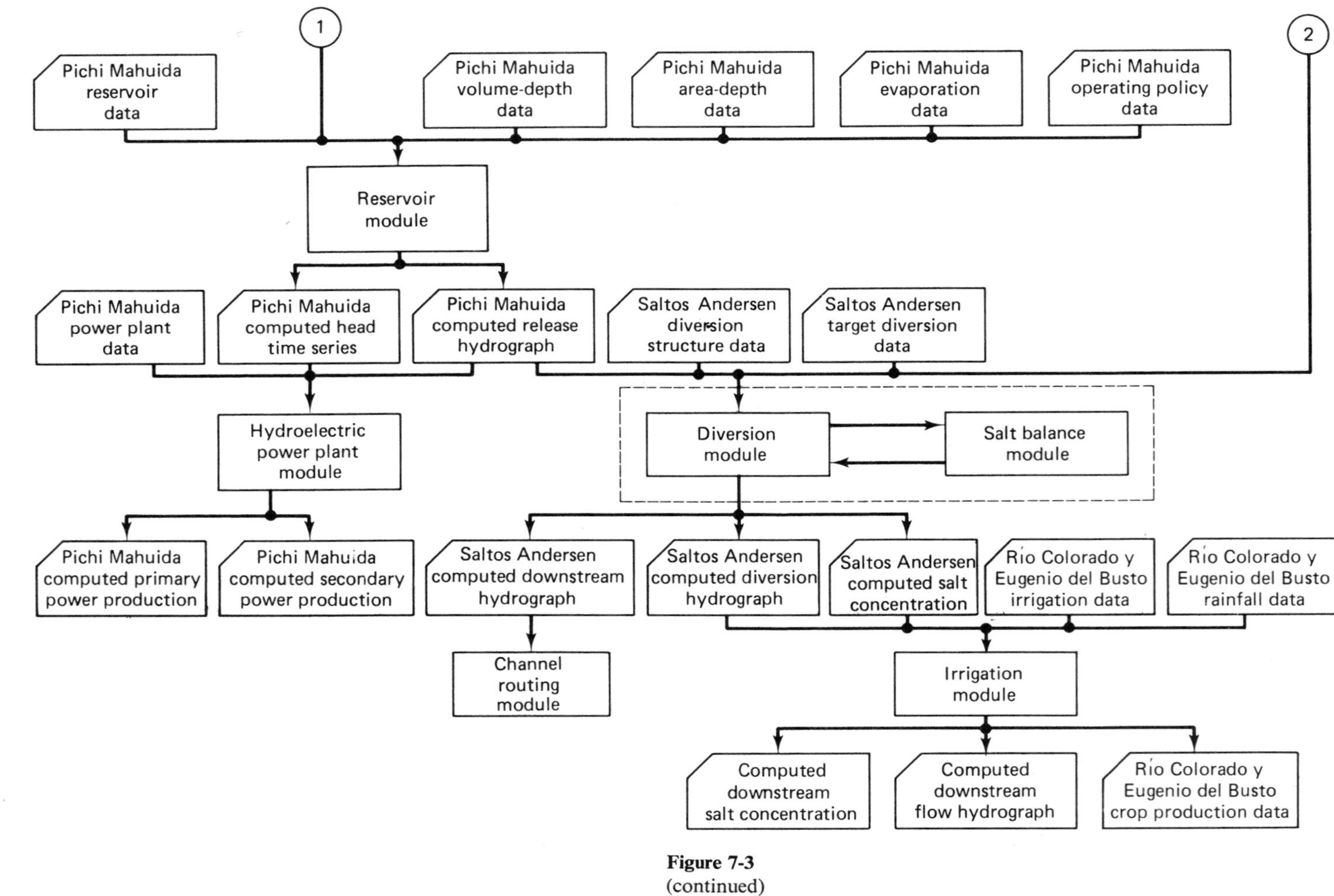

Figure 7-3
(continued)

The module contains two methods of simulating the snowmelt process, to be used depending on the type of data available. The first method is based on temperature, whereas the second is based on the energy balance. The energy balance method applies a detailed approximation of the energy interaction between the snowpack and its surroundings; the temperature method is utilized when there are not sufficient data to use the more exact energy balance method. In the temperature method, the temperature of the air is used as an index of heat transfer.

CHANNEL ROUTING

The objective of this module is to simulate the flow of water through a channel segment. In the Río Colorado, its use was envisioned for analyses at small time steps (hours or days), in particular for flood analyses. Given the upstream input hydrograph, the lateral inflow, and the physical characteristics of the segment, it calculates the output hydrograph at the downstream boundary, taking into account both flood propagation and attenuation effects, and the losses in the segment.

The module provides two different methods for simulating this process, both of which have been widely used. The first is the Muskingum method (McCarthy, 1939), which has in previous applications given satisfactory results, especially in the case of rivers with moderate slopes and without significant lateral inflows (such as is the case for the Río Colorado). This method relates linearly the output hydrograph with the input hydrograph and the segment storage.

The second method of flood routing in the module is the kinematic wave method (Lighthill and Whitham, 1955), which should be used for segments that have important lateral inflow and pronounced slope.

OVERLAND FLOW

Overland flow is the process by which surface runoff from rainfall flows over the ground into rivers or streams. The overland flow module uses the second method of flood routing contained in the channel routing module (see previous section).

INFILTRATION AND EVAPOTRANSPIRATION

The purpose of this module is to simulate the infiltration and evapotranspiration processes. It is most usefully employed in association with the module for simulating irrigation areas (described later), although it was also used in the Río Colorado study for estimating reservoir evaporation (see Chapter 10). It contains two approaches: The first uses the *streamflow synthesis and reservoir regulation* (SSARR) method developed by the U.S. Army Corps of Engineers (Tanovan, 1967). This utilizes empirical relationships between precipitation and surface runoff and infiltration based on parameters of which the most important are indices of soil humidity and infiltration capacity. The second method uses equations that describe the dynamics of physical phenomena. In this case, the losses by evapotranspiration are modeled by physically based equations, either the Penman modified equation (Penman, 1948), the Blaney and Criddle (1950) equation, or the Kohler equation (Kohler, Nordenson, and Fox, 1955), whereas the infiltration process is simulated by means of the equation of diffusion (Eagleson, 1971, pp. 280–282).

GROUNDWATER

This module simulates the behavior of water flow in a groundwater system. It was designed for use in the Río Colorado primarily in conjunction with the irrigation module, which is described later. The behavior of the water flow is described by two separate submodules. The first focuses on basin-wide applications, emphasizing the entire groundwater aquifer; the second considers shallow zone systems (e.g., the drainage system of an irrigation area).

The basis of the basin-wide module is the continuity equation for one-dimensional flow in conjunction with a modified form of Darcy's law on the flow of water through porous media. This model is used to calibrate a simple linear model which is then used to obtain results.

For shallow zone systems, a finite difference representation of the groundwater level was derived using Darcy's law in conjunction with the continuity equations, whose solution required the division of the aquifer into a series of cells. The resulting expression permits the determination of the groundwater elevation in a given cell at a given time as a function of the groundwater elevation in the previous time step, the groundwater elevation in adjacent cells, the flow into the cell, and the physical characteristics of the aquifer.

SALT BALANCE

Intensive use of irrigation in a river basin in many cases may modify the water quality of the river, principally with respect to the concentration of salts. The purpose of the salt balance module is to take this factor into account. The module is based on an accounting of the total volume of salts in the river using simple mass balance equations.

The initial volume of salts for each time period at a given point in the river is calculated as a function of recorded observations of salt concentration and flow. The salt volume at a downstream point, given the salt volume at an upstream point, is calculated by including in the mass balance equation the salt contributions of intermediate tributaries and irrigation return flows.

RESERVOIRS

In simulating the operation of a reservoir, the function of the model is to determine the release from the reservoir as specified by the operating policy. The policy assumed here was the standard operating policy (Chapter 6). However, the detailed model simulates this policy more realistically than the basic model by taking into account the capacity of the outfalls (which can be located at different depths) and the characteristics of the spillway. This last factor enables it to simulate discharge over the spillway in times of flood and, thus, to analyze the effect of alternative spillway designs on the downstream flood wave.

IRRIGATION AREAS

Both the screening model and the basic simulation model utilize substantial simplifications to model irrigation systems. The purpose of the irrigation module in the detailed model is to represent the irrigation processes at a greater level of detail than was possible in the other models. One of its primary roles is to verify and calibrate the simplifying assumptions incorporated in the other models. This module is described in detail by Elinger and Schaake (1972) and is represented in Figure 7-4.

The irrigation module is of considerable size and complexity. It consists of four principal components, which can be run separately or together: water balance, salt balance, crop production, and water allocation. These are run for the cells, representing irrigation plots, into which each irrigation area can be divided for the purposes of detailed simulation.

The water balance component first routes the flow of water from the diversion structure to the irrigation cells, and then, taking into account evapotranspiration, groundwater losses to adjacent cells, and the drainage process, calculates the movement of water from each cell.

The salt balance component follows a similar approach, based on a mass balance of dissolved solids. The crop production component relates the growth of crops to soil moisture, salt concentration, and other physical parameters. In the water allocation component, the water is allocated among cells of homogeneous characteristics in such a way that short-term losses are minimized within each growing season; this is achieved by means of a set of decision rules that takes into account the condition of crops and the condition of the plot in which they are grown.

The irrigation module was always used in conjunction with the groundwater module described earlier to account for return flows and their corre-

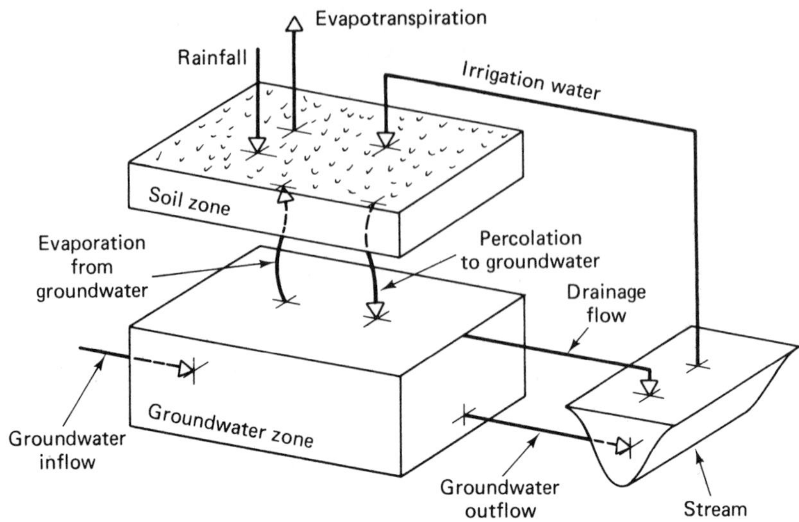

Figure 7-4
Representation of a typical irrigation cell in the detailed simulation model.

sponding salinity at the point of return to the river. The irrigation module routes water through the canal network, soil, drainage network, and groundwater zone back to the river and also accounts for the changes in water quality due to the concentration of salts. The irrigation module also had to be associated with a diversion module, which will be discussed below.

The irrigation module was also designed for use, if required by the characteristics of the basin, in association with the infiltration/evapotranspiration module described earlier.

HYDROELECTRIC PLANTS

The generation of hydroelectric energy is a relatively straightforward technical process that can be modeled simply for planning purposes. Thus, the power plant module in the detailed simulation model is the same as the set of corresponding equations in the basic model, except that smaller time steps are permitted.

DIVERSIONS, IMPORTS, AND EXPORTS

Exports of water from and imports of water to the basin and diversion of water within the basin are modeled with the use of the diversion module. When diversions within the basin are studied this module is used in conjunction with the irrigation and/or power modules.

The module operates with externally specified targets for exports of water from the basin. In the case of imports of water to the basin the import is specified and the module simply adds this flow to the existing flow in the basin. When diversions within the basin are considered, targets are external to the module for diversions to hydroelectric power plants; for diversions to irrigation areas the targets are computed internally based on the water requirements for irrigation.

As mentioned previously, the basic model computed diversion releases on the basis of the continuity equation. The detailed model operates in essentially the same way except in the case of fixed-outlet diversions that are not controlled by a dam or diversion structure. In these cases the module takes into account the dependence of the diversion flow on the flow in the river at the time of diversion. This is important for the Río Colorado, where some diversions are of the fixed-outlet type.

In the basic model, diversion releases in each time step can be modified on the basis of current downstream demands, and this capability can be utilized for such purposes as implementing the shortage allocation rule discussed in Chapter 6. Because of the modular structure of the detailed model, diversion releases cannot be modified on the basis of current downstream demands. However, the diversion module does provide for constraining diversion releases according to prespecified downstream low flow targets. The module also provides for the computation of salt concentrations in diverted flows.

SIMULATION MODULE FOR HYDROLOGIC DATA

As mentioned in the previous chapter, the basic model was designed for use with a homogeneous set of time series of streamflow data. The use of synthesized streamflow for system design studies has been widely accepted since the first applications by Maass et al. (1962), Hufschmidt and Fiering (1966), and Fiering (1967). The capability for synthesizing streamflow for both simulation models was incorporated as a module in the detailed simulation model.

The module for synthetic data generation involved a major departure from traditional modes of streamflow synthesis. Previously, daily, monthly, or seasonal data were generated sequentially. However, the method used in the detailed model was to generate annual data in a sequential manner first and then to disaggregate to obtain seasonal, monthly, or daily values.

The disaggregation scheme, described in Appendix 7A, maintains relevant statistics at all levels of aggregation owing to the fact that the model preserves all linear relationships between variables at successive levels of aggregation. When sequences corresponding to a certain level of aggregation are generated with autoregressive models, relevant statistics of higher levels of aggregation are not necessarily preserved.

The module incorporated into the detailed model contains a routine with two alternative methods for annual generation: The first uses the multivariate, autoregressive Matalas (1967) model, and the second uses the broken-line model developed by Mejía, Rodríguez-Iturbe, and Dawdy (1972). The module also contains three routines for disaggregation to be used sequentially when needed: In a first step annual values are disaggregated into seasonal values; then monthly values are obtained from seasonal values; and finally monthly values are disaggregated into daily values. These are complemented by routines for parameter estimation based on the historical data and by routines for data augmentation of short records, based on longer records within the same basin.

REFERENCES

Blaney, H. F., and W. D. Criddle. "Determining Water Requirements in Irrigated Areas from Climatological and Irrigation Data." Technical Paper 96. United States Department of Agricultural and Soil Conservation Service, Washington, D.C., 1950.

Crawford, H. H., and Ray K. Linsley. "Digital Simulation in Hydrology: Stanford Watershed Model IV." Technical Report 39. Department of Civil Engineering, Stanford University, Stanford, Calif., 1966.

Eagleson, Peter S. *Dynamic Hydrology*. New York: McGraw-Hill, 1970.

Elinger, Marcos M., and John C. Schaake, Jr. "Physical and Economic Simulation of an Irrigation System." Presented at the 53rd Annual Meeting of the American Geophysical Union, Washington, D.C., April 1972.

Fiering, Myron B. *Streamflow Synthesis*. Cambridge, Mass.: Harvard University Press, 1967.

Harley, Brendan M., Frank E. Perkins, and Peter S. Eagleson. "A Modular Distributed Model of Catchment Dynamics." Technical Report No. 133. Ralph M. Parsons Laboratory for Water Resources and Hydrodynamics, MIT, Cambridge, Mass., December 1970.

Hufschmidt, Maynard M., and Myron B Fiering. *Simulation Techniques for Water Resource Systems*. Cambridge, Mass.: Harvard University Press, 1966.

Kohler, M. A., T. J. Nordenson, and W. E. Fox. "Evaporation from Pans and Lakes." Technical Paper 38. United States Department of Commerce Weather Bureau, Washington, D.C., 1955.

Laramie, Richard L., and John C. Schaake, Jr. "Simulation of the Continuous Snowmelt Process." Technical Report No. 143. Ralph M. Parsons Laboratory for Water Resources and Hydrodynamics, MIT, Cambridge, Mass., January 1972.

Lighthill, M. J., and G. B. Whitham. "On Kinematic Waves. 1—Flood Movement in Long Rivers." *Proc. Roy. Soc.* (*London*), Ser. A, **229**, May 1955, pp. 281–316.

MAASS, ARTHUR, MAYNARD M. HUFSCHMIDT, ROBERT DORFMAN, HAROLD A. THOMAS JR., STEPHEN A. MARGLIN, and GORDON MASKEW FAIR. *Design of Water-Resource Systems.* Cambridge, Mass.: Harvard University Press, 1962.

MCCARTHY, G. T. "The Unit Hydrograph and Flood Routing." United States Army Corps of Engineers, Providence, R.I., 1939.

MATALAS, N. C. "Mathematical Assessment of Synthetic Hydrology." *Water Resources Research,* **3** (*4*), 1967, pp. 937–946.

MEJIA, JOSE M., I. RODRIGUEZ-ITURBE, and D. R. DAWDY. "Stream-flow Simulation, 2, The Broken Line Process as a Potential for Hydrologic Simulation." *Water Resources Research,* **8** (*4*), 1972, pp. 931–941.

PENMAN, H. L. "Natural Evaporation from Open Water, Base Soil and Grass." *Proc. Roy. Soc.* (*London*), Ser. A, **193**, 1948, pp. 120–145.

TANOVAN, B. "Notes on Generalized Basin Runoff Characteristics in the SSARR Program for IBM 360." United States Army Corps of Engineers, Mekong Committee, Portland, Ore., 1967.

VALENCIA, DARIO, and JOHN C. SCHAAKE, JR. "Disaggregation Processes in Stochastic Hydrology." *Water Resources Research,* **9** (*3*), 1973, pp. 580–585.

APPENDIX 7A THE DISAGGREGATION MODEL[1]

DARIO VALENCIA
JOHN C. SCHAAKE, JR.

THE MODEL

The disaggregation model takes the simple mathematical form

$$\mathbf{Y} = \mathbf{AX} + \mathbf{W} \tag{7A.1}$$

where **Y** is an $(n \times 1)$ vector of correlated random variables, **X** is an $(m \times 1)$ vector of correlated random variables, **A** is an $(n \times m)$ coefficient matrix, and **W** is an $(n \times 1)$ vector of correlated random variables and is independent of **X**. It is assumed that all random variables have been transformed to have zero mean. Although it may be helpful to assume that the appropriate data transformations have been made to render the data Gaussian, it is not always necessary. It can be shown that the model preserves first- and second-order moment properties regardless of the types of underlying probability distributions.

An important application of this model is to generate series of seasonal streamflow volumes from a given series of annual streamflow volumes. In this case, the vector **X** is a vector of annual streamflow volumes at m different sites

[1]This appendix has been taken from Valencia and Schaake (1973).

$$\mathbf{X} = \begin{bmatrix} x_1 \\ \cdot \\ \cdot \\ \cdot \\ x_m \end{bmatrix}$$

The vector **Y** is a vector of seasonal volumes—that is, an $n \times 1$ vector, where $n = 3m$ assuming three 4-month seasons in a year.

$$\mathbf{Y} = \begin{bmatrix} y_{11} = y_1 \\ y_{12} = y_2 \\ y_{13} = y_3 \\ y_{21} = y_4 \\ y_{22} = y_5 \\ y_{23} = y_6 \\ \cdot \quad \cdot \\ \cdot \quad \cdot \\ \cdot \quad \cdot \\ y_{m3} \quad y_n \end{bmatrix}$$

The element y_{ij} denotes the streamflow volume at site i during season j. The seasonal runoff volumes at the m sites for a year are represented by the y_{ij} in a **Y** vector.

Certain subsets of the y_{ij} bear a simple relation to the x_i. Specifically,

$$x_i = \sum_{j=1}^{3} y_{ij} \tag{7A.2}$$

or, in general,

$$\mathbf{X} = \mathbf{CY} \tag{7A.3}$$

where

$$\mathbf{C} = \begin{bmatrix} 111 & 000 & \cdots & 000 \\ 000 & 111 & \cdots & 000 \\ \cdots & \cdots & \cdots & \cdots \\ 000 & 000 & \cdots & 111 \end{bmatrix}$$

DISAGGREGATION OF ANNUAL STREAMFLOW DATA

The strategy for using the model is first to generate values of **X** for a number of years by using a fractional noise model or an autoregressive model. Then, given the generated value of **X** for a particular year, the proposed model is used to generate **Y**.

Because historically the relation between $\mathbf{X}$ and $\mathbf{Y}$ given by Eq. (7A.3) is always maintained, it is important that this relation be maintained in the generated data. In other words, the sum of the three generated seasonal volumes at any site should be exactly equal to the given annual volume. It is shown in Valencia and Schaake (1973) that this important relationship is maintained. This central property of the model guarantees that the disaggregation preserves all the statistics considered in the annual generation.

In the case of annual disaggregation, the value of each seasonal runoff volume at a particular site is computed as the sum of terms depending on the annual runoff volumes at the different sites plus a random component. The random components may be generated by the relation

$$\mathbf{W} = \mathbf{B}\mathbf{V} \tag{7A.4}$$

where $\mathbf{V}$ is a vector of n independently distributed standard normal deviates and $\mathbf{B}$ is a coefficient matrix selected to preserve the proper covariance structure of $\mathbf{W}$. In a second step, the disaggregation model could be used to disaggregate seasonal values into monthly values.

PARAMETER ESTIMATION

The parameter estimation problem is to use historical data to estimate numerical values of $\mathbf{A}$ and $\mathbf{B}$ so that the generated values of $\mathbf{Y}$ resemble the historical values of $\mathbf{Y}$ according to an appropriate resemblance criterion. A widely used criterion is that expected means, variances, and covariances of the generated data are equal to the historical means, variances, and covariances. Expressions for the generated means, variances, and covariances in terms of the parameters $\mathbf{A}$ and $\mathbf{B}$ are derived in Valencia and Schaake (1973), resulting in a pair of equations for the matrix estimators $\hat{\mathbf{A}}$ and $\hat{\mathbf{B}}$.

EXTENSION OF THE MODEL

Equation (7A.1) can be seen in a broader perspective as representing a whole class of models. The disaggregation model already discussed is a member of this class; other models proposed in the field of stochastic hydrology, such as the Matalas (1967) model or, in general, multivariate autoregressive models of any order, are also included in the class. The question in each case is to define in a proper way the meanings of $\mathbf{X}$ and $\mathbf{Y}$; the model is applicable when the relevant statistics to be reproduced in the generation are those related to means, variances, and covariances.

As a result of this generalization, all the properties exhibited by the disaggregation model, such as those related to estimation and existence of parameters and to preservation of linear transformations [see Valencia and Schaake (1973)], are also valid for the other models of the class.

An illustration of the flexibility of the general model is presented in Appendix 10A, where Eq. (7A.1) is used to augment hydrologic data.

REFERENCES

Matalas, N. C. "Mathematical Assessment of Synthetic Hydrology." *Water Resources Research*, **3** (*4*), 1967, pp. 937–946.

Valencia, Dario, and John C. Schaake, Jr. "Disaggregation Processes in Stochastic Hydrology." *Water Resources Research*, **9** (*3*), 1973, pp. 580–585.

CHAPTER EIGHT THE MATHEMATICAL PROGRAMMING SEQUENCING MODEL

TOMAS FACET
JARED COHON
DAVID MARKS

The purpose of this chapter is to describe the model used to sequence alternative development plans for the Río Colorado.

The planning methodology that we used for the river begins with the application of the screening model and continues with the use of the basic simulation model. The result of applying these two models is a set of projects, or basin configurations, of determined sizes and locations. In the sequencing model, (the third and last of the three models used to generate alternative plans for the river), such a set of projects is scheduled optimally in four future time periods. Thus, the question addressed with the sequencing model is not what projects to build, or what sizes these projects should be, but, rather, during which time periods they should be constructed.

The model takes into account in the scheduling decision benefits over time, budget constraints, constraints on the number of farmers available to work new irrigation areas, and project interrelationships such as the necessity to ensure that an irrigation area is not built before the construction of a dam to supply it. Just as the simulation model permitted us to relax the assumption of steady-state hydrology in the screening model, so the sequencing model allows us to relax the assumption in both the screening and the simulation models that all projects would be constructed at once, and at the beginning of the period of analysis.

In this chapter, we first provide a description of the general characteristics of the sequencing model, and then we discuss the particular aspects of the model: continuity constraints; the representation of irrigation and power projects; conditionality constraints; budget and population constraints; and the objective function. [Theoretical discussions of scheduling can be found in Maass et al. (1962); Marglin (1963), (1967); and Major (1977). An alternative approach to scheduling that was examined in the project is described in Appendix A. Another approach to sequencing and scheduling is that of Manne (1967). Goreux and Manne (1973) describe applications of programming models to planning over time for energy and agriculture.]

GENERAL CHARACTERISTICS OF THE SEQUENCING MODEL

The way in which the sequencing model is formulated is a direct reflection of the nature of the problem that it is designed to examine. It is a mixed-integer programming model (see Chapter 3), as is the screening model. In such models, some of the decision variables are "continuous" variables that can take on any real value in the solution within given constraints. For example, in the screening model, the size of an irrigation area can be any value between zero and some upper limit on hectares. Other variables are "integer" (0–1) variables. These can take a value of either 0 or 1, but no other value; such variables represent decisions in the sequencing model such as the construction (or not) of a project whose size has already been determined (an either/or decision). The formulation of the sequencing model differs from that of the screening model in that whereas most of the variables in the latter are continuous variables—irrigation areas, power plant sizes, dam heights—all of the variables in the sequencing model are integer variables except for the flow variable representing flow downstream of a site. The reason why the variables in the sequencing model are integer variables, except for flow, is that they all represent projects whose sizes are already determined, and for which the only remaining decisions, in the methodology used here, are whether to construct a particular project within a given time period. Such decisions are appropriately represented by integer variables.

The formulation of the sequencing model differs from that of the screening model in another way that reflects its function of dealing with projects already sized and selected. In the screening model, all of the projects in the system were potential projects in every run, even though, of course, many projects were not selected in each run. That is, the screening model looked at the entire schematic shown in Chapter 4 (Figure 4-1) in every run. The sequencing model, on the other hand, considers the construction (or not) of a fixed set of projects of determined sizes. It looks not at the entire schematic but, rather, at a schematic containing the fixed set of projects. Thus, the formulation of the model for each run is problem-specific.

The sequencing model as it was used for the Río Colorado assumed that projects would be constructed during four time periods, each of equal length (10 years). Each project was assumed to have a life of 40 years from the time of construction. The selection of the initial time period in particular seemed reasonable given the planning horizons and implementation capabilities of the authorities in the basin. Alternative sets of time periods might be suitable for other planning problems. For example, a short run of 5 years might constitute the first period; then an intermediate planning period of years 6-15 might constitute the second period; and a long run of years 16-40 might constitute the third and last period. And, of course, the total number of years in the construction periods can differ from 40 if desired.

A difference between the screening model and the sequencing model relating to hydrology is that, in the sequencing model, the flow equations within each planning period are not written for average seasonal flows as in the screening model but, rather, are written for "critical" season flows. There are two reasons for this. First, because the sizes of projects studied in the sequencing model are fixed, there is no need to consider seasonal streamflow variations for purposes of project sizing (as was required in the screening model). Second, the nature of the sequencing model makes it difficult to write continuity constraints as between planning periods if seasonal average flows are utilized. This problem does not arise in the screening model, because every year is assumed to be the same over the entire time horizon. With the sequencing model, each year is the same only within each planning period; flows change between time periods because of the construction of projects.

In the sections to follow, particular aspects of the model are described. A formulation of the model for a simple hypothetical basin configuration of projects is given in Appendix 8A. A list of symbols used in the formulation of the sequencing model is given in Appendix 8B. In reading the sections to follow it will be helpful to note that in the sequencing model parameters are written with bars over the letters. Some of the parameters in each run of the sequencing model, such as project sizes, were, of course, decision variables in the screening model.

CONTINUITY CONSTRAINTS

Continuity constraints in the sequencing model maintain the links in space and over time between water uses for the proposed projects. These constraints ensure that when a project is built, the water it will use will be available during the critical season of every year from construction onward. On the other hand, in the periods preceding that in which a project is built, the water will be available for any other use. That is to say, the continuity constraints in the sequencing model are an accounting system for water use in the river basin.

A typical reservoir site is shown in Figure 8-1. The continuity constraint for this site is slightly different from the constraint that would have been formulated for the same site in the screening model: The inclusion of reservoir yield replaces explicit consideration of storage volume. For the first period, $i = 1$, the continuity constraint is

$$D_{s,1} = \bar{Q}_s + \bar{Y}_s R_{s,1} - \bar{E}_s I_{s,1} + \bar{I}_s M_{s,1} \qquad \forall_s \tag{8.1}$$

which says that the release out of the reservoir in the critical period ($D_{s,1}$) is equal to the flow coming into the reservoir in the critical season ($\bar{Q}_s$), plus the yield from the reservoir if it is built in Period 1 ($\bar{Y}_s$) plus the import into the reservoir ($\bar{I}_s$) if the import is built in Period 1, minus the diversion to the irrigation site ($\bar{E}_s$) if it is built in Period 1. The symbols $R_{s,1}$, $I_{s.1}$, and $M_{s,1}$ are integer decision variables and take values of either one (if the reservoir, irrigation area, or import at site s is built in Period 1) or zero (if it is not).

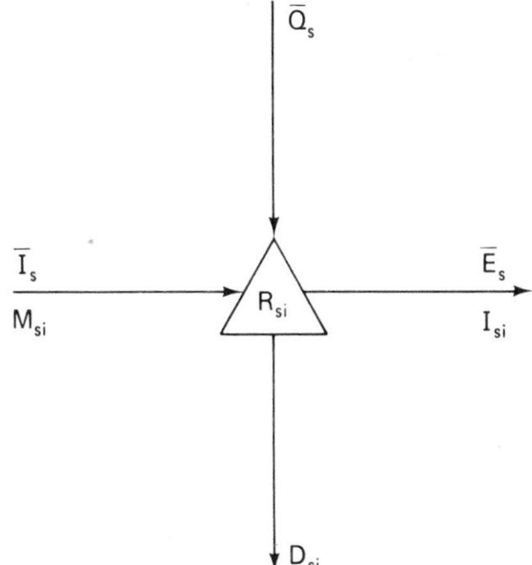

Figure 8-1
A typical reservoir site.

Using Eq. (8.1), one can see how the continuity constraint takes into account decisions such as building the reservoir and irrigation site during the first period (which implies that $R_{s,1} = 1$ and $I_{s,1} = 1$) and not building the import (which implies $M_{s,1} = 0$). In this case, the release in the first period, $D_{s,1}$, is given by

$$D_{s,1} = \bar{Q}_s + \bar{Y}_s - \bar{E}_s \qquad \forall_s \tag{8.2}$$

In order to extend the effect of the continuity constraint to all periods, another type of constraint must be introduced. It is termed a *construction constraint* and is a consequence of the use of a 0–1 variable for each period in the planning horizon. That variable takes only the value one or zero to represent the construction (or not) of a project during each period. To guarantee that each project will be constructed at most once, a constraint is added of the form

$$\sum_i \text{PROJECT}_{si}^k \leq 1 \qquad \forall_{sk} \tag{8.3}$$

where PROJECT refers to the integer decision variable corresponding to a particular project at site s, k to the project type, and i to the time period. (The superscript k is required because projects of different types can be built at the same site s.)

In the case of a reservoir, Eq. (8.3) becomes:

$$\sum_i R_{si} \leq 1 \qquad \forall_s \tag{8.4}$$

where s refers to the site number.

The construction constraint says that a project can be built at most once. Only one term at most can be different from zero (equal to one) in that sum. With this constraint it is possible to extend the continuity constraint to more than one period and, therefore, to incorporate the effect of a decision made in any one period into the remaining periods (i.e., a project that exists in Period 1 also exists in subsequent periods). Extending Eq. (8.1) to many periods gives

$$D_{si} = \bar{Q}_s + \sum_{j=1}^{i} \bar{I}_s M_{sj} + \sum_{j=1}^{i} \bar{Y}_s R_{sj} - \sum_{j=1}^{i} \bar{E}_s I_{sj} \qquad \forall_{si} \tag{8.5}$$

In Eq. (8.5) there is a sum of terms for each type of project at each site; at most one term in each sum can be different from zero. Once a decision variable takes a value of one, the effect of that construction on the continuity of the system ($\bar{I}_s$, $\bar{Y}_s$, or $\bar{E}_s$) will be taken into account for the rest of the planning horizon.

A further important consideration is the representation of continuity in space. Site s in Figure 8-2 is the same site shown in Figure 8-1. The site immediately upstream of site s, $s - 1$, is also included in Figure 8-2. As previously discussed in Chapter 5, $\bar{Q}_s$ in Eq. (8.5) is affected by upstream development as well as natural changes in streamflow. By continuity,

$$\bar{Q}_s = \Delta\bar{F}_s + D_{s-1,i} \qquad \forall_{si} \tag{8.6}$$

where $\Delta\bar{F}_s$ represents the difference between streamflow at sites s and $s - 1$ in the critical season; that is,

$$\Delta\bar{F}_s = \bar{F}_s - \bar{F}_{s-1} \qquad \forall_s \tag{8.7}$$

Substituting Eqs. (8.6) and (8.7) into Eq. (8.5) gives

$$D_{si} - D_{s-1,i} - \sum_{j=1}^{i} \bar{I}_s M_{sj} - \sum_{j=1}^{i} \bar{Y}_s R_{sj} + \sum_{j=1}^{i} \bar{E}_s \bar{I}_{sj}$$
$$= \bar{F}_s - \bar{F}_{s-1} \qquad \forall_{si} \tag{8.8}$$

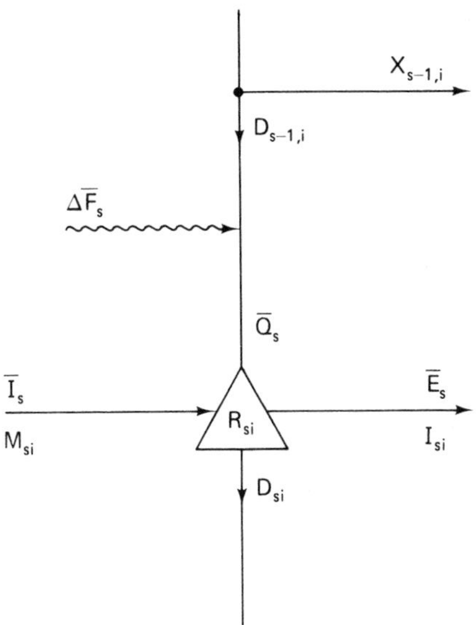

Figure 8-2
The effect of an upstream site on the inflow to a reservoir.

Equation (8.8) thus links flow at site s with flow at the upstream site $s - 1$.

An additional factor that must be considered in the continuity equation between sites is that during the filling of a dam, flow is required to accumulate storage. The parameter $\bar{c}_s$ represents that part of the critical flow to be used during the construction period to ensure a full dam at the beginning of the next period, during and after which yield from the reservoir can be made available. These considerations can be included in Eq. (8.8) to give

$$D_{si} - D_{s-1,i} - \sum_{j=1}^{i} \bar{I}_s M_{sj} - \sum_{j=1}^{i-1} \bar{Y}_s R_{sj} + \bar{c}_s R_{si} + \sum_{j=1}^{i} \bar{E}_s I_{sj} = \bar{F}_s - \bar{F}_{s-1} \qquad \forall_{s,i} \tag{8.9}$$

Note that the summation over j for the reservoir yield term is from 1 to $i - 1$, which represents the requirement that the dam be built in a previous period to obtain yield from it in the present period.

Equation (8.9) is the complete form of the continuity equation. The precise form of Eq. (8.9) varies from site to site, depending on the types of possible alternatives at the site.

IRRIGATION

The irrigation process is important in the sequencing model in terms of volumes of water diverted from the stream and the corresponding return flows.

The continuity constraint at site s is

$$D_{si} - D_{s-1,i} + \sum_{j=1}^{i} \bar{E}_s I_{sj} = \bar{F}_s - \bar{F}_{s-1} \qquad \forall_{si} \tag{8.10}$$

The continuity constraint at site $s + 1$, to which the irrigation return flow goes, is

$$D_{s+1,i} - D_{si} - \sum_{j=1}^{i} (1 - \bar{u}_s)\bar{E}_s I_{sj} = \bar{F}_{s+1} - \bar{F}_s \qquad \forall_{si} \tag{8.11}$$

where $\bar{u}_s$ is the irrigation coefficient defined in Chapter 5, the percentage of diverted water that is consumptively used and does not return to the stream. Figure 8-3 shows the representation of an irrigation area in the sequencing model.

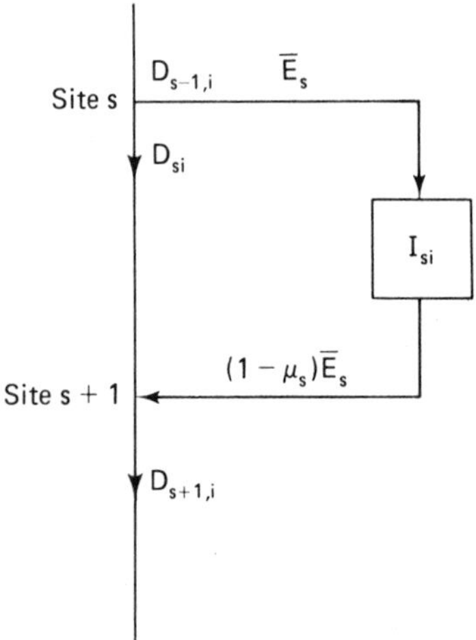

Figure 8-3
Representation of an irrigation site in the sequencing model.

HYDROELECTRIC ENERGY

The technical process of hydroelectric energy production need not be represented explicitly in the sequencing model because plant capacities and energy targets are previously set by the screening and simulation models. However, we do need to consider the required flow through turbines. The representation of energy production in the sequencing model differs depending on whether the power plants are fixed-head or variable-head plants. The representation of a site with a fixed-head power plant is shown in Figure 8-4. A new variable and a new parameter are defined:

- P_{si}: Integer variable indicating the construction (or not) of a fixed-head power plant (of a given capacity) at site s in period i.
- $\overline{DD}_s$: Required flow through the turbines to produce a prespecified amount of energy in the critical season.

The continuity constraint for this site is, thus,

$$D_{si} - D_{s-1,i} + \sum_{j=1}^{i} \overline{DD}_s P_{sj} = \bar{F}_s - \bar{F}_{s-1} \qquad \forall_{si} \tag{8.12}$$

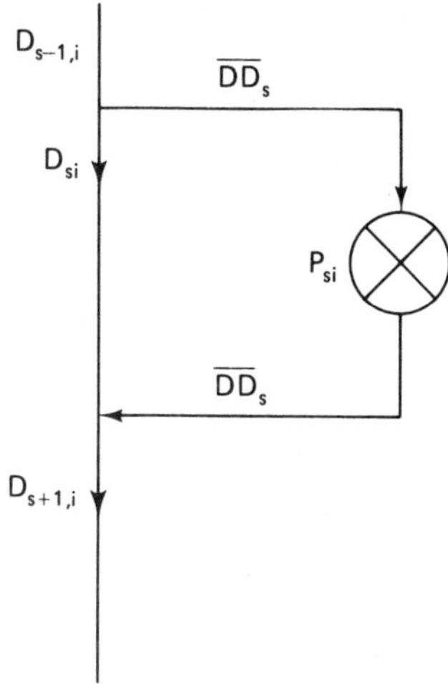

Figure 8-4
Representation of a fixed-head power plant in the sequencing model.

This is analogous to the case of an irrigation site, but with a return flow equal to the total diverted, because there is no consumptive use. The continuity constraint at site $s + 1$ is

$$D_{s+1,i} - D_{si} - \sum_{j=1}^{i} \overline{DD}_s P_{sj} = \bar{F}_{s+1} - \bar{F}_s \qquad \forall_{si} \tag{8.13}$$

Variable-head plants, which are associated with a reservoir site, are also required to have a given flow through the turbines to produce a prespecified amount of energy. However in the sequencing model it is assumed that this required flow will be determined by the associated reservoir at the same site. Thus the only constraints required for this type of power plant are the conditional constraints discussed in the next section.

CONDITIONALITY CONSTRAINTS

As we have seen, in the sequencing model, every proposed project is represented by 0–1 variables. In this section, we discuss how this property allows specification of important interrelationships among these projects. The use of constraints on these variables for the three main activities within the model—hydroelectric energy production, irrigation, and exports to or imports from other basins—is described here.

Hydroelectricity. Fixed-head power plants and the manner in which they are incorporated into the continuity constraint are described earlier in the chapter. The purpose of the fixed-head constraints is to indicate to the system that before the plant can produce the prespecified energy level, it is required to have a prespecified level of flow in the river. In the case of variable-head plants, the required flows are assumed to be provided by reservoir releases inherent in the operating rules used in the simulation model. Thus, the only additional constraint needed is one that says that the reservoir must be built during or before the period of construction of the hydroelectric power plant so that the required releases can be provided.

PPV_{si} is defined as a 0–1 integer variable that represents the construction (or not) of a variable-head power plant at site s in period i. Because the reservoir at site s must be built by the time the power plant begins operation (in the period in which it is constructed) we can write the required constraint as

$$PPV_{si} \leq \sum_{j=1}^{i} R_{sj} \qquad \forall_{si} \tag{8.14}$$

If PPV_{si} takes on a value of 0, representing no construction of a power plant, constraint Eq. (8.14) shows that this has no impact on whether or not the reservoir is built. If, on the other hand, PPV_{si} takes a value of 1, representing construction of the power plant, the sum at the right must be at least equal to 1, indicating that the reservoir is built either in the same or a previous period. Constraint Eq. (8.3) prevents the reservoir from being built more than once, so that the operation of Eqs. (8.3) and (8.14) together ensures that the right-hand side of Eq. (8.14) will be either 0 or 1.

Irrigation. The total size of the irrigation area at each site is given by the screening and simulation processes. In the sequencing model, the total size of each of the irrigation areas can be divided into subareas, and the model can opt to build only part of the total irrigated acreage at each site during a particular time period. This capability, which requires conditionality constraints, is important for two reasons. First, some portions of some sites are already constructed. By allowing the model to consider these separately, at zero costs (because costs are sunk) these existing areas can all enter the solution during the first time period, because no additional funds or farmers are required for them. Second, in the presence of constraints on budgets and population, it will often be optimal in terms of maximizing net benefits to build only part of an area in a given time period. The subdivision of areas in the model permits this to occur.

The hypothetical site shown in Figure 8-5 can be considered as an example. This site has been divided into three subareas, each of which has a 0–1 integer variable associated with it, denoted respectively as IA_{si}, IB_{si}, and IC_{si}. The flow to be diverted ($\bar{E}_s^A$, $\bar{E}_s^B$, $\bar{E}_s^C$) and the return flow from each subarea are considered separately. The continuity constraint at site s for this case is:

$$D_{si} - D_{s-1,i} + \sum_{j=1}^{i} \bar{E}_s^A IA_{sj} + \sum_{j=1}^{i} \bar{E}_s^B IB_{sj} + \sum_{j=1}^{i} \bar{E}_s^C IC_{sj}$$
$$= \bar{F}_s - \bar{F}_{s-1} \qquad \forall_{si} \tag{8.15}$$

However, this constraint by itself does not tell the model the order in which it should build the different parts. In order to ensure desired priority,

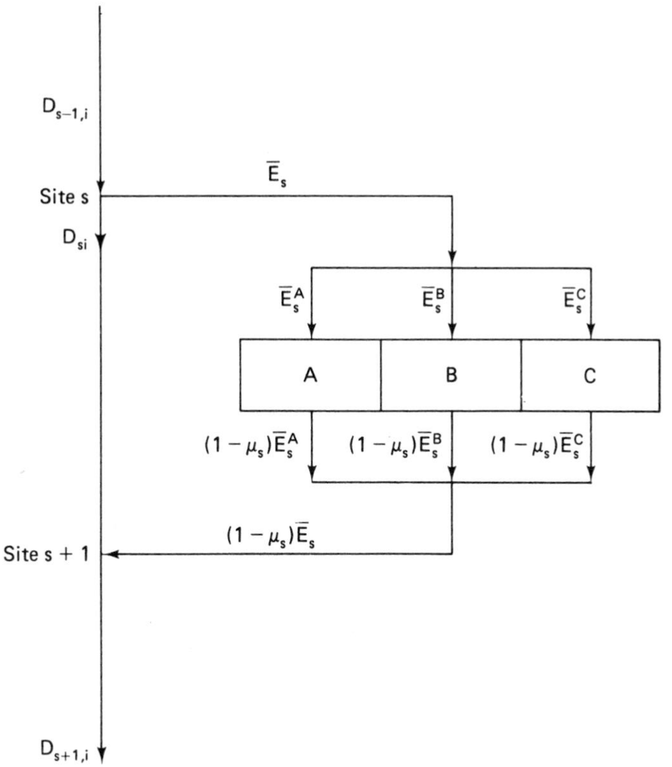

Figure 8-5
Subdivision of an irrigation site.

conditionality constraints have to be written. Assuming that Part A must be built before B, and B before C, these constraints are

$$IB_{si} \leq \sum_{j=1}^{i} IA_{sj} \qquad \forall_{si} \tag{8.16}$$

$$IC_{si} \leq \sum_{j=1}^{i} IB_{sj} \qquad \forall_{si} \tag{8.17}$$

In this way, two effects are obtained: priority of development within an area, and better allocation of people and capital as between the subareas of the various development sites.

Interbasin Transfers. Conditionality constraints are also provided in the sequencing model to govern the construction of exports from and imports to the basin. These can be used in the model to reflect time-dependent policy constraints relating to transfers, such as an agreement not to build an export without first providing for an import. An example is shown in Figure 8-6.

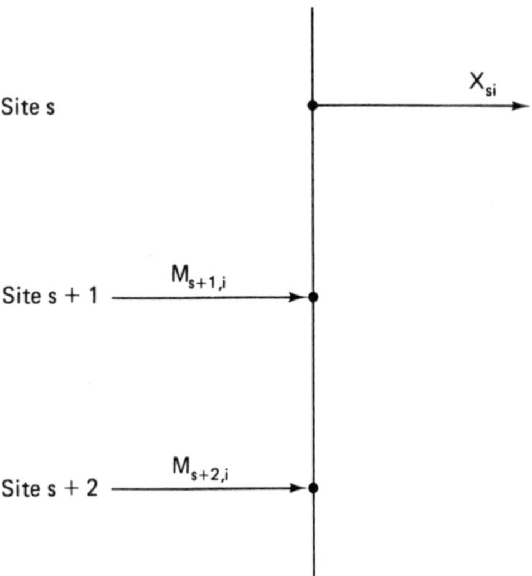

Figure 8-6
Example for representation of policy constraints on interbasin transfers.

Here, we assume that the policy constraints are: no export until the construction of at least one import, and only one, not both, of the imports may be constructed. These constraints are written,

$$X_{si} \leq \sum_{j=1}^{i} M_{s+1,j} + \sum_{j=1}^{i} M_{s+2,j} \qquad \forall_{si} \tag{8.18}$$

and

$$\sum_{i} M_{s+1,i} + \sum_{i} M_{s+2,i} \leq 1 \qquad \forall_{s} \tag{8.19}$$

Note that the continuity constraint does not differ from the general form shown in Eq. (8.9).

Of course, these are not the only types of projects affected by policy constraints. For other types of projects, relationships of mutual exclusivity or complementarity can be expressed in similar ways.

BUDGET AND POPULATION CONSTRAINTS

In the sequencing model, budget and population restrictions are treated as constraints. In both cases, there is a scarce resource that determines an upper bound on potential projects in every period during the planning horizon. In order to take these factors into account, each integer decision variable representing the construction (or not) of a project is multiplied by a coefficient that represents the total expenditures or people required for construction or operation of the project. Expenditure coefficients are defined for every type of project (power plants, reservoirs, irrigation areas, exports, imports) during each period. Population coefficients are defined only for those projects that need that resource in substantial amounts in order to be operated; it is assumed in the model that this holds only in the case of irrigation areas.

The expression of the budget constraint is

$$\sum_s \overline{\mathrm{BUD}}^k_{si}\mathrm{PROJECT}^k_{si} \leq \bar{B}_i \qquad \forall_{ik} \tag{8.20}$$

where $\bar{B}_i$ is the total budget available in period i, and $\overline{\mathrm{BUD}}^k_{si}$ is the total capital cost of the project of type k built at site s during period i.

The population constraint is defined in a similar way but only for irrigation projects:

$$\sum_s \overline{\mathrm{POP}}_{si} I_{si} \leq \overline{\mathrm{TP}}_i \qquad \forall_i \tag{8.21}$$

where $\overline{\mathrm{TP}}_i$ is the total population available in period i, and $\overline{\mathrm{POP}}_{si}$ represents the total number of persons required to farm an irrigation area at site s during period i.

OBJECTIVE FUNCTION

The general form of the objective function is the maximization of the sum of the net present value of benefits toward a given planning objective. As we have seen, each 0–1 variable in this model refers to the construction of some project in a period i; for each decision variable, cost and/or benefit values, which depend on prespecified capacities and production levels, are defined for every period, assuming a given number of years as the project life. Thus, a stream of net benefits is associated with each project, and that stream is discounted to the present.

Figure 8-7, parts (a) and (b), illustrates how these net present values are introduced into the objective function in the case of an irrigation area. Both new and existing irrigation areas are considered. A fixed project life of 40 years from the date of construction is assumed, and the stream of net benefits is defined. Figure 8-7(a) shows the shape of the stream of net benefits for the new portion assuming a 15-year build-up period. If this part of the project is built during the first period, the coefficient for IB_{s1} in the objective function will be the net present value as of year 0 of $ABCD$ in Figure 8-7(a); if it is built during the second period, the coefficient of IB_{s2} will be the present value as of year 0 of $A'B'C'D'$ in Figure 8-7(a); and so on. In the same manner, if an existing portion receives water during the first period, the coefficient of IA_{s1} in the objective function is the net present value of $ABCD$ in Figure 8-7(b); if the water is obtained during the second period, the coefficient will be the present value of $A'B'C'D'$. The coefficients for the rest of the periods are obtained in the same way.

In the objective function, a decision variable will be included for each type of area (new and existing) and for each period (1, 2, 3, 4) and will be

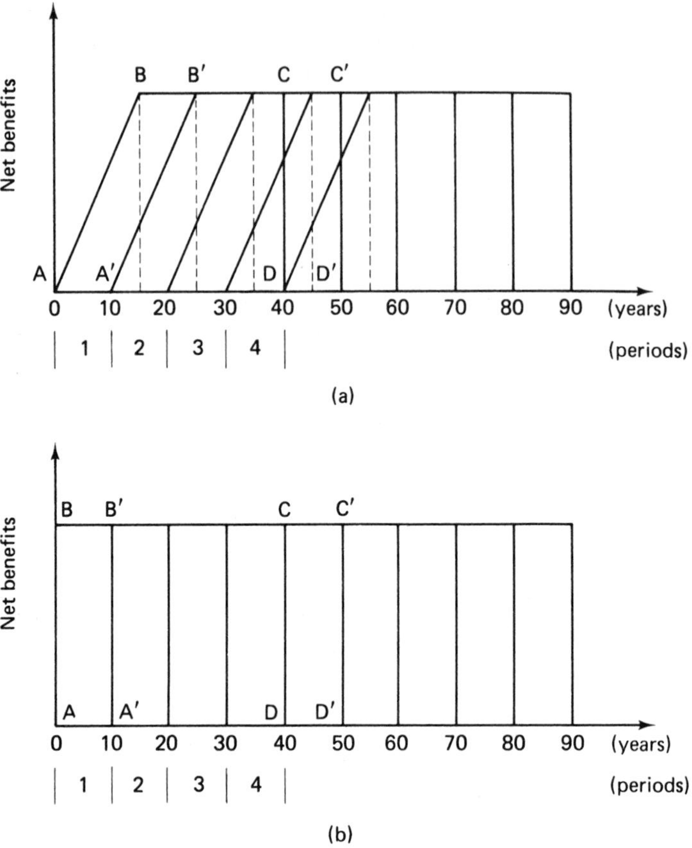

Figure 8-7
(a) Time stream of net benefits for the new portion of the irrigation area. (b) Time stream of net benefits for the existing portion of the irrigation area.

multiplied by a coefficient that represents the net present value of future benefits and costs. Note that the requirement that capital costs as well as benefits be counted only once is guaranteed by the construction constraints of Eq. (8.3).

Taking into account all the foregoing considerations, the mathematical form of the objective function for national income can be written as:

$$\begin{aligned}\text{Max } Z = \sum_s \sum_i [&(\beta_{si}^{\text{PPV}} - \alpha_{si}^{\text{PPV}})\text{PPV}_{si} + (\beta_{si}^{P} - \alpha_{si}^{P})P_{si} \\ &+ (\beta_{si}^{X} - \alpha_{si}^{X})X_{si} + (\beta_{si}^{M} - \alpha_{si}^{M})M_{si} + (\beta_{si}^{IA} - \alpha_{si}^{IA})IA_{si} \\ &+ (\beta_{si}^{IB} - \alpha_{si}^{IB})IB_{si} - \alpha_{si}^{\text{R}}\text{R}_{si}]\end{aligned} \tag{8.22}$$

where α_{si}^{k} is the present value of capital and operation and maintenance costs for a project of type k at site s constructed in period i, and β_{si}^{k} is the present value of the stream of benefits for a project of type k at site s constructed in period i.

It should be mentioned that it is not necessary to define the same level of net benefit for all periods in the sequencing model; benefits may vary from period to period. Thus, it is possible to consider benefits that are a function of calendar as well as of project time (Marglin, 1967).

REFERENCES

GOREUX, LOUIS M., and ALAN S. MANNE, eds. *Multi-level Planning: Case Studies in Mexico.* Amsterdam and New York: North-Holland and American Elsevier, 1973.

MAASS, ARTHUR, MAYNARD M. HUFSCHMIDT, ROBERT DORFMAN, HAROLD A. THOMAS JR., STEPHEN A. MARGLIN, and GORDON MASKEW FAIR. *Design of Water-Resource Systems.* Cambridge, Mass.: Harvard University Press, 1962.

MAJOR, DAVID C. *Multiobjective Water Resource Planning.* American Geophysical Union Water Resources Monograph 4, Washington, D.C., 1977.

MANNE, ALAN S. *Investments for Capacity Expansion: Size, Location and Time Phasing.* Cambridge, Mass.: MIT Press, 1967.

MARGLIN, STEPHEN A. *Approaches to Dynamic Investment Planning.* Amsterdam: North-Holland, 1963.

——— *Public Investment Criteria.* Cambridge, Mass.: MIT Press, 1967.

APPENDIX 8A SEQUENCING MODEL FORMULATION FOR AN EXAMPLE CONFIGURATION

An example site is shown in Figure 8-8. The formulation of the sequencing model is presented below for two reservoirs, one variable-head power plant, one fixed-head power plant, one irrigation area (divided into two subareas), and one export. In addition to the conditionality constraints previously discussed, another constraint is included to require the construction of the reservoir at Site 1 before the export is constructed. It is assumed that Part A of Site 3 is an existing irrigation area and that Part B is a new area.

CONTINUITY CONSTRAINTS

$$D_{1,i} - \sum_{j=1}^{i-1} \bar{Y}_1 R_{1,j} + \bar{c}_1 R_{1,i} + \sum_{j=1}^{i} \bar{E}_1 X_{1,j} = \bar{F}_1 \qquad \forall_i$$

$$D_{2,i} - D_{1,i} - \sum_{j=1}^{i} \bar{Y}_2 R_{2,j} = \bar{F}_2 - \bar{F}_1 \qquad \forall_i$$

$$D_{3,i} - D_{2,i} + \sum_{j=1}^{i} (\bar{E}_3^A IA_{3,j} + \bar{E}_3^B IB_{3,j}) = \bar{F}_3 - \bar{F}_2 \qquad \forall_i$$

$$D_{4,i} - D_{3,i} + \sum_{j=1}^{i} \overline{DD}_{4,j} P_{4,j} = \bar{F}_4 - \bar{F}_3 \qquad \forall_i$$

$$D_{5,i} - D_{4,i} - \sum_{j=1}^{i} \overline{DD}_4 P_{4,j} - \sum_{j=1}^{i} (1 - \mu_3)(\bar{E}_3^A IA_{3,j} + \bar{E}_3^B IB_{3,j}) = \bar{F}_5 - \bar{F}_4 \qquad \forall_i$$

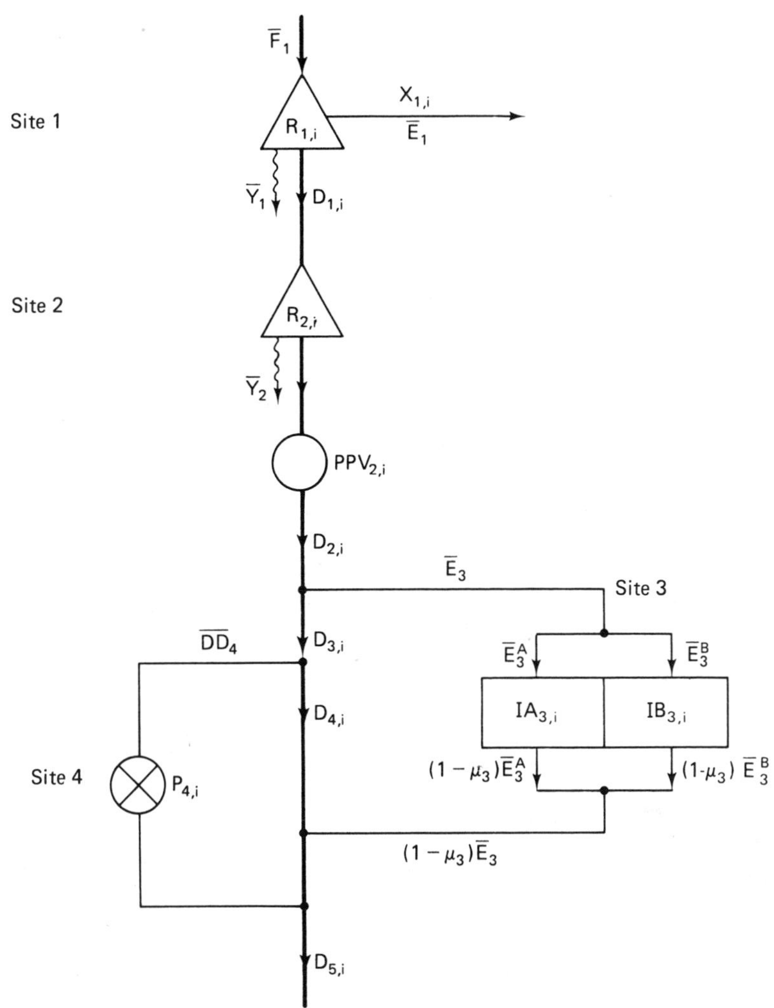

Figure 8-8
Example configuration.

CONSTRUCTION CONSTRAINTS

$$\sum_i R_{1,i} \leq 1$$

$$\sum_i X_{1,i} \leq 1$$

$$\sum_i R_{2,i} \leq 1$$

$$\sum_i \text{PPV}_{2,i} \leq 1$$

$$\sum_i IA_{3,i} \leq 1$$

$$\sum_i IB_{3,i} \leq 1$$

$$\sum_i P_{4,i} \leq 1$$

CONDITIONALITY CONSTRAINTS

$$X_{1,i} - \sum_{j=1}^{i} R_{1,j} \leq 0 \qquad \forall_i$$

$$\text{PPV}_{2,i} - \sum_{j=1}^{i} R_{2,j} \leq 0 \qquad \forall_i$$

$$IB_{3,i} - \sum_{j=1}^{i} IA_{3,j} \leq 0 \qquad \forall_i$$

BUDGET CONSTRAINTS

$$\overline{\text{BUD}}^{R}_{1,i}R_{1,i} + \overline{\text{BUD}}^{X}_{1,i}X_{1,i} + \overline{\text{BUD}}^{R}_{2,i}R_{2,i} + \overline{\text{BUD}}^{\text{PPV}}_{2,i}\text{PPV}_{2,i} + \overline{\text{BUD}}^{IA}_{3,i}IA_{3,i} + \overline{\text{BUD}}^{IB}_{3,i}IB_{3,i} + \overline{\text{BUD}}^{P}_{4,i}P_{4,i} \leq \bar{B}_i \qquad \forall_i$$

POPULATION CONSTRAINTS

$$\overline{\text{POP}}^{A}_{3,i}\, IA_{3,i} + \overline{\text{POP}}^{B}_{3,i}\, IB_{3,i} \leq \overline{\text{TP}}_i \qquad \forall_i$$

OBJECTIVE FUNCTION

$$\text{Max } Z = \sum_i [(\beta^{X}_{1,i} - \alpha^{X}_{1,i})X_{1,i} + (\beta^{\text{PPV}}_{2,i} - \alpha^{\text{PPV}}_{2,i})\text{PPV}_{2,i} + (\beta^{IA}_{3,i} - \alpha^{IA}_{3,i})IA_{3,i} + (\beta^{IB}_{3,i} - \alpha^{IB}_{3,i})IB_{3,i} + (\beta^{P}_{4,i} - \alpha^{P}_{4,i})P_{4,i} - \alpha^{R}_{1,i}R_{1,i} - \alpha^{R}_{2,i}R_{2,i}]$$

APPENDIX 8B LIST OF SYMBOLS USED IN THE SEQUENCING MODEL

Integer Decision Variables

Variable	*Definition*	*Units*
X_{si}	Construction (or not) of an export to another basin from site s during period i	—
M_{si}	Construction (or not) of an import from another basin at site s during period i	—
I_{si}	Construction (or not) of an irrigation site at site s during period i	—
P_{si}	Construction (or not) of a fixed-head power plant at site s during period i	—
PPV_{si}	Construction (or not) of a variable-head power plant at site s during period i	—
R_{si}	Construction (or not) of a reservoir at site s during period i	—

Continuous Decision Variables

Variable	*Definition*	*Units*
D_{si}	Critical season release from reservoir site s during period i, for reservoir built prior to or during period i. (Otherwise, D_{si} represents critical streamflow at s during i)	m^3/sec

Parameters

Variable	*Definition*	*Units*
$\overline{B}_i$	Budget available in period i	\$*
$\overline{c}_s$	Flow in critical season to reservoir at site s which is consumptively used during its construction and filling	m^3/sec
$\overline{BUD}^k_{si}$	Capital cost of a project of type k constructed at site s in period i	\$*
$\overline{DD}_s$	Required flow to operate a fixed-head power plant of given capacity at site s during critical season	m^3/sec
$\overline{E}_s$	Diversion for irrigation or for export at site s during critical season (assumed to be the diversion capacity)	m^3/sec
$\overline{F}_s$	Streamflow measured at site s during critical season	m^3/sec
$\overline{I}_s$	Import at site s during critical season (assumed to be the import capacity)	m^3/sec
$\overline{TP}_i$	Total number of persons available to farm irrigation areas during period i	# of persons
$\overline{POP}_{si}$	Number of persons required to farm an irrigation area at site s during period i	# of persons
$\overline{Q}_s$	Inflow to site s during critical season	m^3/sec
$\overline{Y}_s$	Yield from a reservoir at site s during critical season	m^3/sec
α^k_{si}	Present value of capital and operation and maintenance costs for a project of type k constructed in period i at site s	\$*
β^k_{si}	Present value of time stream of benefits resulting from the construction of a project of type k in period i at site s	\$*
$\bar{u}_s$	Irrigation loss coefficient at site s	—

*See Chapter 9 for the monetary unit used in model runs.

Part III Parameter Inputs, Model Results, and Interpretations

CHAPTER NINE

ECONOMIC PARAMETERS

JAVIER PASCUCHI
WALTER GRAYMAN
JOSE SUAREZ
DAVID C. MAJOR

This chapter provides explanations of the methods used to derive the principal economic parameters required by the models. These parameters include benefits for irrigation and energy, including benefits from the export of water to the Río Atuel basin, Mendoza; the opportunity costs of imports from the Río Negro system; regional income costs and benefits; the shadow price on foreign exchange; and budget and population limits on development.

The values of the parameters in each section are presented in terms of the model parameter notation used for the screening and simulation models. Because these parameters are essentially the same in both models (except for streamflow), we have used the notation in each case from the screening model (see Chapter 5). The values of the parameters given in this chapter are those used for final runs.

The unit of Argentine currency used is called the *peso moneda nacional*; its symbol is m$n. The benefit and cost estimates in this chapter and Chapter 10 are given in m$n indexed to 1970 as a base year. For these constant-peso estimates, we have used the symbol: m$n (1970). (One US$ (1970) = 400 m$n (1970). It should be noted that Argentina has since converted to a new currency unit, given the symbol $A, which is worth 100 units of m$n.) Where estimates in Chapters 9 and 10 were based on information in pesos other than m$n (1970), or in US$, these figures were converted to m$n (1970) using implicit Argentine price deflators and exchange rates, as shown in Figures 9-1 and 9-2.

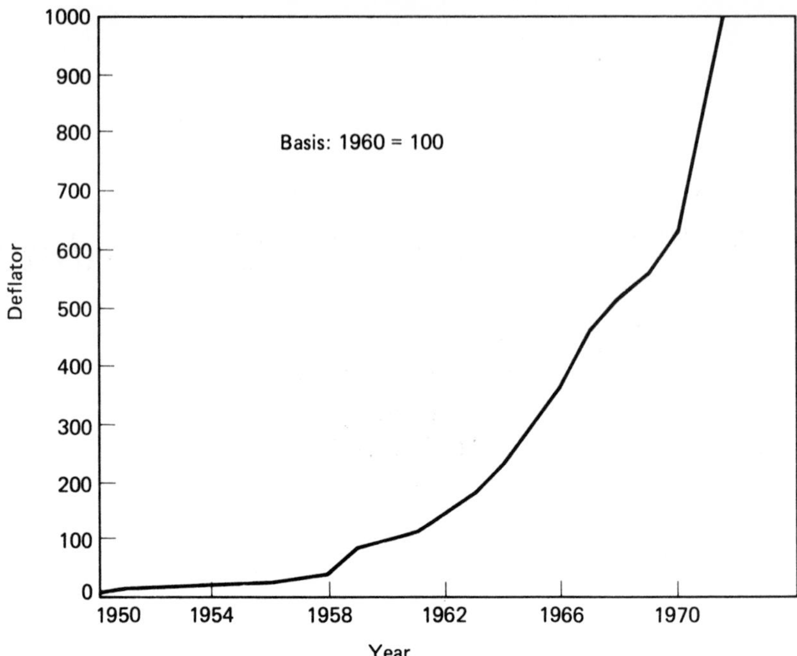

Figure 9-1
Implicit deflators.

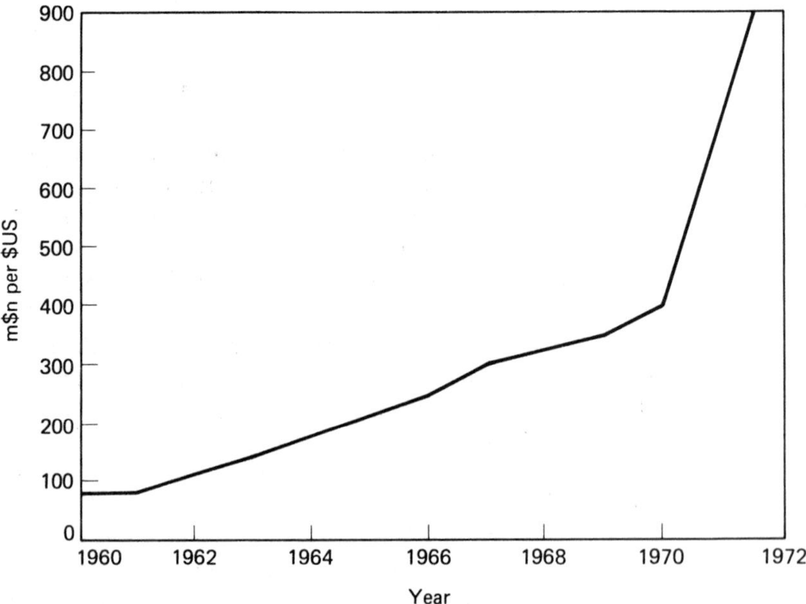

Figure 9-2 Dollar-peso exchange rates.

The planning horizon used for the calculation of benefits and costs in this chapter and Chapter 10 and in the running of the screening and simulation models is 50 years. The interest rate used for discounting national income benefits and costs in most of the model runs is 8%. This value was estimated on the basis of our analysis of the productivity relationships in the Argentine economy, taking into account the judgments of Argentine officials. Although the value of 8% was used in most of the model runs, we also made runs of the screening model using rates of 4% and 16% (see Chapter 11) in order to test the sensitivity of the results to changes in the interest rate. The 8% rate was also used for discounting regional income benefits and costs, although in principle the same rate need not be used for both national and regional income benefits. [On the theory of the interest rate, particularly the social rate of discount, see Marglin (1967) and the references cited therein.]

ESTIMATION OF BENEFITS FROM THE USE OF WATER FOR IRRIGATION

Irrigation is one of the two principal purposes of development on the Río Colorado (energy production is the other), and, accordingly, a substantial effort was made to estimate benefits from the use of water for irrigation in the valley (Pascuchi, 1972a).

The approach taken was that of calculating willingness to pay, both private and social, for irrigation water. This approach requires, from the private point of view, the calculation of farm revenues and of all farm-level costs, including direct input costs (including normal wages) and normal returns to capital. The net difference between revenues and all costs is the surplus that the farmer could in principle be charged for the supply of irrigation water. This is the farmer's private willingness to pay for water. The estimate changes when the social viewpoint is taken, because, to the extent that outputs are exported or inputs are imported, their costs must be adjusted by means of a foreign exchange premium that reflects the true rather than the official value of foreign exchange. (The basis of this approach is explained in a later section of this chapter.) The social willingness to pay for water is the basis of the benefit coefficient entered into the models (β_s^I in the screening model objective function). However, the private willingness to pay must also be calculated, because situations can arise in which social willingness to pay is positive and private willingness to pay is negative. In such cases, basin configurations can be implemented only in conjunction with appropriate financial transfers to farmers.

The benefit calculations were made on the assumption that grain would be grown on irrigated hectares for the purpose of fattening beef cattle for export. This assumption was made on the basis that the production of beef would generally remain a viable option for farmers in the area because of the characteristics of the world market for beef, in which Argentina participates.

The quantity of beef produced in the Río Colorado would be small relative to this world market: This permits the use of a constant price per unit of output in our benefit calculations. Insofar as other crops might be more profitable over the life of the Río Colorado developments, farmers would be likely to shift to these.

The benefit calculations, adjusted for build-up periods for new irrigation areas, and for sunk capital costs for existing areas, yield the benefit coefficient β_s^I in the objective function of the screening model. This coefficient is defined for each site; however, because of the general similarity of the sites in the Río Colorado, the benefit estimates used in the runs were taken as the same for each site.

The benefit estimating approach requires (1) the estimation of a production function—the relationship between inputs and outputs—for beef production using irrigated crops, and (2) the estimation of prices of inputs and the prices of outputs. A simple linear production function was utilized for the estimates.

Three crop-raising activities were defined: alfalfa, sorghum, and corn. These are the crops that we judged most appropriate for cultivation, given the conditions in the Río Colorado basin, for the purpose of fattening beef cattle. It was assumed that these three crops would be grown in fixed proportions on each hectare of irrigated land. These proportions were 20%, 40%, and 40%, for alfalfa, sorghum, and corn, respectively. The activity of producing beef with these inputs was also defined. Each activity requires the use of a number of inputs per year and per hectare as a result of the various operations that are required in the production process.

Total costs of production for direct inputs (such as labor and fuel) were estimated by first defining a vector of operations for each activity. The elements of this vector are the number of times each operation must be carried out per year. The operations considered were ploughing, harrowing, sowing, irrigating, cutting, transporting, and spraying. For each activity, a matrix was defined whose elements are the amount required of each input by each operation.

The product of the vector of operations and the matrix of inputs for a given activity is a vector whose elements are the total requirements of each input, per hectare and per year, for the activity. The vectors of total requirements per activity are weighted according to the share of each activity in the crop mix and then added. The result is a vector of total requirements of inputs per hectare and per year. When this vector is multiplied by a vector that contains the prices of inputs, we obtain the total direct costs of production.

Capital good requirements per hectare were estimated on the basis of assuming lots of 100 hectares of size. Because capital inputs are not linearly related to size, it is necessary to linearize around some reasonable size, and 100 hectares seemed the best choice on the basis of previous studies on beef production in irrigated areas. Depreciation charges were estimated for capital goods on the basis of service life, and estimated maintenance charges were also included. Where irrigated areas were already in existence, an adjustment was made for sunk costs.

On the basis of the yield of each crop, in terms of kilograms of dry fodder, and of a conversion factor for the latter into kilograms of beef (live weight), total output per hectare and per year was computed. Value of output was obtained by multiplying the beef production by its price. The difference between value of output and the sum of direct and fixed costs is then the long-run willingness to pay for water per hectare.

This procedure yields both the private willingness to pay for water and, when the foreign exchange premium is used to adjust the earnings from the export of beef and the costs for importing fertilizer, the social willingness to pay for water, which is the basis for the value of β_s^I entered in the objective function of the screening model. (Note that when the foreign exchange premium is 0%—that is, the shadow price is 1—the private and social willingness to pay for water are the same.) A summary of irrigation benefit calculations for foreign exchange premiums of 0%, 150%, and 300%, and for farmer financial costs of capital of 4% and 8%, is given in Table 9-1.

Table 9-1 Irrigation Benefits [m$n (1970)/year/ha.]

	Foreign Exchange Premium	0%	150%	300%
	Gross Revenue	55,936	139,840	223,744
	Direct cost	33,058	49,348	65,638
	Depreciation and maintenance	7,586	7,586	7,586
	Subtotal	15,292	82,906	150,520
4% *Cost of Capital*	Capital costs	7,392	7,392	7,392
	Willingness to pay	7,900	75,514	143,128
8% *Cost of Capital*	Capital costs	14,757	14,757	14,757
	Willingness to pay	535	68,149	135,763

The values presented in Table 9-1 are steady-state values. During the period when a farm is being developed, the steady-state benefits cannot be attained immediately, and so, in the models, the social willingness to pay benefits calculated as just described were adjusted to reflect a build-up period. This period was assumed to last 15 years; during this time, benefits were assumed to rise linearly from 0 at the start of the first year to the steady-state value in the fifteenth year. For existing areas no build-up period was used.

Willingness to pay for water, reflected by the case in which there is no premium on the exchange rate, indicates how much the farmers can be charged for the use of irrigation water, assuming that they have personally financed all investments at the farm. Sensitivity analysis showed that, under certain conservative assumptions regarding yields and prices, private profitability becomes mildly negative. But, because it is reasonable to assume that the farmers will themselves finance only a small fraction of total investments at the farm level, this problem can be easily avoided by reducing the financial obligations that the farmer will have with the government. This simply implies that, because social profitability is quite high given the assumptions, it is possible to make the activity profitable to farmers by means of appropriate transfers. The value of water from the social point of view is reflected in the result that is based upon the use of the 2.5 coefficient on the exchange rate (a premium of 150%). This is the number used in the models to represent irrigation benefits. The other cases presented were studied for purposes of sensitivity analysis.

The benefit estimation procedures were carried out in a simple computer program, which made the vector and matrix manipulations required to obtain the benefit estimates. The output of the program was arranged to provide the user with (1) all the data inputs for a particular run, and (2) a summary of the results for various foreign exchange shadow prices.

The benefit and cost figures estimated according to the procedures described above were entered differently into the screening and simulation models. The net benefit coefficient β^I_s is used in the screening model, adjusted where required for sunk costs in existing irrigation areas. The costs of large-scale irrigation works, not included in the above estimates, and of social infrastructure, were entered separately into the screening model in the function $\phi(L_{sm})$.

In the basic simulation model, all of the costs associated with irrigation are assumed to be fixed costs, including the costs of farm-level inputs (which are netted out in calculating the benefit coefficient β^I_s for the screening model objective function), as well as the large-scale irrigation costs and social infrastructure costs entered as ϕ_s in the screening model objective function. This procedure reflects the assumption that, within a given year, the farmer makes investments in input costs and treats these as fixed, adjusting his water use accordingly in the face of short-term deficits. Thus, net irrigation benefits per hectare as used in the basic simulation model are equal to the gross benefits shown in Table 9-1, minus losses from short-term deficits, and minus all fixed costs, including input costs treated as fixed in the short run.

ENERGY BENEFITS

Energy benefits enter the objective functions of the screening and basic simulation models as the product of a benefit coefficient, β^P_{st} in m$n (1970)/MWh, and the output of hydroelectric energy at a site, P_{st} in MWh. In this section, we explain our methodology for estimating β^P_{st}.

The energy benefits were based on the alternative cost method of estimation. This approach is strictly valid if two conditions are met: first, that there is a likely alternative source that will be built if the project under consideration is not built; and, second, that the gross benefits of the alternative will be equal to the gross benefits of the project under consideration. Under these conditions, the benefits of the project are equal to the costs foregone by preventing the construction of the alternative (Steiner, 1967).

These two conditions hold approximately for power planning for the Río Colorado. Power systems in Argentina appear to be expanded to meet demands, minimizing the costs of the required facilities rather than maximizing net benefits. If power is not supplied from one source, it will be supplied from another; the power supplied by alternatives will provide approximately the same gross benefits as the projects under consideration.

Although β^P_{st} is defined by site s and by season t, it seemed appropriate, using the alternative cost measure of benefits, to utilize generalized estimates of β^P_{st} for the basin and for all seasons. Thus, we usually used the same values for each region of the basin in our production runs; and we always used the same value for every season for a given site.

Water in the Río Colorado can be used to produce energy in two areas. If there is a diversion to the Atuel basin included in the chosen configuration, energy can be generated at power installations in the Atuel basin. With water kept within the Río Colorado basin, energy can be generated at new plants; and, because of the obligation of HIDRONOR (Hidroeléctrica Norpatagónica), an autonomous power authority, to supply power from the large hydroelectric plant at El Chocón to the basin (see the maps in Chapter 1), such water use would substitute for this power and allow additional amounts of power from El Chocón to be sent to the Buenos Aires market. This power could, in general, be used as peaking or shoulder power in conjunction with thermal base power in the Buenos Aires market. An additional factor to be considered in estimating power benefits for the Río Colorado is that within the likely time frame of implementation of Río Colorado power production, Argentina will be approaching a national grid system.

Using a variety of assumptions as to (1) the proportion of alternative power that would be required for peak and shoulder periods, (2) the growth of the Buenos Aires interconnected market, (3) the daily demand curve, and (4) other factors explained by Suarez (1972), we concluded that the likely alternative cost of the Río Colorado addition to the system (via the supply of additional El Chocón power to the Buenos Aires market) would be about 8 or 9 pesos m$n (1970) per kWh. This estimate was confirmed by discussions with Argentine power experts. Depending on alternative assumptions, a very wide range of benefit estimates would be possible. For example, an updating of an estimate for peak-only alternative costs yielded an estimate for power benefits of 24 pesos m$n (1970); whereas calculations for base-only alternative costs yielded estimates substantially below 8 or 9 pesos m$n (1970). We did not differentiate, in general, between Río Colorado and Río Atuel alternative costs for power, because we did not have systematic grounds for doing so and because the ultimate advent of a national grid for power would tend to make the estimates the same; however, some sensitivity runs were made with different estimates for the Río Atuel and the Río Colorado.

The specific figure used in most of the model runs was 8.6 pesos m$n (1970). In runs for sensitivity purposes, values from 8.6 to 24 were used (see Chapter 11).

Energy benefits from each potential project were assumed to occur over a 50-year time horizon following the construction of the project. In making the present value calculation, there was assumed to be a time lag between the decision to initiate power plant construction and the time when benefits begin. In the Río Colorado, it was assumed that the construction of the facilities required approximately 4 years and that at the end of that time the full steady-state benefits could be reaped. Therefore, benefits were calculated assuming zero benefits for the first 4 years and constant benefits from year 5 to year 50.

BENEFITS FROM THE EXPORT OF WATER TO THE RIO ATUEL BASIN, MENDOZA

In the objective function of the screening model, benefits from irrigation and energy production in the Río Colorado basin are considered separately. Benefits for exports of water to the Río Atuel basin in Mendoza province, on the other hand, enter the objective function as the product of a coefficient, v_{st} in m\$n/m^{3}sec^{-1}, and the amount of water diverted, EX_{st} in m^3/sec. The energy and irrigation benefit coefficients are utilized (net of additional site development costs in the Atuel basin associated with the use of the diverted water) to obtain a single benefit estimate per unit of water diverted. The costs of the diversion structures themselves enter separately into the objective function. Although the benefit coefficient for water diverted is permitted to vary in the models by site and by season, for production runs we utilized the same values of v_{st} for alternative diversion sites and for each season.

The Atuel basin was not explicitly modeled in our study, so the use of the water diverted to the Atuel basin was based upon the study conducted by Harza (1972). The unit benefit values developed in the present study for irrigation and power were used, making the estimates consistent with those used in the Río Colorado.

Three basic alternative diversions were studied by Harza. These correspond to average diversions of 24 m^3/sec, 38 m^3/sec, and 105 m^3/sec. In each case, the diversion from the Río Colorado was assumed to remain constant throughout the year; any changes in the flow pattern needed to satisfy demands were to be made by the dams in the Atuel basin. For each alternative, estimates were made in the Harza Report of (1) the additional energy that could be generated in the Atuel basin, (2) the amount of new irrigation area that could be developed, and (3) the amount of existing area that could be improved through the use of larger quantities of water and more dependable flow patterns. These values are summarized in Table 9-2.

Table 9-2 Proposed Development in the Atuel Basin*

Average Diversion	*Additional Energy*	*Additional Irrigation Area*	*Improvement of Existing Area*
m^3/sec	GWh/year	ha	ha
24	636	13,100	52,700
38	1,001	33,100	72,200
105	2,628	106,400	72,200

**Source:* Harza (1972).

Because a single benefit coefficient for water diversion was to be estimated, it was necessary to assume a distribution of water between energy production, new irrigation areas and existing irrigation areas. For this purpose we used the distribution given in the Harza study.

Harza presented irrigation development plans for both lined and unlined canals. In the present study, the amount of area that can be irrigated and the cost of development reflect the lined canal alternative, which is consistent with the plans for development of the Río Colorado.

Cost estimates for the site development costs in the Atuel basin associated with the use of diverted water were also taken from Harza (1972, chap. 11 and 15). The cost of social infrastructure was not considered in Harza (1972), so costs for social infrastructure investments were added using the estimates for the Río Colorado (see Chapter 10). The resulting costs are summarized in Table 9-3.

Table 9-3 Summary of Costs in the Atuel Basin*

	Energy		*Irrigation*		
Average Diversion m^3/sec	*Capital Cost* 10^9 m\$n (1970)	*O & M Cost* 10^9 m\$n (1970)/Year	*Capital Cost* 10^9 m\$n (1970)	*Social Infrastructure Cost* 10^9 m\$n (1970)	*O & M Cost* 10^9 m\$n (1970)/Year
24	3.39	0.0339	9.30	0.46	0.093
38	8.77	0.0877	12.35	2.29	0.123
105	46.30	0.4630	26.91	8.99	0.269

**Source:* Harza (1972); Pascuchi (1972a).

Unit energy benefits for most runs were taken at the same value used in the Río Colorado: 8.6 m\$n (1970)/kWh. In addition, a build-up period of 4 years, during which time no power is produced, was used. This is the same assumption used for the Río Colorado.

It was decided that irrigation benefits per hectare should be based on the values used for the Río Colorado. For new areas, the per hectare benefits were identical to those used in the Río Colorado. For currently existing areas, the additional benefits per hectare derived from the larger quantity and reliability of the water were taken as proportional to the per-hectare benefits in new areas, using Harza's (1972, chap. 9) coefficient of proportionality. For new areas, the same 15-year linear build-up period used in the Río Colorado was employed in the Atuel basin.

The present worth of a 50-year time stream of benefits and costs is summarized in Table 9-4 for the case of an 8% interest rate and 150% foreign exchange premium. The effects of build-up periods are incorporated in these calculations.

Table 9-4 Summary of Benefits and Costs in the Atuel Basin for an 8% Interest Rate and 150% Premium

	Irrigation			*Energy*			
Average Diversion (m^3/sec)	*Gross Benefits*	*Capital Costs for Site Development Including Social Infrastructure*	*O & M Costs*	*Gross Benefits*	*Capital Costs for Site Development*	*O & M Costs*	*Gross Benefits Net of Site Development*
24	16.14	9.76	1.14	48.78	3.39	0.41	50.22
38	29.50	14.64	1.51	76.77	8.77	1.07	80.28
105	65.23	35.90	3.29	201.55	46.30	5.66	175.63

Note: All benefits and costs in 10^9 m$n (1970).

THE OPPORTUNITY COSTS OF IMPORTS

Imports from the Río Negro system to the Río Colorado are permitted in the models at two points: from the Río Neuquén at the site of a proposed compensating dam for the Cerros Colorados system, and from the Río Negro itself near the town of Chelforó (see Figure 1-1). The opportunity costs for uses of water in the Río Negro system must be taken into account in the analysis of imports of water from the system to the Río Colorado. These opportunity costs were taken into account in two ways:

1. The import from the Río Neuquén that was chosen for incorporation into the models replaces a formerly proposed diversion from farther up the Río Neuquén at Portezuelo Grande (Grayman, 1972, p. 114). The reason for this choice is that the Portezuelo Grande import would have affected power production at the Cerros Colorados site, whereas the diversion included in the models does not. In this case, the choice of import site was based on the assumption of high opportunity costs at the rejected diversion site.

2. For the two diversions included in the models, at the Cerros Colorados site and from Chelforó, we assumed zero opportunity costs for the amounts of water that were permitted to be diverted to the Río Colorado in the models. This decision was based on discussions with local officials, on consideration of the development levels of the Río Negro basin, and on the question of Buenos Aires province's right to Río Negro water as a consequence of its being a riparian province in that basin. However, developments are possible in the Río Negro system that would entail a positive opportunity cost for imports to the Río Colorado. Should these occur, they can be studied in the models by including an opportunity cost coefficient for imports analogous to the benefit coefficient for exports ν_{st}.

REGIONAL INCOME BENEFIT AND COST ESTIMATION

The interprovincial nature of the Río Colorado decision problem is one of its most notable aspects. Several of the objectives used in the study relate to regional goals: equitable distribution of water; "territorial integration," meaning the development of relatively unpopulated areas in the basin; a preference for irrigation over power; and concerns about interbasin transfers. The use of regional income benefit and cost estimates, described in this section, represents another aspect of the regional nature of the objectives for the river.

The screening model objective function including regional income benefits and costs is written [Eq. (5.37)] as

$$\text{Max}\, Z = \lambda_{NI}\text{NIB} + \sum_i \lambda_i \text{RIB}_i$$

where NIB, the net national income benefits, are as in Eq. (5.38a), (5.38b) and (5.38c), and where RIB_i, the net regional income benefits to province i, are:

$$\text{RIB}_i = \text{RB}_i - \text{RC}_i$$

where

$$\text{RB}_i = \sum_s \beta_{si}^{IR}(L_{sm})$$

and

$$\text{RC}_i = \sum_s \phi_{si}^{R}(L_{sm})$$

where RB_i and RC_i are the regional income benefits and costs to province i, $\beta_{si}^{IR}(L_{sm})$ is the function relating discounted regional income benefit per hectare to province i and hectares of irrigation development at site s, $\phi_{si}^{R}(L_{sm})$ is the function relating discounted cost to province i and hectares of irrigation development at site s, and L_{sm} is the size in hectares of the irrigation project at site s. As explained later, regional income accounting benefits in the objective function are related to irrigation development in the basin but not to power development.

An additional term for regional income benefits is included in the objective function in order to capture the regional income benefits accruing to Mendoza from irrigation areas supplied by exports to the Atuel basin. This term is:

$$v_{st}^{R}\ \mathrm{EX}_{st}$$

where v_{st}^{R} is the net regional income benefit per unit of flow to Mendoza from exports, and EX_{st} is the flow defined in m^3/sec.

Guidelines for counting regional income benefits and costs can be found in UNIDO (1972), Marglin (1967), and Major (1977); and there have been various attempts to estimate regional benefits and costs in practice [see Kalter and Stevens (1971)]. The principal distinction between regional and national income benefit cost accounting is that, for regional benefits and costs, transfer payments of various kinds (e.g., charges, repayments, subsidies) are relevant; whereas for national income benefit–cost accounting only national productivity benefits and costs are countable.

The benefits and costs described here were used in screening model runs (see Chapter 11) to explore the regional aspects of plan formulation in the Río Colorado. Because there is relatively little regional income information in Argentina, and because we did not have a mandate to do detailed investigations of regional income flows, it was decided that the best approach would be to use regional income benefit–cost accounting to illustrate to Argentine decision-makers the substantial effects on the allocation of resources that could occur when regional benefits and costs were included, with varying weights, in the objective function. This was the approach carried out.

Our general method was, first, to list the relevant regional income flows; second, to make rough estimates of the values of flows in terms of coefficients related to decision variables in the screening model (Table 9-5); and, finally, to enter these into the objective function. This task was made simpler by the nature of investment in power generation in the region, referred to previously in the section on national income energy benefits. Power would be supplied to the region whether or not plants were built in the Río Colorado basin itself; hence, the regional income stemming from energy use would not change significantly, it was assumed, because of investments made in the basin itself. Furthermore, it was assumed that the construction and operation benefits should power plants be built within the region would flow largely to firms and employees from outside the region, and that these benefits could also be ignored. Hence, regional income benefit and cost accounting for the basin was related only to irrigation development.

Financing of irrigation projects in the basin was available from three sources—revenue sharing, national subsidies, and loans from the national development bank—and the flow variables considered reflect these sources of funding. Variables were also defined in terms of project-level flows, in addition to regional flows, so that project-level effects could be examined.

Table 9-5 Variables for Regional Benefit and Cost Accounting

	Men-doza	*La Pampa*	*Neu-quén*	*Río Negro*	*Buenos Aires*
Fraction of capital costs paid by province in taxes through national–provincial coparticipation schemes	75%	50% (25% at 25 de Mayo)	50%	50%	75%
Fraction of capital cost paid by bank loans at 8%	25%	25%	25%	25%	25%
Fraction of bank loans repaid by the province	50%	75% (50% at El Sauzal)	50%	50%	50%
Fraction of bank loans repaid by the users	50%	25% (50% at El Sauzal)	50%	50%	50%
Fraction of capital costs paid by subsidy	0%	25% (50% at 25 de Mayo)	25%	25%	0%
Operation and maintenance costs paid by province	0%	100%	0%	0%	0%
Operation and maintenance costs paid by users	100%	0%	100%	100%	100%
Ratio between outflow and inflow of taxes	1.0	0.8	0.9	0.9	1.0
Ratio between taxes paid by a province and the national total	0.15	0.05	0.05	0.05	0.20
Regional multipliers	1.75	1.60*	1.25	1.60**	1.70

*1.50 for Valles Marginales, Valle del Prado, and Bajo de los Baguales.
**1.50 for Huelches and Río Colorado.

However, little information was available about prospective provincial charging and repayment schemes, so the definition of such variables was mainly to provide a decision framework; the values assumed were rough estimates based on a general knowledge of interprovincial and intraprovincial revenue flows and management schemes. These flow variables were combined according to regional income accounting principles to yield the net benefit coefficients entered into the objective function.

FOREIGN EXCHANGE SHADOW PRICE

A principal economic parameter used in our irrigation benefit estimation is the shadow price on foreign exchange. This shadow price is appropriately used for national income accounting in situations where the official rate of exchange of a country, as has been the case in Argentina, does not correctly represent the economic value of foreign exchange earnings.

There are various conceptual bases for the calculation of a foreign exchange shadow price, as discussed in UNIDO (1972) and Pascuchi (1972b). The approach used in UNIDO requires the calculation of a relatively straightforward premium on the foreign exchange rate depending on willingness to pay for the marginal bill of imports. The approach used as the basis of our work involved a more complex attempt to consider the economy in the aggregate as constrained by foreign exchange availability (Pascuchi, 1972b).

The shadow price on foreign exchange was applied to beef, as the expected export resulting from the supply of irrigation water, and to fertilizer, expected to be imported in large part and used in conjunction with irrigation water. In a very detailed analysis of projects, more detailed than would have been appropriate at the prefeasibility level, shadow pricing on foreign exchange can be extended to calculations of the direct and indirect foreign exchange impacts of all inputs and outputs resulting from project development, including those for energy production.

In the runs of the screening model described in Chapter 11, shadow prices of 1 (i.e., a premium of 0%) up to 4 (a premium of 300%) were used. It should be noted again that when foreign exchange shadow pricing is used, the outcome of a run can be that irrigation projects might be privately unprofitable but publicly profitable on an aggregate consumption basis. This situation would then require the application of subsidies to induce farmers to undertake the publicly profitable farming operations. Note also that the gains from exports will depend on the crops produced; the analysis in our work assumes the production of exportable beef. Alternative crop mixes, should they prove more profitable privately to farmers, might not be equally profitable publicly.

POPULATION AND BUDGET LIMITS ON DEVELOPMENT

Two potential limits to the development of the Río Colorado that are considered in our study are limits on population and limits on budgets for project construction. These two potential limits are taken into account in the sequencing model. In the formulation of that model, the two parameters that relate to population are $\overline{\text{TP}}_i$, the total number of persons available to develop irrigation areas in period i, and $\overline{\text{POP}}_{si}$, the number of persons required to develop an irrigation area at site s during period i.

The value of the first parameter was estimated to be at most 10,000 persons per year. This estimate was based on an analysis of population and migration patterns and incentives in Argentina. The value of the second parameter was estimated to be one person per hectare of new irrigation area; this estimate includes farmers and their families and the workers and their families required to develop related infrastructure. Taken together, these estimates yield a maximum value of 100,000 hectares of new irrigation development per 10-year construction period in the sequencing model. These parameter values were applied in the second, third, and fourth 10-year construction periods in the model. Time delays in the development and working of new irrigation areas were taken into account in the model runs by assuming that no new irrigation areas would be developed during the first 10-year construction period.

The parameters that relate to the budget are $\bar{B}_i$, the budget available in period i, and $\overline{\mathrm{BUD}}_{si}^k$, the discounted capital cost of the project of type k at site s when constructed during period i. The latter parameters were estimated on the basis of the cost data for individual projects (see Chapter 10).

The budgets examined during the study were forecast on the basis of historical trends for outlays for public works, in general, and water resources, in particular, in each of the five provinces. For each of the provinces, the proportion of the total funding projected for public works and water resources that would be likely to be available for projects on the Río Colorado was analyzed, based on the relative importance of the development of the river to the other demands for public works outlays in each province. Our calculations indicated that, over a 40-year construction period, the forecast levels of expenditures would be sufficient to meet the investment demands of alternative development schemes for the river; so these financial constraints were not used in the sequencing model runs. However, it should be noted that we analyzed overall financial constraints, and to the extent that there are particular restrictions on the various individual sources of funding, such constraints could be binding (Major, Cohon, and Frydl, 1974).

REFERENCES

GRAYMAN, WALTER M. "Río Colorado Data Report." Ralph M. Parsons Laboratory for Water Resources and Hydrodynamics, MIT, Cambridge, Mass. November 1972.

Harza (Harza Engineering Company). "The Diversion of the Río Colorado to the Atuel Basin." Chicago, 1972.

KALTER, ROBERT J., and T. H. STEVENS. "Resource Investments, Impact Distribution, and Evaluation Concepts." *American Journal of Agricultural Economics*, **53** (**2**), 1971, pp. 206–215.

MAJOR, DAVID C. *Multiobjective Water Resources Planning*. American Geophysical Union, Water Resources Monograph 4, Washington, D.C., 1977.

MAJOR, DAVID C., JARED COHON, and EDWARD FRYDL. "Project Evaluation in Water Resources: Budget Constraints." Technical Report No. 188, Ralph M. Parsons Laboratory for Water Resources and Hydrodynamics, MIT, Cambridge, Mass., September, 1974.

MARGLIN, STEPHEN A. *Public Investment Criteria*. Cambridge, Mass.: MIT Press, 1967.

PASCUCHI, JAVIER. "Métodos de Estimación de los Beneficios de Riego." Ralph M. Parsons Laboratory for Water Resources and Hydrodynamics, MIT, Cambridge, Mass., September 1972a.

PASCUCHI, JAVIER. "Macroeconomic Aspects of Water Resources Planning in Argentina." Ralph M. Parsons Laboratory for Water Resources and Hydrodynamics, MIT, Cambridge, Mass., November, 1972b.

STEINER, PETER O. "The Role of Alternative Cost in Project Design and Selection." *Quarterly Journal of Economics*, 79 (3), 417–430, 1965.

SUAREZ, JOSE. "Iteración Económica en Mercados para la Electricidad." Ralph M. Parsons Laboratory for Water Resources and Hydrodynamics, MIT, Cambridge, Mass., September, 1972.

UNIDO (United Nations Industrial Development Organization). *Guidelines for Project Evaluation*. New York: United Nations, 1972.

CHAPTER TEN ENGINEERING AND COST PARAMETERS

WALTER GRAYMAN

This chapter describes the estimation of the engineering and cost parameters used in the series of three models employed to generate program alternatives for the Río Colorado. The chapter is divided into three sections, relating respectively to streamflow data, physical and structural characteristics of the proposed projects, and project cost estimates. In each section sources of data are given, methods of estimation are described, and the values of the parameters used in the final model runs of the project are presented. In Appendix 10A, an example of the method used to augment streamflow traces is provided.

The parameter values given in this chapter are presented in terms of the parameter notation used for the screening model and the basic simulation model. Because, as noted in Chapter 6, the parameters are essentially the same for both models, we have used the screening model notation from Chapter 5.

The development of the parameter estimates was the result of an iterative procedure. Early in the project, an initial set of parameter values was established using readily available documents. This set of values was used in a preliminary data report and in initial runs of the models. Identification of the parameters to which the models were most sensitive, as well as comments by Argentine officials, led to revised sets of estimates and finally to the set of estimates presented here. Final parameter estimates are based on available maps; on Argentine, United States, and other documents; and on information supplied by Federal, provincial, and local officials in Argentina.

ESTIMATION AND GENERATION OF STREAMFLOW DATA

Both the mathematical programming screening model and the basic simulation models require streamflow data for the upper reaches of the Río Colorado. The former uses average seasonal values (the parameter F_{st} described in Chapter 5); the latter uses time series of seasonal flow. In both cases, the streamflow values were based on the historical records obtained from gaging stations in the basin. The locations of those stations which are in the upper portions of the basin are shown in Figure 10-8. Pichi Mahuida, located in the lower reach of the river, is indicated on the maps in Chapter 1. The periods of record for the stations are listed in Table 10-1.

Table 10-1 Available Data on Streamflow

Site	*Years of Record*	*Comments*
Cobre	1951–52 to 1968–69	Used to estimate streamflow at La Estrechura and Río Valenzuela
Tordillo	1961–52 to 1968–69	
Portezuelo del Viento	1942–43 to 1955–56	Augmented records used in models
Potimalal	1947–48 to 1951–52	Not used
Bardas Blancas	1947–48 to 1968–69	Augmented records used in models
Buta Ranquil	1939–40 to 1968–69	Augmented records used in models
Pichi Mahuida	1918–19 to 1968–69	Used to augment data at other stations

The locations at which streamflow was assumed to enter the river in the models do not in all cases correspond to the locations of the stream gages. The streamflow entry locations considered in the screening model were La Estrechura, Río Valenzuela, Portezuelo del Viento, Bardas Blancas, and Buta Ranquil. Streamflow records at the entry locations that do not coincide with gaging stations were estimated from streamflow records at other locations. (One set of streamflow records, that of Potimalal, was not used either for streamflow estimation or augmentation.)

It will be remembered from our description of the basic simulation model that the flow records at each of the "start" nodes of the river basin system must be of the same length. In the Río Colorado, one station (Pichi Mahuida) had 51 years of available records; the remaining stations had shorter records. For this reason, the disaggregation component of the detailed simulation model, described in Chapter 7, was used to augment the historical record so that 51-year series of monthly streamflow values were available at five principal locations. These locations are, in addition to Pichi Mahuida, the confluence of Ríos Cobre and Tordillo (obtained from the Cobre and Tordillo records), Portezuelo del Viento, Bardas Blancas, and Buta Ranquil. All the stations exhibited a strong correlation with Pich. Mahuida (about 0.9 for annual values), which was selected as the pivotal station, and each one of the others was treated as a satellite station. The augmentation procedure is illustrated in Appendix 10A for the case of Buta Ranquil.

Of the four augmented records at the locations indicated above, three were used directly in the models. The record at Pichi Mahuida itself was used only for augmentation and for determining streamflow losses in the lower portions of the river (see below). The record at the confluence of the Cobre and Tordillo rivers was used to estimate the streamflow records at La Estrechura and Río Valenzuela, which were then used in the models. Streamflow at La Estrechura was calculated as the sum of the flow at the Cobre–Tordillo confluence plus an amount due primarily to the discharge from two small streams, Santa Elena and Las Cargas. On the basis of Harza (1972), the flow in these streams was related to the flow at the Cobre–Tordillo confluence by:

$$F_E = F_{CT}(1 + 0.71C) \tag{10.1}$$

where F_E is the monthly flow at La Estrechura, F_{CT} is the flow at the confluence, and C is a monthly coefficient given in Harza (1972). The resulting values are listed in Table 10-2.

Table 10-2 Coefficients for Determining Flow at La Estrechura from Flow at the Cobre–Tordillo Confluence

Month	*C*
January	0.47
February	0.51
March	0.50
April	0.40
May	0.36
June	0.33
July	0.34
August	0.34
September	0.33
October	0.38
November	0.42
December	0.44

Source: Harza (1972).

Streamflow in the Río Valenzuela (F_V) was also assumed to be proportional to the flow in the small upstream rivers. The following equation was used:

$$F_V = 1.77CF_{CT} \tag{10.2}$$

The screening model requires mean seasonal flows as input. The values used in the screening model for the upper basin were estimated on the basis of the augmented 51-year streamflow records, taking the mean value of the augmented record for each station. The resulting seasonal streamflow averages at each inflow site considered in the screening model are shown in Table 10-3. Note that the flow in the growing seasons (September–April) is much higher than in the nongrowing winter months (May–August).

Table 10-3 Mean Seasonal Flows (m^3/sec) Used in the Screening Model

Location	*Season I* *May–Aug.*	*Season II* *Sept.–Dec.*	*Season III* *Jan.–April*
La Estrechura	9.6	32.8	33.6
Río Valuezuela	4.7	27.4	21.2
Portezuelo del Viento	43.9	159.3	96.4
Bardas Blancas	53.8	187.2	104.7
Buta Ranquil	83.0	217.0	137.0

Two further streamflow parameters are required by both models. These are the parameters a_s and b_s of Eq. (5.8) to (5.11), which are used to determine streamflow losses in the central and lower reaches of the river. These coefficients were estimated by regression methods, the results of which are shown in Table 10-4.

Table 10-4 River Loss Parameters for the Colorado Basin

Location	a_s	b_s
Buta Ranquil	2.41	0.014
Mendoza Zone II	0.41	0.002
Las Torrecillas	0.38	0.002
Rincón Colorado	0.51	0.003
Agua del Piche	1.02	0.006
Peñas Blancas	0.33	0.002
El Sauzal	0.05	0
Punto Unido	2.49	0.015
25 de Mayo	0.08	0
25 de Mayo (Lower Intake)	1.50	0.009
Casa de Piedra	4.65	0.028
Huelches	0.05	0
El Chivero	1.30	0.008
Pichi Mahuida	0.36	0.002
Saltos Andersen	0.61	0.004
Valle del Prado	0.99	0.006
Valle Interior (Intake)	0.43	0.003
Bajo de los Baguales (LP)	1.50	0.009
Bajo de los Baguales (BA)	0.86	0.005
Pedro Luro	2.84	0.017
Atlantic Ocean		

ESTIMATION OF PHYSICAL AND STRUCTURAL PARAMETERS OF THE POTENTIAL PROJECTS IN THE BASIN

This section describes the estimation of the model parameters relating to the physical and structural characteristics of the potential projects in the basin: reservoir area–depth and volume–depth curves, reservoir evaporation data, irrigation parameters, hydroelectric power plant parameters, and upper bounds on project sizes.

RESERVOIR AREA–DEPTH AND VOLUME–DEPTH CURVES

The relationships between the area and depth of a reservoir (the "area–depth" curve) and between the volume and depth of a reservoir (the "volume–depth" curve) are required both for direct use in the models and for the estimation of other model parameters such as the evaporation losses per unit of water in storage (described in the following subsection).

The volume–depth curve, for example, is used in the case of the relationship $S_{st} = \sigma_s(A_{st})$ in Eq. (5-15) of the screening model. This equation expresses the relationship between storage (S_{st}) and depth of water behind the dam (A_{st}) and is thus given directly by the volume–depth curve. The volume–depth curve is entered in the models in piece-wise linear form (see Figure 5-6).

Volume–depth and area–depth curves were available from the preliminary studies of each of the reservoirs in the Río Colorado basin. These curves are shown in Figures 10-1 and 10-2. The sources of information were Harza (1972) for La Estrechura; COTIRC (1967) for Portezuelo del Viento, Las Torrecillas, Casa de Piedra, and Huelches; COTIRC (1967, 1971) for Agua del Piche; Harza (1972) for Bardas Blancas; and ITALCONSULT (1961) for Pichi Mahuida.

RESERVOIR EVAPORATION DATA

Evaporation from reservoirs was calculated in both the mathematical programming and the simulation models on the basis of the evaporation depth per time period at the various reservoir locations. Where available, average monthly evaporation depths were obtained from data collected at nearby sites. The evaporation stations nearest to each reservoir are listed in Table 10-5 (See also the basin map in Chapter 1). No evaporation data were available for the proposed reservoir at La Estrechura. In this case, average monthly evaporation values were estimated using the infiltration and evapotranspiration module of the detailed simulation model (Chapter 7). The basic data required to calculate evaporation are daily temperature, humidity, sunlight, and wind velocity, which were available at neighboring stations.

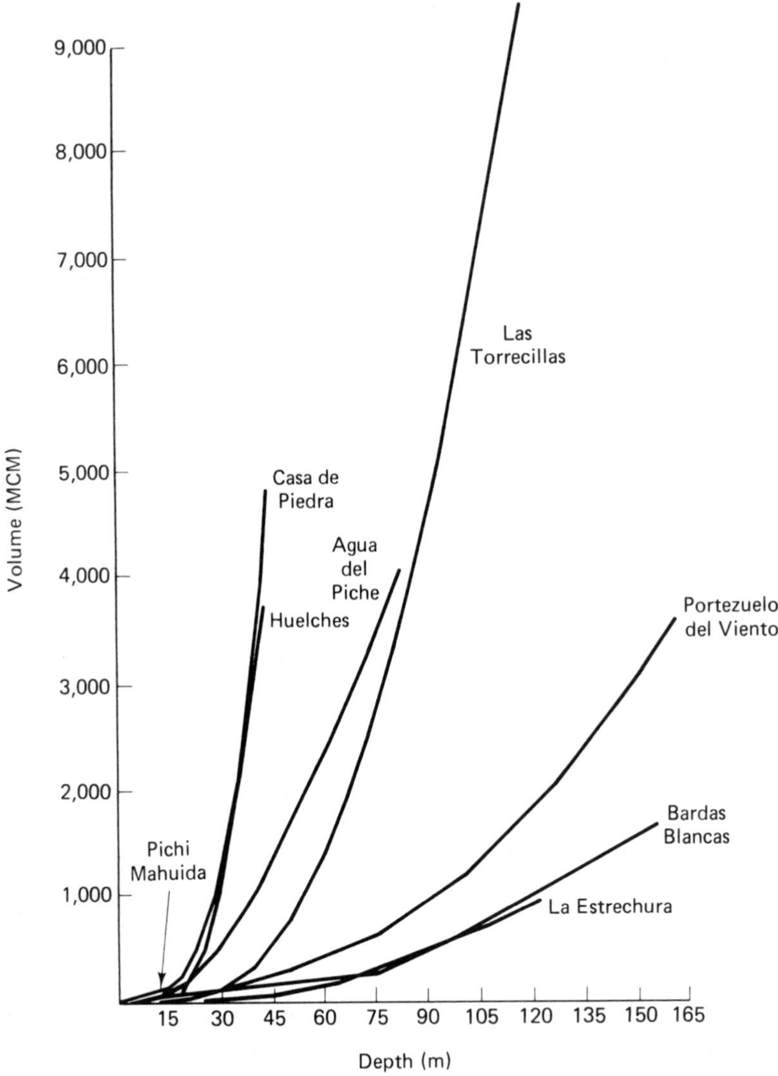

Figure 10-1
Reservoir volume-depth curves.

In the screening model, seasonal evaporation was assumed to be a function of reservoir storage rather than reservoir area [see Eq. (5.7)]. Linear relationships were determined between reservoir storage and surface area, from which the parameters $EVAP_{st}$ (the ratio of the volume evaporated and the volume in the reservoir for each reservoir s and season t) were estimated using the evaporation depth data. The resulting parameter estimates for $EVAP_{st}$ are listed in Table 10-6. Note that, at most, evaporation accounts for 6–7% losses at some reservoirs in the peak summer months and therefore is likely

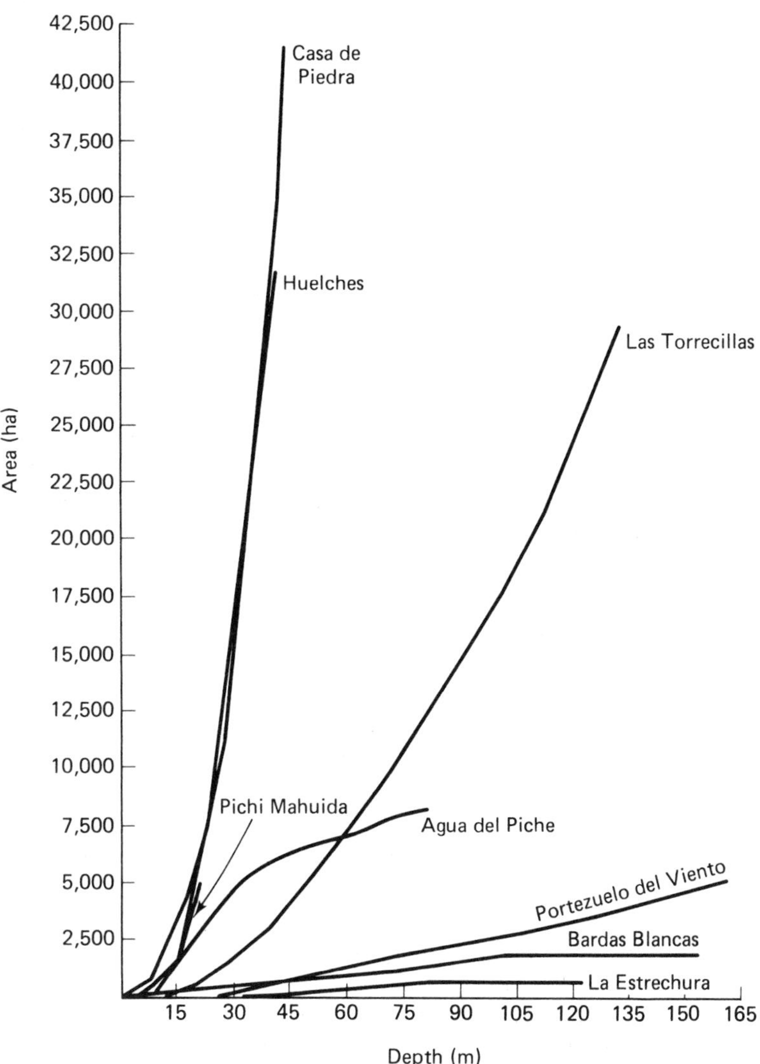

Figure 10-2
Reservoir area-depth curves.

Table 10-5 Location of Evaporation Measurement Stations for Determining Reservoir Evaporation

Reservoir	*Evaporation Station Used*
La Estrechura	Calculated on the basis of climatological data
Portezuelo del Viento	Bardas Blancas
Bardas Blancas	Bardas Blancas
Las Torrecillas	Cipolletti and Chos Malal*
Agua del Piche	Cipolletti
Casa de Piedra	Cipolletti
Huelches	Pichi Mahuida
Pichi Mahuida	Pichi Mahuida

*Weighted average of both stations.

Table 10-6 Estimated Values of $EVAP_{st}$ Based on Linear Relationships Between Reservoir Storage and Surface Areas

Reservoir	*Season I May–Aug.*	*Season II Sept.–Dec.*	*Season III Jan.–April*
La Estrechura	0.0014	0.0031	0.0046
Portezuelo del Viento	0.0068	0.0114	0.0116
Bardas Blancas	0.0091	0.0151	0.0154
Las Torrecillas	0.0052	0.0129	0.0132
Agua del Piche	0.0046	0.0135	0.0128
Casa de Piedra	0.0138	0.0405	0.0382
Huelches	0.0185	0.0549	0.0659
Pichi Mahuida	0.0185	0.0549	0.0659

to have little effect on the results. It can be seen that the relatively shallow proposed reservoirs at Huelches and Pichi Mahuida are somewhat worse off from this perspective than the deeper ones at the remaining locations.

IRRIGATION PARAMETERS

The irrigation data requirements of the screening model and the basic simulation model consisted of:

1. Water requirements at the field level (τ_{st} and ρ_{st}).
2. Losses in the delivery of water to the fields (ϵ_{st}).
3. Return flow from the fields to the river (ω_{sti} and χ_{sti}),

A description of the procedures used to estimate each of these parameters follows.

The principal irrigation constraint [Eq. (5.16)] relates irrigated land to the volume of water supplied for irrigation by means of a set of seasonal water-use coefficients (τ_{st}) that vary from site to site. These coefficients represent the unit amount of water required to produce the target yield per hectare and are thus a function of the crops that are planted. In the Río Colorado, the cropping pattern at all sites was assumed to be 20% alfalfa, 40% corn, and 40% sorghum (see Chapter 9).

The coefficient τ_{st} in m^3/ha can be estimated by means of

$$\tau_{st} = 10\left(\frac{U_{st}}{EF_{st}} - RF_{st}\right) \tag{10.3}$$

where U_{st} is the crop consumptive use at site s during season t (mm); EF_{st} is the irrigation efficiency at site s during season t; and RF_{st} is the rainfall (mm) at site s during season t. The factor 10 is used to convert mm to m^3/ha.

The term U_{st} was calculated on the basis of monthly consumptive use, which was estimated by the Blaney–Criddle (1950) method:

$$U_{sn} = 25.4T_{sn}PD_{sn}K_{sn} \tag{10.4}$$

where U_{sn} is the consumptive use in mm in month n (site s), T_{sn} is the average temperature in °F in month n (site s), PD_{sn} is the percentage of total daylight hours per year occurring during month n (site s), and K_{sn} is the Blaney–Criddle crop factor for month n (site s). Seasonal values were determined by aggregation of monthly values.

In order to estimate consumptive use in the Rio Colorado, the basin was divided into five climatic zones (Table 10-7). Average temperature values for the growing months in these five zones are presented in Table 10-8, together with the monthly percentages of total daylight hours, the average monthly rainfall values, and the Blaney–Criddle crop factors based on the assumed cropping pattern.

Table 10-7 Climatic Zones of the Rio Colorado

Zone 1	Mendoza Zone I and II
	Buta Ranquil y Rincón de los Sauces
	Rincón Colorado
Zone 2	25 de Mayo I–V
	El Sauzal
	Peñas Blancas y Valle Verde
	Colonia Catriel
Zone 3	Casa de Piedra
	Planicie de Curacó
Zone 4	Río Colorado y Eugenio del Busto
	Valle del Prado y Valles Marginales
	Bajo de los Baguales
	Huelches
	Valles Interiores
Zone 5	Pedro Luro

The use of Eq. (10.3) and (10.4) with the parameter estimates given above and an assumed irrigation efficiency of 50% for all seasons and sites yields the final estimates of the parameter τ_{st} given in Table 10-9. (With respect to irrigation efficiency, note that this is one of the many instances in planning in which the choice of technology is an important determinant of model input.)

A second important parameter that is related to τ_{st}, but which is used primarily in determining the return flow, is the consumptive use coefficient for irrigation at site s during season t, denoted ρ_{st} [Eq. (5.20)]. This represents the fraction of water supplied by irrigation that is consumed by the crops and thus can be estimated directly by

$$\rho_{st} = \frac{U_{st}}{\tau_{st}} \qquad \rho_{st} \leq 1. \tag{10.5}$$

The resulting estimates of ρ_{st} for the five climatic zones are presented in Table 10-9.

Equation (5.18) of the screening model relates water supplied for irrigation

Table 10-8 Parameters Used for Estimation of Consumptive Use Requirements

		Climatic Zones														
		1			2			3			4			5		
		T	*PD*	*RF*	*T*	*PD*	*RF*	*T*	*PD*	*RF*	*T*	*PD*	*RF*	*T*	*PD*	*RF*
Month	*K*	(°C)	(%)	(mm)	(°C)	(%)	(mm)	(°C)	(%)	(mm)	(°C)	(%)	(mm)	(°C)	(%)	(mm)
September	0.116	10.0	8.34	12.2	11.6	8.34	6.0	11.6	8.34	6.0	12.0	8.33	27.7	11.3	8.33	35.8
October	0.122	14.5	8.90	17.7	15.7	8.90	17.0	15.7	8.92	17.0	16.3	8.93	43.8	15.1	8.94	49.4
November	0.602	18.3	9.92	10.6	19.4	9.92	7.0	19.4	9.95	7.0	20.4	9.97	35.4	18.8	10.00	29.0
December	0.806	20.8	9.95	11.8	21.7	9.95	12.0	21.7	9.98	12.0	22.9	10.01	30.2	21.5	10.05	39.0
January	0.960	21.9	10.10	9.7	22.6	10.10	10.0	22.6	10.13	10.0	24.1	10.16	26.2	22.6	10.19	28.0
February	0.910	20.8	9.47	8.2	21.3	9.47	9.0	21.3	9.49	9.0	22.7	9.51	36.0	21.7	9.52	38.4
March	0.802	17.7	8.38	12.8	18.0	8.38	13.0	18.0	8.38	13.0	18.8	8.38	42.9	18.3	8.38	46.3
April	0.134	12.8	7.80	18.7	13.3	7.80	23.0	13.3	7.77	23.0	15.3	7.77	27.4	15.0	7.76	27.0

Table 10-9 Irrigation Requirements

Climatic Zone	τ_{st} *Irrigation Requirement* (m³/ha)		ρ_{st} *Consumptive Use Factor*	
	Season II Sept.–Dec.	*Season III Jan.–April*	*Season II Sept.–Dec.*	*Season III Jan.–April*
1	4,843	8,536	0.55	0.53
2	5,097	8,605	0.54	0.53
3	5,113	8,631	0.54	0.53
4	4,440	8,176	0.64	0.58
5	4,243	7,871	0.65	0.59

to water diverted for irrigation by means of a coefficient ϵ_{st}, which represents the fraction of diverted water lost in transport between the river and the irrigation site. Although in principle this coefficient can vary from season to season (hence the subscript t), it is assumed in the model runs to remain constant through the year.

Canal losses arise from two different causes: (1) losses from delivery canals and principal canals, and (2) losses from farm-level canals. Delivery canals and principal canals are lined in all but two of the existing irrigation areas, and it was assumed that canals in all future systems would be lined. For lined canals, losses are assumed to be 1% of the total water diverted. Losses for the two sites with unlined canals, Río Colorado y Eugenio del Busto and Pedro Luro, were estimated at 7% and 5%, respectively (Agua y Energía Eléctrica, 1962; Edison Consult S.A., n.d.). Losses from farm-level canals were estimated at 3%, based on assumed canal configurations, seepage rates, and average percent usage of the canal. The total value of ϵ_{st} used in the models is summarized as follows:

Río Colorado y Eugenio del Busto: $\epsilon_{st} = 0.10$

Pedro Luro: $\epsilon_{st} = 0.08$

All other sites: $\epsilon_{st} = 0.04$

Part of the water that enters the soil in an irrigation area either through canal losses or as excess water applied to the fields returns to the river. This is represented in the screening model by means of Eq. (5.20), where the return flow RI_{st} from the irrigation site s during season t is seen to depend on the parameters ϵ_{st} and ρ_{st} (described above) and the water diverted to the irrigation area. This equation assumes that all water used for irrigation, except that lost through consumptive use, eventually returns to the river. Because it can be assumed that most return flow in the Río Colorado will be via drainage canals, where there are few losses, and because evidence suggests that the groundwater system slopes toward the river, causing additional water to return via that system, this assumption is representative of the physical situation at all but one of the Río Colorado sites.

The one exception is the irrigation area at Valles Interiores, which is located away from the river. In this case, because of the distance from the river and the terrain and geology of the area, drainage can be accomplished most easily by running drainage canals away from the river to nearby low areas north of the site. For this reason, it was assumed that no flow returned to the river. This is represented in the model by setting $RI_{st} = 0$ for this site.

The time distribution of return flow is represented in the screening model by means of (5.21), which contains the parameters ω_{sti} and χ_{sti} (the portions of the intake canal losses and the drainage losses at site s in season i, respectively, that return to the stream in season t). The assumption was made that both parameters, for equal values of s, t, and i, took on the same value. Both coefficients were estimated by using the groundwater module of the detailed simulation model, which routes the water applied to the field through the ground to the drainage canals, determining an average hydrograph for each season i in which the water is applied. These hydrographs were then translated into weights by linearization.

The weights for each site corresponding to the application of water during Season II (September–December) and Season III (January–April) are listed in Table 10-10. No water is applied during Season I (May–August), although water may return during that season. The resulting values of ω_{sti} and χ_{sti} were normalized to reflect the screening model assumption that all water returns within the same year [Eq. (5.22)].

Table 10-10 Return Flow Weights

	Season II Weights			*Season III Weights*		
Irrigation Area	ω_{s12} χ_{s12}	ω_{s22} χ_{s22}	ω_{s32} χ_{s32}	ω_{s13} χ_{s13}	ω_{s23} χ_{s23}	ω_{s33} χ_{s33}
Buta Ranquil y Rincón de los Sauces Mendoza Zone I and II, Rincón Colorado, Casa de Piedra	0.55	0.40	0.05	0.64	0.32	0.04
Peñas Blancas y Valle Verde, El Sauzal, Colonia Catriel, Huelches, Río Colorado y Eugenio del Busto, Bajo de los Baguales	0.49	0.43	0.08	0.57	0.36	0.07
25 de Mayo I–V, Planicie de Curacó	0.46	0.44	0.10	0.54	0.37	0.09
Valle del Prado y Valles Marginales	0.41	0.44	0.15	0.48	0.38	0.41

HYDROELECTRIC POWER PLANT PARAMETERS

Three parameters enter directly into the equations for energy production used in the models. Two represent the generation of hydroelectric energy: e_s, the power plant efficiency at plant s [Eq. (5.24)], and Y_{st}, the ratio between average daily generation and peak daily generation at plant s during season t

[Eq. (5.28)]. The third, A_{st}, is the turbine head of water at plant s during time t [Eq. (5.24)]. A_{st} is a parameter only in the case of fixed-head plants (i.e., plants whose flow is not regulated by a reservoir), because for variable-head plants the value of A_{st} is determined by the model through the reservoir continuity equation [Eq. (5.11)] and the storage-head relationship [Eq. (5.15)].

The first parameter, e_s, is composed of two parts: *hydraulic efficiency* and *plant efficiency*. Hydraulic efficiency is defined as the ratio between net head and gross head and accounts for the hydraulic losses between the reservoir and the turbines. Plant efficiency accounts for losses within the power plant and may be defined as the ratio between the actual energy produced and the potential energy of water at the turbine inlet. This value depends on the turbine design and operation. For plants in the Río Colorado, an average value for plant efficiency of 0.75 was assumed. The overall efficiency including both hydraulic and plant efficiency was assumed to be 0.65.

The parameter Y_{st}, defined to include reserve capacity requirements, was estimated on the basis of the load factor and the factor of utilization. The load factor for the Río Colorado basin was estimated using the historical demand patterns for the Comahue interconnected system, which includes all or parts of the provinces of Neuquén, Río Negro, La Pampa, and Buenos Aires. From 1965 through 1969, the average value of use of thermal and hydroelectric plants was 3592 kWh per kW installed capacity per year (Secretaría de Energía, 1968) for a load factor of 0.41. This value was used for the load factor in our calculations, assuming no changes in consumption patterns and no interconnection of the Comahue grid with the national grid.

The estimation of the load factor for the Atuel basin in Mendoza was complicated by the probability of an interconnection between the local grid and the national grid. A final estimate of 0.86 was used in our calculations, based not only on this interconnection but also on studies of tariff policy and changing consumption patterns.

The factor of utilization is defined as the ratio between capacity in regular use and total installed capacity and reflects the need for reserve power capacity to account for breakdowns and routine maintenance procedures. For the lower basin, a factor of utilization of 0.85 was used based on the situation in the Comahue interconnected grid. In the Atuel basin a factor of utilization of 0.675 was used in the models based on the average reserve in the Cuyo Interconnected System (which includes the province of Mendoza) for the period 1960–1970 (Harza, n.d.).

The final estimate of Y_{st} used in the models was obtained as a product of the load factor and the factor of utilization. Although Y_{st} varies between regions, it was assumed to remain constant from season to season.

The remaining power parameters required by the models—the turbine heads for the fixed-head plants—were estimated from preliminary engineering studies for the plants. The estimates of power parameters as used in the models are summarized in Table 10-11.

Table 10-11 Power Plant Head and Efficiency Data

Power Plant	Type	Gross Head	Efficiency	Load Factor	Factor of Utilization
Los Morros	FH	110	0.65	0.86	0.675
Portezuelo del Viento	VH	*	0.65	0.41	0.85
Las Chacras	FH	60	0.65	0.86	0.675
Las Torrecillas	VH	*	0.65	0.41	0.85
Agua del Piche	VH	*	0.65	0.41	0.85
Los Divisaderos	FH	17†	0.75	0.41	0.85
Tapera de Avendaño	FH	57†	0.75	0.41	0.85
Loma Redonda	FH	10†	0.75	0.41	0.85
Casa de Piedra	VH	*	0.65	0.41	0.85
Huelches	VH	*	0.65	0.41	0.85
El Chivero	FH	15	0.65	0.41	0.85
Pichi Mahuida	VH	*	0.65	0.41	0.85
Saltos Andersen	FH	6.75†	0.75	0.41	0.85

FH = Fixed-head plants.
VH = Variable-head plants.
* = For all power plants with variable head, the gross head used to calculate power production is the difference between the water level and the bed of the river at the dam.
† = Net head.

UPPER BOUNDS ON PROJECT SIZES

The screening model formulation requires that maximum values be placed on the possible sizes of irrigation areas and reservoirs. For this reason, two parameters were defined: $CAPL_s$, the upper bound on the irrigation area at site s, and $CAPD_s$, the upper bound on the storage capacity of the reservoir at site s. Power plant capacities are not constrained in themselves, although their maximum size is determined by the maximum head and flow available at the site. Import and export capacities were constrained according to the particular import/export policy alternatives considered in each run.

In the case of reservoirs, estimates of the upper bounds were generally assumed to be equal to the largest reservoir size considered in previous engineering studies. In the case of irrigation areas, upper bounds were primarily derived by an analysis of soil maps of the area, measuring the maximum irrigable area in each case. The final upper bound estimates for each type of project are summarized in Tables 10-12 and 10-13.

ESTIMATED COST PARAMETERS

This section describes the cost relationships that were estimated for the potential projects in the basin. All cost data were reduced to 1970 Argentine pesos (m$n) using the implicit deflators and dollar–peso exchange rates shown in Figs. 9-1 and 9-2.

The cost estimates included in this section were incorporated into the models in linear or piece-wise linear relations between the cost of the project

Table 10-12 Upper Bounds on Irrigation Areas

Irrigation Area	*Province*	*Upper Bound* (ha)
Buta Ranquil y Rincón de los Sauces	Neuquén	3,500
Mendoza Zone I, II	Mendoza	5,020
Rincón Colorado	Neuquén	500
Peñas Blancas y Valle Verde	Río Negro	20,000
El Sauzal	La Pampa	2,600
25 de Mayo I	La Pampa	4,300
25 de Mayo V	La Pampa	4,000
Colonia Catriel	Río Negro	25,400
25 de Mayo II, III, IV	La Pampa	54,720
Casa de Piedra	Río Negro	78,000
Planicie de Curacó	La Pampa	25,600
Huelches	Río Negro	150,000
Río Colorado y Eugenio del Busto	Río Negro	17,000
Valle Interior	La Pampa	110,000
Valles Marginales y Valle del Prado	La Pampa	4,040
Bajo de los Baguales	La Pampa-Buenos Aires	40,000
Pedro Luro	Buenos Aires	218,000
Total		762,680

Table 10-13 Upper Bounds on Reservoir Storage Capacities

Reservoir	*Upper Bound* (MCM)
La Estrechura	960
Portezuelo del Viento	3,600
Bardas Blancas	1,680
Las Torrecillas	13,400
Agua del Piche	4,050
Casa de Piedra	5,000
Huelches	4,250
Pichi Mahuida	300
Total	33,240

and its corresponding design variable, as required by the cost expression [Eq. (5.38c)] used in the models:

$$C = \sum_s [\alpha_s(V_s) + \delta_s(H_s) + \phi_s(L_{sm}) + \gamma_s^E(EX_{sm}) + \gamma_s^I(I_{sm})]$$

The function $\alpha_s(V_s)$ denotes the reservoir cost as a function of the reservoir capacity V_s; the function $\delta_s(H_s)$ denotes the power plant cost as a function of installed capacity H_s; the function $\phi_s(L_{sm})$ denotes the irrigation cost as a function of irrigated area L_{sm}; and the functions $\gamma_s^E(EX_{sm})$ and $\gamma_s^I(I_{sm})$ denote the export and import costs as functions of the export diversion capacity EX_{sm} and the import diversion capacity I_{sm}, respectively. The estimation of each of these functions is discussed in the following subsections.

RESERVOIR COSTS

All the proposed reservoirs in the Río Colorado basin had been subjected to cost analyses prior to our study (see Table 10-14). The cost curves for each of the eight proposed regulating dams in the basin were estimated on the basis of these studies. The capital cost curves as a function of storage capacity for each of the reservoirs are presented in Figure 10-3. Annual operation and maintenance costs for all reservoirs were estimated at 1% of the capital cost per year (Harza, 1972).

Table 10-14 Engineering Studies Used in Estimating Reservoir Costs

Reservoir	*Reference*
Bardas Blancas	Harza (1972)
Portezuelo del Viento	Harza (1972)
Agua del Piche	COTIRC (1967, 1971)
Las Torrecillas	COTIRC (1967)
Huelchas	COTIRC (1967)
Casa de Piedra	COTIRC (1967)
La Estrechura	Harza (1972)
Pichi Mahuida	ITALCONSULT (1961)

POWER PLANT COSTS

The cost of a power installation is composed of capital, operation, and maintenance costs for the power plant itself, the substations, the transmission lines, and the hydraulic components. Cost data for proposed power plants in the Río Colorado were few. General relationships were developed for each of the various components in order to estimate cost curves for the proposed power installations as a function of installed capacity.

The capital cost of the power plant is a function primarily of installed capacity, head, and type of installation. In estimating the general cost curves, information from a large number of plants of varying types in the United States was used, yielding an average value based on different types of plants. The effects of maximum operating head on cost were incorporated by a priori grouping of all proposed plants into three categories: low-head plants (around 15 m); medium-head plants (around 50 m); and high-head plants (around 120 m). (This method requires reasonable correspondence between the assumed operating head values of each plant and the values in the screening model solutions.) Cost curves were then estimated for each category based on a study by the United States Federal Power Commission (1968).

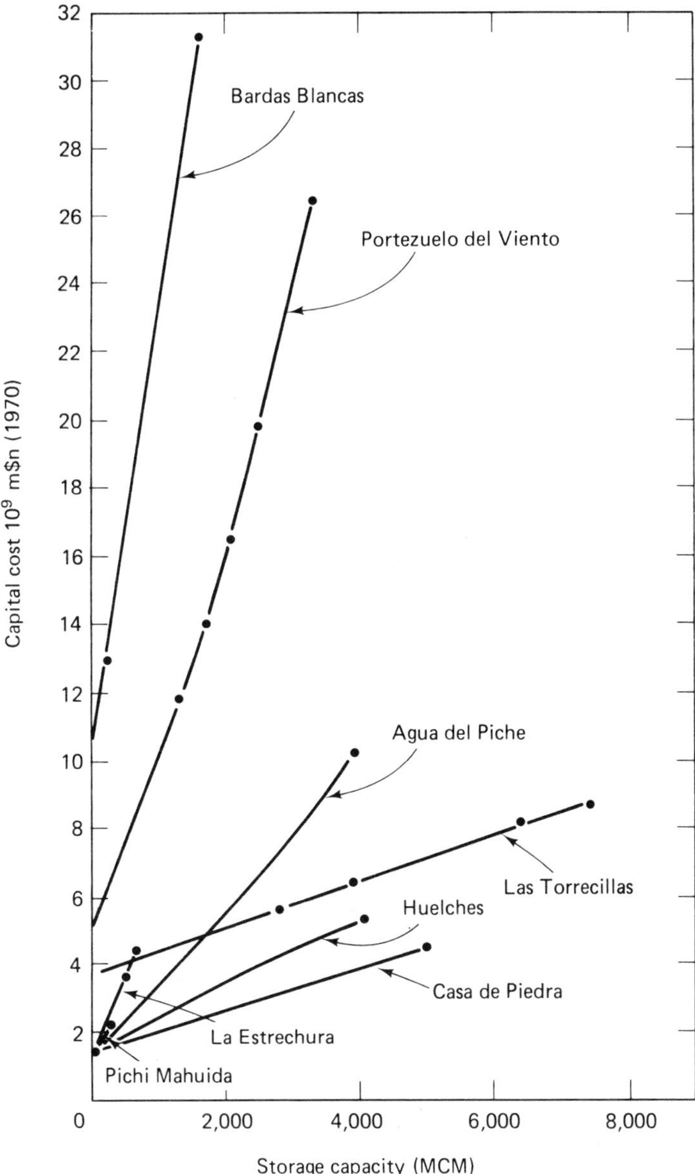

Figure 10-3
Reservoir capital cost curves.

These curves, converted into metric units and Argentine currency, are presented in Figure 10-4 for the three head categories. A comparison of costs predicted by these curves to estimates made in Argentina for the few power plants on the Río Colorado for which cost data were available showed close agreement, suggesting that these curves were approximately valid for use in

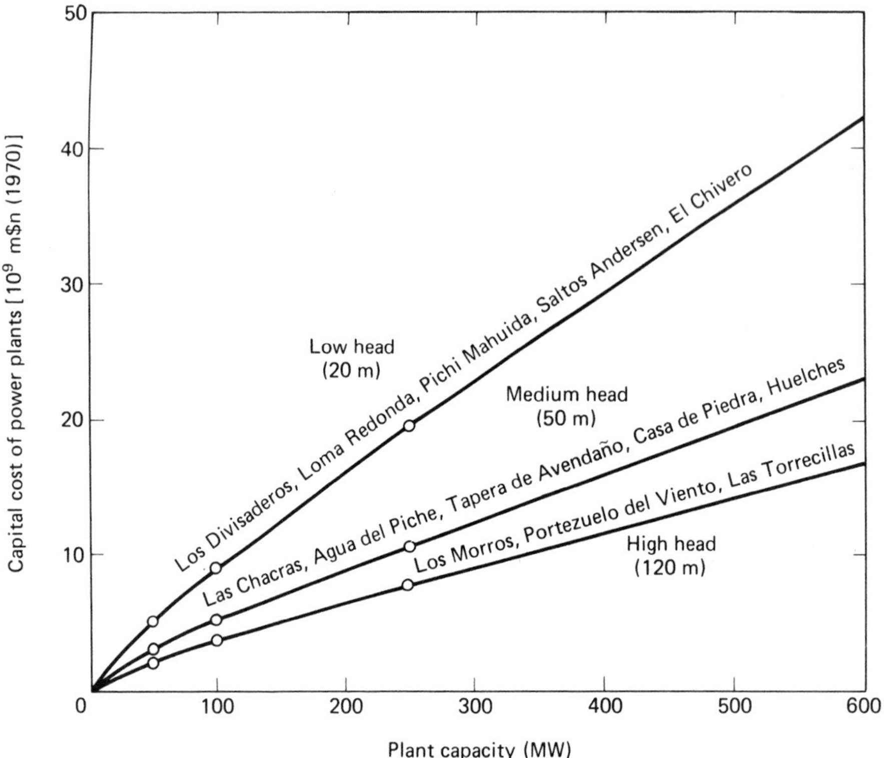

Figure 10-4
Hydroelectric power plant capital cost curves classified by head category.

Argentina. The operation and maintenance cost functions of the plants were estimated on the basis of another study conducted by the United States Federal Power Commission (1970).

For purposes of estimating the substation costs, it was assumed that one substation was required at each power plant. Both the capital and operation and maintenance costs of substations were determined from a United States Federal Power Commission study (1968).

The transmission line costs were estimated as a function of the installed capacity of the plant being served and the length of the line. Although actual design of such lines requires a systematic investigation of all plants and their interaction, in our study the transmission costs were estimated assuming that each plant had a separate transmission line whose length depended on the location of the plant. The capital and operation and maintenance cost functions used to calculate transmission line costs were based on the United States Federal Power Commission (1970) study.

Some plants require additional expenditures. Costs in this category include the cost of the diversion works and dams for the fixed-head plants at Tapera de Avendaño, Los Divisaderos, and El Chivero. At other sites, dam costs were either calculated separately, included in the calculation of the export to Mendoza, or treated as sunk costs.

The overall power plant cost functions as used in the models were obtained by aggregating the plant, transmission, substation, and other capital costs (where applicable) and adding the discounted operation and maintenance costs for an 8% discount rate and 50-year planning horizon. For runs testing sensitivity to the interest rate, operation and maintenance costs were discounted at the rate used in the test run rather than at 8%.

IRRIGATION COSTS

Irrigation costs can be broken down into large-scale costs and farm-level costs. Large-scale irrigation costs include the costs of diversion dams or intakes, primary and secondary delivery canals, principal drainage canals, and the social infrastructure associated with irrigation development. Farm-level costs include the costs of direct inputs, such as labor and fuel and the cost of capital good inputs, and are accounted for as described in Chapter 9. In this section, we describe the estimation of large-scale irrigation costs.

The methods used for estimating large-scale irrigation costs varied according to the availability of data at each particular site; the types of information available for each irrigation area are shown in Table 10-15. The potential

Table 10-15 Data Availability for Irrigation Areas*

Site	*Cost Data*	*Soil Map*	*Proposed Canal Configuration Map*	*Detailed Topo-graphical Map*	*Rough Topo-graphical Map Only*
Mendoza Zone I		x		x	
Buta Ranquil					x
Rincón de los Sauces		x			
Mendoza Zone II		x		x	
Rincón Colorado					x
Valle Verde			x		
Peñas Blancas				x	
25 de Mayo	x		x		
Colonia Catriel				x	
Casa de Piedra					x
Planicie de Curacó	x	x	x	x	
Huelches					x
Río Colorado	x		x		
Valle del Prado			x		
Valles Marginales				x	
Valles Interiores		x			
Bajo de los Baguales (LP)		x	x		
Bajo de los Baguales (BA)					x
Pedro Luro	x	x	x	x	

*Omitting El Sauzal and Eugenio del Busto.

irrigation areas in the Colorado basin can be divided into three categories based on the amount of data available:

1. *Appropriate cost data available.* This category includes those sites at which appropriate cost data of good quality were available. In this case, the existing cost data were used, adjusted to 1970 prices.

2. *No appropriate cost data available; good physical data available.* Many sites had data on the physical characteristics that affect large-scale irrigation costs. This information included soil studies, detailed topographical and geological characteristics, or actual designs of canal networks. In these cases, such information was used together with the general cost relationships used in category 3 to determine cost estimates.

3. *Few data available.* At several sites, there were few or no data available on soil or geological characteristics and only large scale topographical maps or no maps at all. In these cases, judgment in conjunction with the general cost relationships described below was used to make cost estimates.

The general relationships based on information available from other sources used to make cost estimates for irrigation canals, diversion works, and siphons, and to estimate social infrastructure costs, are now described.

Unit cost curves for lined and unlined irrigation canals were first estimated as a function of canal length and design flow. These curves are shown in Figure 10-5. They were based on estimates obtained from studies of proposed Río Colorado canals. Although canal costs are also a function of other variables such as slope, type of lining, topography, etc., these variables were not considered, because within a reasonable range they are of secondary importance compared to length and capacity.

The spacing of transportation canals, primary delivery canals, and principal drainage canals depends on the specific area. However, a reasonable estimate of the number of secondary delivery canals could be obtained by assuming them to be spaced at intervals of 4 to 5 km (Rueda, 1967). The size of the secondary canals and hence their cost was estimated by assuming that the capacity of these canals was 1 m^3/sec per 1,000 hectares irrigated. Delivery canals were assumed to be lined with the exception of the two areas that currently exist with unlined canals. Drainage canals were assumed to be unlined.

Costs for siphons were estimated as a function of siphon capacity. Length was not considered as an independent variable because it was assumed that all siphons would be approximately the same length. The cost curve used was based on the estimated cost of a 20 m^3/sec capacity siphon at Pedro Luro.

The final estimates of the total capital costs for each irrigation site (excluding social infrastructure costs) as a function of area are shown in Figure 10-6. The upper bounds of the irrigation areas in the cost curves correspond to the upper bounds in the screening model formulation. These cost

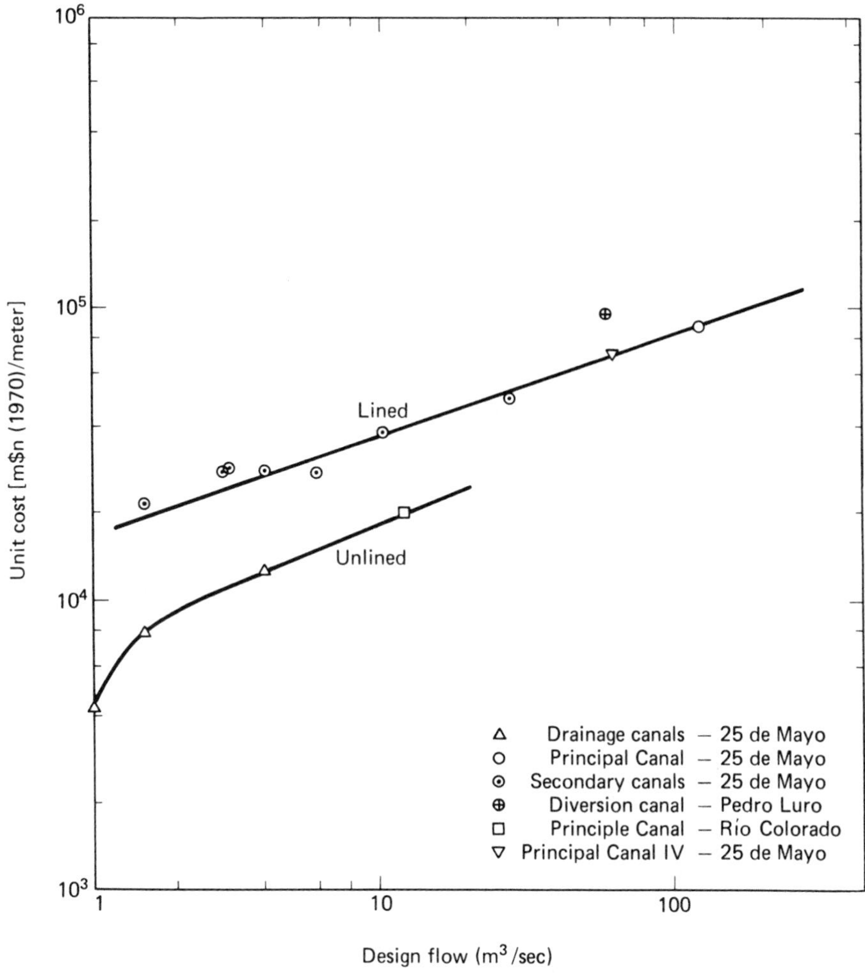

Figure 10-5
Irrigation canal costs.

curves should be kept in mind while reviewing the model results presented in Chapter 11. The unit slopes of the curves together with the relative locations of the areas are the principal determinants of whether an area enters a screening model solution or not. (The gross unit benefits of all irrigation areas are assumed to be the same and thus do not affect the model solutions as between irrigation areas.)

The cost curves in Figure 10-6 do not include annual operation and maintenance costs. These were estimated at 3% per year for unlined canals (CEPAL–CFI, 1969, p. 32) and 1% per year for lined canals (Harza, 1972, chap. 15).

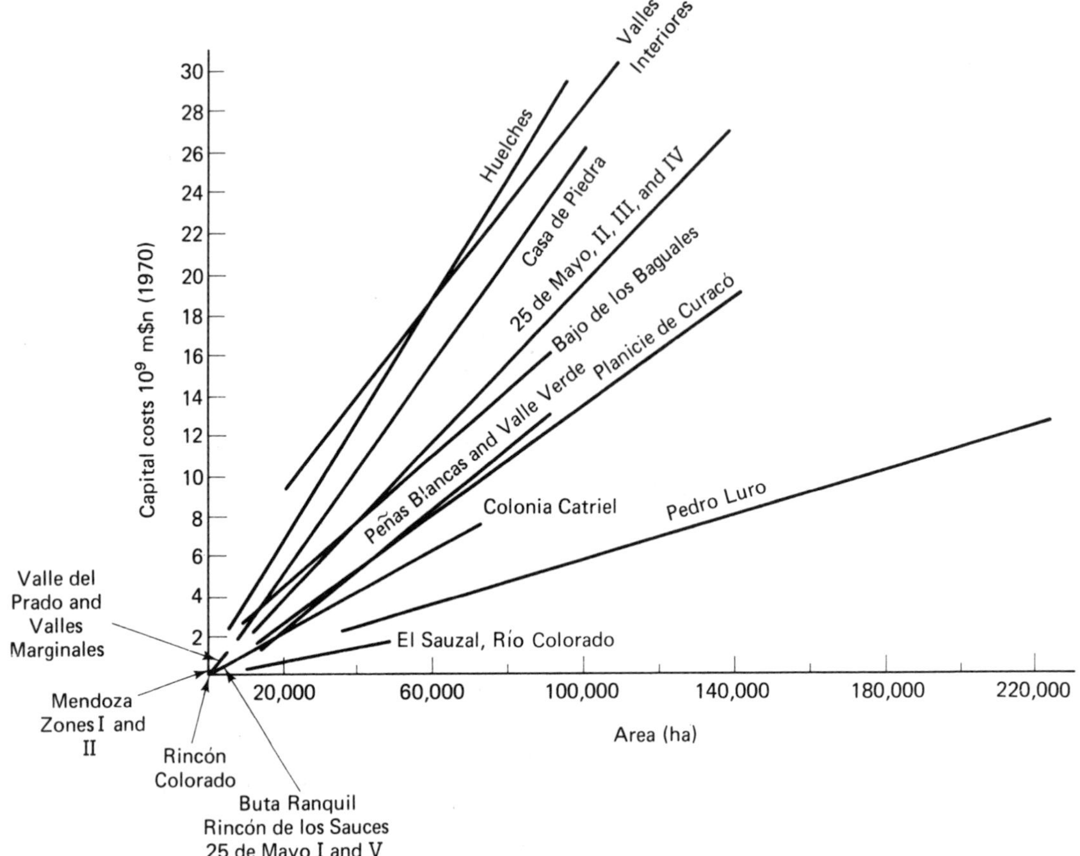

Figure 10-6
Capital costs of irrigation works.

The creation of new irrigated areas requires not only investment in diversion dams, irrigation networks, and land improvement, but also expenditures for housing and public services. Sometimes new towns must be built in order to provide farmers with a minimum of services. These expenditures may represent a substantial fraction of the total investments required by the irrigation projects.

Social infrastructure costs per capita for new irrigated areas were estimated as three times the per capita agricultural income per year of the population of an area (Pascuchi, 1972). This relationship appears to be reasonably consistent with data for the United States and a group of European countries (Stone, 1964). No charges for social infrastructure for existing irrigated areas were imputed, because it was assumed that such facilities already exist.

IMPORT AND EXPORT COSTS

Estimates of the capital costs of the conveyance structures for importing and exporting water were based primarily on the available cost information for each diversion. The geological and topographical features varied significantly enough between sites to warrant the development of separate cost curves for each site.

In most cases, detailed engineering studies existed that provided cost estimates for at least one and usually two design capacities. These studies are described in the following paragraphs, and the resulting cost estimates are plotted in Figure 10-7.

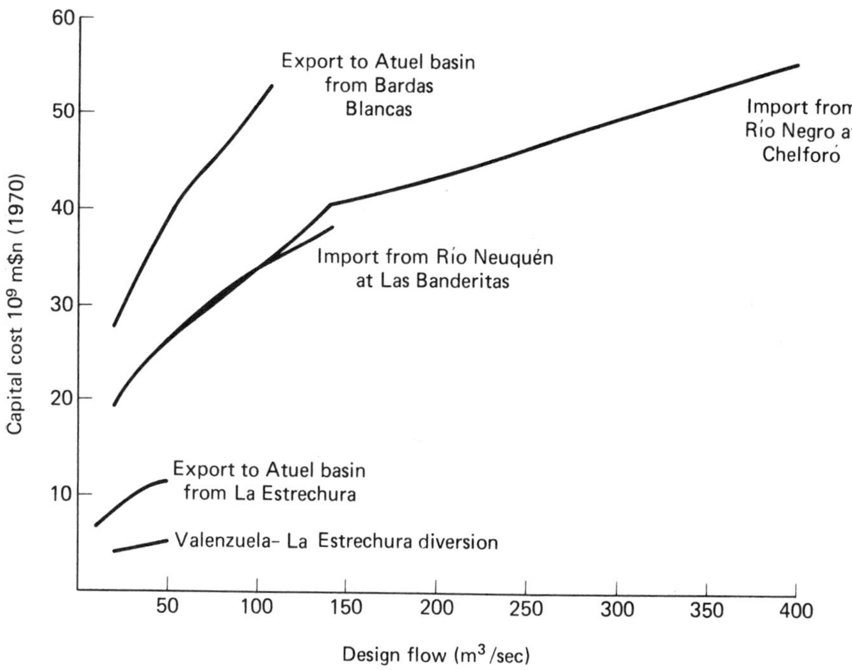

Figure 10-7
Capital cost curves for imports and exports.

The Valenzuela–Estrechura export diversion is described in detail in Harza (1972). The cost of the Río Valenzuela diversion dam, not included in Figure 10-7, was estimated in the same report as 1.1×10^9 m$n (1970) for the entire range of diversion capacities.

The diversion from La Estrechura dam to the Río Atuel Basin was investigated in Harza (1972) utilizing two alternative flows. The costs of La Estrechura dam are not included in these estimates because they are considered separately in the models.

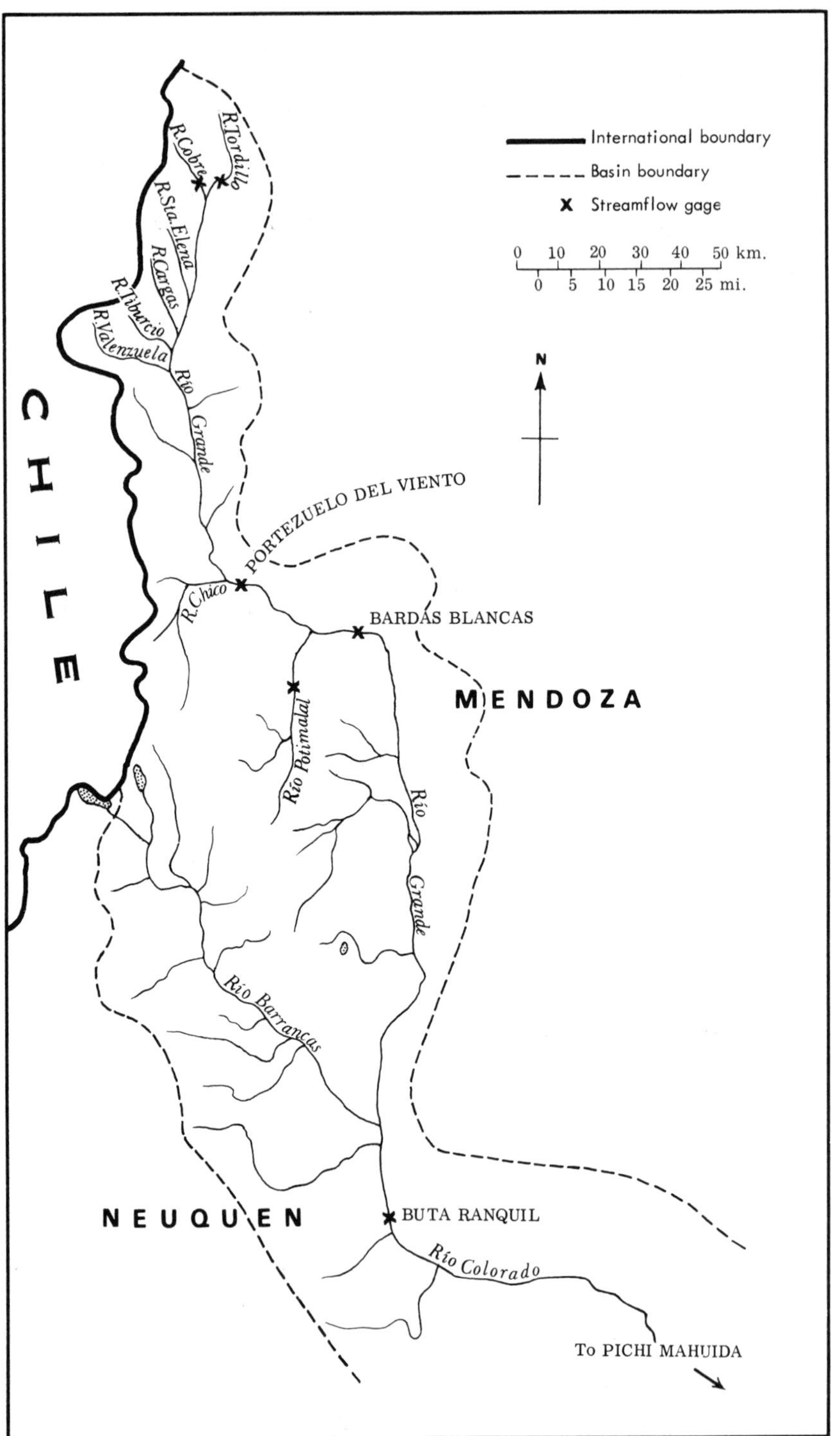

Figure 10-8
Location of streamflow gages.

The diversion at Bardas Blancas to the Atuel basin is also described in Harza (1972), for capacities of 80 m³/sec and 105 m³/sec. Cost estimates derived in this report were used directly to obtain the costs in Figure 10-7.

Preliminary engineering studies of the diversion from the Río Neuquén at Las Banderitas were performed by HIDRONOR (1971). These studies investigated the possible alternative routes but contain no cost data. However, cost estimates for the canals and tunnels of a previously proposed but discarded diversion from the Río Neuquén at Portezuelo Grande were available (Ente Provincial del Río Colorado, n.d.). Due to the geographical proximity of the Las Banderitas and Portezuelo Grande alternatives and due to their apparent similarity in topography, the unit tunnel and canal costs from the Portezuelo Grande alternative were used to estimate the cost of the Las Banderitas alternative.

The import diversion from the Río Negro at Chelforó to the Río Colorado was studied by COTIRC (1967). The cost figures from this report were used directly to estimate the cost curve presented in Figure 10-7.

REFERENCES

Agua y Energia Electrica, Republica Argentina. "Proyecto de la Red de Riego para la Zona de Río Colorado y Eugenio del Busto." 1962.

Blaney, H. F., and W. D. Criddle. "Determining Water Requirements in Irrigated Areas from Climatological and Irrigation Data." Technical Paper 96. United States Department of Agriculture, Soil Conservation Service, Washington, D.C., 1950.

CEPAL-CFI (Comisión Económica para la América Latina and Consejo Federal de Inversiones). "Los Recúrsos Hidráulicos de Argentina." **5**, 1969.

COTIRC (Comisión Técnica Interprovincial del Río Colorado). Informe No. 9/67, July 1967.

COTIRC (Comisión Técnica Interprovincial del Río Colorado). Informe No. 2/71, February 1971.

Edison Consult S. A. "Estudio Técnico, Económico y Social: Valle Bonaerense Río Colorado". Primera Fase, Tomo I, n.d.

Ente Provincial del Río Colorado. "Transvasamiento del Río Neuquén al Río Colorado," n.d.

Harza (Harza Engineering Company). "The Diversion of the Río Colorado to the Atuel Basin." Chicago, 1972.

Harza (Harza Engineering Company). "Gerencia Regional Cuyo." Chicago, n.d.

HIDRONOR (Hidroeléctrica Norpatagónica). "Transvase Neuquén—Colorado Alternativas." Plano No. 1, 1971.

ITALCONSULT. "Río Colorado: Development of Water Resources, Preliminary Report" (prepared for the Comisión Técnica Interprovincial del Río Colorado). Rome, 1961.

PASCUCHI, JAVIER. "Métodos para la Estimación de los Beneficios del Riego." Ralph M. Parsons Laboratory for Water Resources and Hydrodynamics, MIT, Cambridge, Mass., September, 1972.

RUEDA, OSCAR DÍAZ. "Problemas en el Trazado de Redes de Riego de Gran Magnitud y Evaluación del Costo de las Mísmas." Conferencia Internacional sobre Agua para la Paz, Vol. 7, pp. 528–544, Washington, D.C., 1967.

Secretaría de Energía, República Argentina. "Energía Eléctrica." 1968.

STONE, P. A. "Financing the Construction of New Towns." Background Paper #8, prepared for the United Nations Symposium on the Planning and Development of New Towns, Moscow, August 24–September 9, 1964.

United States Federal Power Commission. "Hydroelectric Power Evaluation." 1968.

United States Federal Power Commission. "The 1970 National Power Survey, Part II."

APPENDIX 10A ILLUSTRATION OF THE STREAMFLOW AUGMENTATION PROCEDURE

DARIO VALENCIA
JOHN C. SCHAAKE, JR.

This appendix illustrates the streamflow augmentation procedure (Valencia and Schaake, 1972) used in the study. The example is the augmentation of the streamflow record at Buta Ranquil, using the record at Pichi Mahuida. Buta Ranquil has records from 1940 to 1969, and Pichi Mahuida from 1919 to 1969.

GENERATION OF ANNUAL VALUES

A particular case of the general model is used:

$$x_{t+1} = [a_1 \quad a_2 \quad a_3] \begin{bmatrix} x_t \\ y_t \\ y_{t+1} \end{bmatrix} + bv_{t+1} \tag{10A.1}$$

where x_t is the annual value at Buta Ranquil corresponding to year t after the mean has been subtracted, and y_t is the annual value at Pichi Mahuida corresponding to year t after the mean has been subtracted.

The estimation of the matrices **A** (in this case, a row vector of three elements) and **B** (a scalar) is based upon the overlapping interval of the two stations from 1940 to 1969. The sample mean at each station must be subtracted from the historical values in order to obtain zero mean data.

When x_t, y_t, and y_{t+1} are known, and a random value of v_{t+1} is generated, a value of x_{t+1} is estimated. If the historical traces at Pichi Mahuida and Buta Ranquil are inverted, it is possible to calculate x_{1939}, because x_{1940}, y_{1939}, and y_{1940} are known; x_{1939} is then the first augmented value. With x_{1939}, y_{1938}, and y_{1939}, it is possible to estimate x_{1938}, and so forth until x_{1919} is estimated. The values to be used in the model require the addition of the sample mean of the annual values at Buta Ranquil.

The values of x_{t+1} thus generated will preserve (1) the annual mean and the annual variance at Buta Ranquil, (2) the lag-one serial correlation at Buta Ranquil, and (3) the lag-zero and lag-one cross correlations between Buta Ranquil and Pichi Mahuida.

GENERATION OF MONTHLY VALUES

The model for the generation of monthly values is:

$$r_{tj} = [a_{1j} \quad a_{2j} \quad a_{3j} \quad a_{4j} \quad a_{5j}] \begin{bmatrix} r_{t,j-1} \\ s_{t,j-1} \\ s_{tj} \\ x_t \\ y_t \end{bmatrix} + b_j v_{tj} \tag{10A.2}$$

where r_{tj} is the monthly value at Buta Ranquil corresponding to year t, month j, after the mean of month j at this station has been subtracted; s_{tj} is the monthly value at Pichi Mahuida corresponding to year t, month j, after the mean of month j at this station has been subtracted; x_t and y_t are the same as in Eq. (10A.1).

The matrices $\mathbf{A}_j$ (row vector of five elements) and $\mathbf{B}_j$ (scalar) are now estimated by the standard procedure using annual and monthly values of the overlapping interval between the two stations. A set of parameters $\mathbf{A}_j$ and $\mathbf{B}_j$ is required for each month of the year.

After the annual values at Buta Ranquil are generated by means of the model given by Eq. (10A.1), the monthly values for the same station are generated by means of Eq. (10A.2), following a recursive procedure similar to that described for annual values. The actual monthly values to be used require the addition of the corresponding sample means.

The values of r_{tj} thus generated will preserve (1) the mean and variance of each month at Buta Ranquil, (2) the lag-one serial correlation of the monthly values at Buta Ranquil, (3) the lag-zero and lag-one cross correlation of monthly values between the two stations, and (4) the correlations of monthly values at Buta Ranquil with the annual value at both the same station and Pichi Mahuida.

REFERENCE

VALENCIA, DARIO, and JOHN C. SCHAAKE, JR. "A Disaggregation Model for Time Series Analysis and Synthesis." Technical Report No. 149. Ralph M. Parsons Laboratory for Water Resources and Hydrodynamics, MIT, Cambridge, Mass., June, 1972.

CHAPTER ELEVEN OUTPUTS OF THE MODELS

JARED COHON
TOMAS FACET
WALTER GRAYMAN
GUILLERMO VICENS

In this chapter, we describe outputs of the system of models used to generate program alternatives for the Río Colorado. Our purpose is to illustrate how the models reflect the physical and policy choices relevant to the development of the basin and to provide insight into the trade-offs among these choices.

The chapter is organized as follows. First, we review briefly the process and meaning of model use in our methodology. Then, outputs of each of the three models are described and discussed in separate sections. The outputs selected for discussion—21 screening runs, 4 simulation analyses, and 3 sequencing runs—are those that we think best illuminate important aspects of the choice problem, taking into account the Argentine objectives for development of the river. Figure 4-1, the schematic of the basin used in the models, has been reproduced as Figure 11-1 as an aid in interpreting the results. The full results of the runs discussed are presented in tabular form in Appendix 11A for the reader who wishes to analyze aspects of the results not discussed in this chapter. The complete set of results are in Vol. I of the project's Final Report (see Introduction). The outcome of the Argentine decision-making process on the Río Colorado, taking into account the information from our project, including the outputs discussed in this chapter, is described in Chapter 12.

PROCESS OF MODEL USE: REVIEW

The models chosen for the selection of alternatives were the mathematical programming screening model, the basic simulation model, and the sequencing model. It was felt that by analyzing alternatives with these three models the results of the analyses could be regarded as workable draft programs for the Río Colorado at the prefeasibility level. (Prefeasibility studies identify projects in a proposed development program but not the final project designs and sizes, which are determined by detailed engineering, economic, and other analyses of each project.) The methodology used was that described in Chapter 4; the engineering, benefit, and cost parameters used in the models were those described in the two previous chapters.

To develop a sense of the key choices in the planning process, the screening model was used to examine a large number of alternatives, reflecting both the physical and the policy choices to be made in the Río Colorado. The simulation model was designed to analyze the best of these configurations—"best" in the sense of being most responsive to Argentine objectives. The best of these development configurations—using "best" again in the same sense—were run in the sequencing model with the aim of presenting them as realistic prefeasibility programs for the river.

The model runs discussed in this chapter are multiobjective (recognizing that objectives can be incorporated as constraints as well as in the objective function). Thus, each run output is in fact a point in n-dimensional net benefit space, where n is the number of objectives considered in each run. We dealt with the presentation of multiobjective information in various ways in the project. For many runs during the course of the project, we developed impact matrices (the tabular version of a point in net benefit space) showing the impacts of a run in terms of various dimensions of interest to decision-makers. In some cases, we developed explicit transformation curves (as for the two objectives of national income and equality of water distribution among provinces—Figure 11-5). For certain objectives, such as the objective of territorial integrity, we did not use explicit numerical scales but, rather, recognized that a given run either did or did not meet that objective in a reasonable way. In the case of territorial integrity, meeting the objective meant having a reasonably uniform distribution of development sites throughout the basin. In this chapter, some of the principal policy and physical trade-offs shown by the various runs are described.

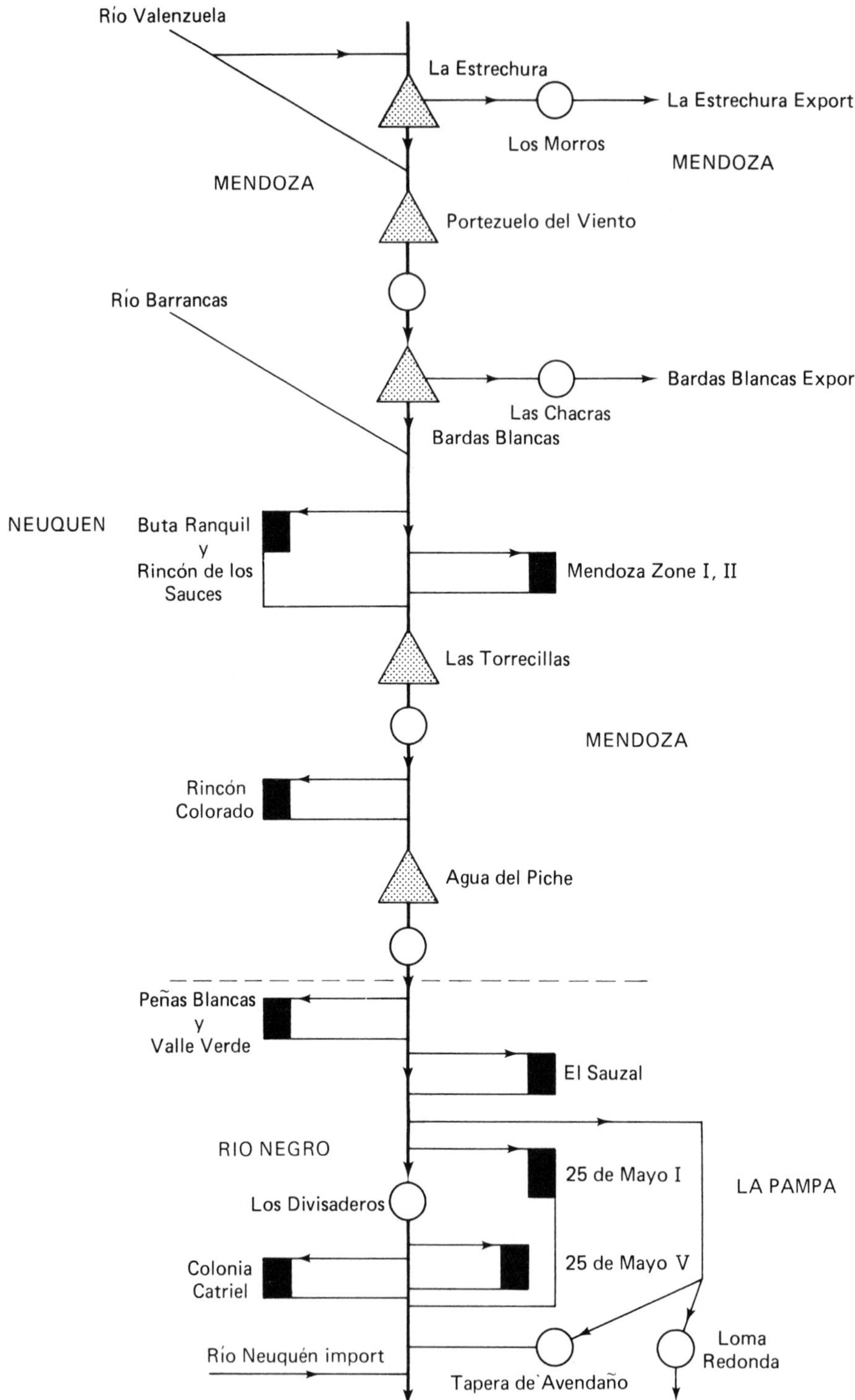

Figure 11-1
Schematic of the Río Colorado basin.

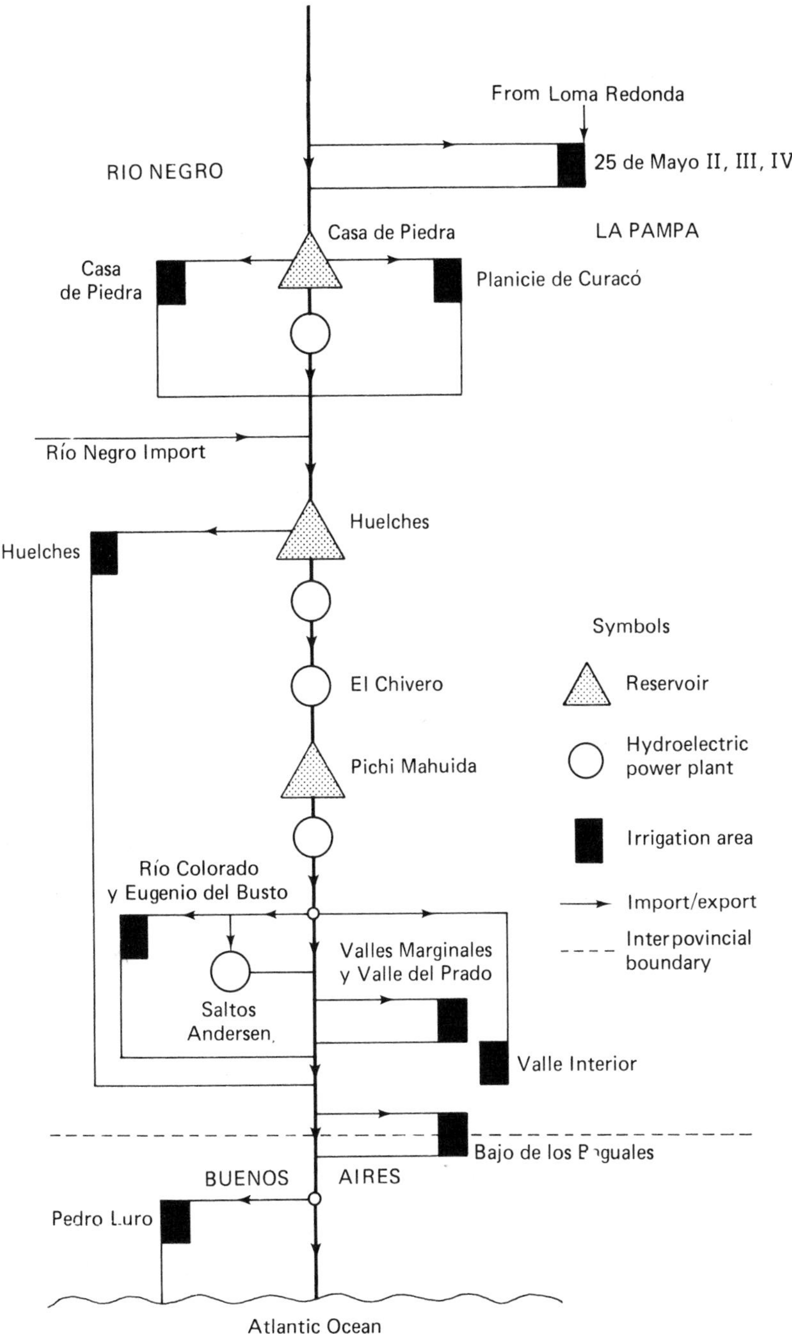

Figure 11-1
(continued)

SCREENING MODEL OUTPUTS

The runs described here have been grouped into four categories for convenience in presentation and discussion. The first three groups of runs are multiobjective runs; the last is a group of runs testing sensitivity to the values of key economic parameters. We call the four groups of runs, for short, *efficiency runs*, *irrigation/power runs*, *regional income runs*, and *sensitivity runs*.

The runs in the first group are multiobjective runs, with national income as the only term in the objective function and with regional objectives incorporated by means of various restrictions on imports and exports of water to and from the basin. The question of the existence and sizes of diversions is among the most important of the regional matters relating to the selection of a development plan for the river.

The second group of runs are multiobjective runs, with national income in the objective function and with the regional preference for the use of water for irrigation rather than for power incorporated by constraint. These runs, for various import/export policies, were carried out in two stages. First, reflecting the emphasis of the interprovincial treaty on the use of water for irrigation rather than for power, the runs were made for irrigation only, with power constrained out. Then, in a second step, the optimum irrigation configuration found in the first step was constrained into the solution, and only power complementary to the irrigation configuration was permitted into the new solution.

The third group of runs are multiobjective runs, with six terms in the objective function: national income and regional income to each of the five provinces. These runs were made with various sets of weights on national and regional incomes to explore the effects of different preferences as to regional income distribution on the outputs.

The fourth set of runs is a set of runs that examines the sensitivity of the solution of an efficiency run to changes in the values of three economic parameters: the interest rate, the premium on foreign exchange earnings, and the energy benefit coefficient.

EFFICIENCY RUNS

The runs in this group are multiobjective runs, with national income in the objective function and regional objectives incorporated by means of constraints on export and import possibilities (Table 11-1). These constraints were chosen on the basis both of policy considerations described by Argentine decision-makers and on the basis of the physical import/export possibilities judged to be reasonably feasible in the basin. The complete results of the efficiency runs are shown in Appendix 11A, Tables 11A-1 through 11A-6.

Table 11-1 Efficiency Runs

Efficiency Run No.	*Net National Income Benefits [10^9 m$n (1970)]*	*Imports*	*Exports*
1	254.20	Restricted to 100 m^3/sec	Unrestricted
2	251.10	Restricted to 100 m^3/sec	None permitted
3	249.30	Restricted to 100 m^3/sec	Over 100 m^3/sec
4	242.30	None permitted	None permitted
5	231.70	Exactly 300 m^3/sec in growing seasons	Unrestricted
6	227.20	None permitted	Exactly 43 m^3/sec

The most efficient run of the series (#1) was that in which exports were unrestricted and imports were allowed up to 100 m³/sec. In the least efficient run (#6), imports were not permitted and the permitted export to the Atuel basin competes both with upper basin use for power and irrigation and with later reuse in the central and lower basin.

The sizes of most irrigation projects depend on the combination of exports and imports in a given run, as shown in Table 11-2.

Table 11-2 Size of Irrigation Projects (ha) as Affected by Import/Export Relationships

Efficiency Run No.	1	2	5	3	4	6
		Imports > Exports			*Imports ≤ Exports*	
Buta Ranquil y Rincón de los Sauces	3,500	3,500	3,500	500	500	500
Mendoza Zone I, II	4,460	4,460	4,460	1,000	1,000	1,000
Rincón Colorado	500	500	500	0	0	0
Peñas Blancas y Valle Verde	20,000	20,000	20,000	6,400	6,400	20,000
Colonia Catriel	25,400	25,400	25,400	21,400	21,400	21,400
25 de Mayo I	4,300	4,300	4,300	0	0	800
25 de Mayo II, III, IV	54,720	54,720	54,720	0	0	0
Casa de Piedra	78,000	78,000	78,000	0	0	0
Valles Marginales y Valle del Prado	3,040	1,040	3,040	0	0	0
Bajo de los Baguales	40,000	40,000	40,000	0	0	0
Pedro Luro	218,000	218,000	218,000	20,830	21,210	12,320

Note: For corresponding import/export limits, see Table 11-1.

Some irrigation sites (El Sauzal, Planicie de Curacó, and Río Colorado y Eugenio del Busto) appeared at their maximum limits in all of the runs, regardless of what limits were placed on imports and exports. Similarly, some reservoirs and power plants (Portezuelo del Viento, Casa de Piedra, and Huelches, plus the power plant at Los Divisaderos) appeared, at various sizes, in all of the solutions. Other projects never entered the run solutions. These were the Pichi Mahuida reservoir and power plant, the Valle Interior irrigation area, and the Loma Redonda power plant. (For the importance of these results, see the discussion on uncertainty and investment strategy in the section on sensitivity runs, below).

An interesting aspect of the results is that the objective function often varies by only a small amount between runs, whereas the configuration that is optimal as governed by the import/export constraints in the run can vary a great deal. This is illustrated in Figure 11-2 for the case of Efficiency Runs #2 and #3 (an export to the Atuel basin is permitted in Run 3 but not in Run 2.) The difference in net benefits between the two runs is less than 1%, yet the irrigation area in #2 is 65% of the total irrigable area in the basin, and the irrigable area in #3 is 38% of the total because of the export requirements in Run #3. To the extent that the model and the parameter values are correct, this suggests that in deciding between these two configurations, regional objectives rather than national income might be the deciding factor.

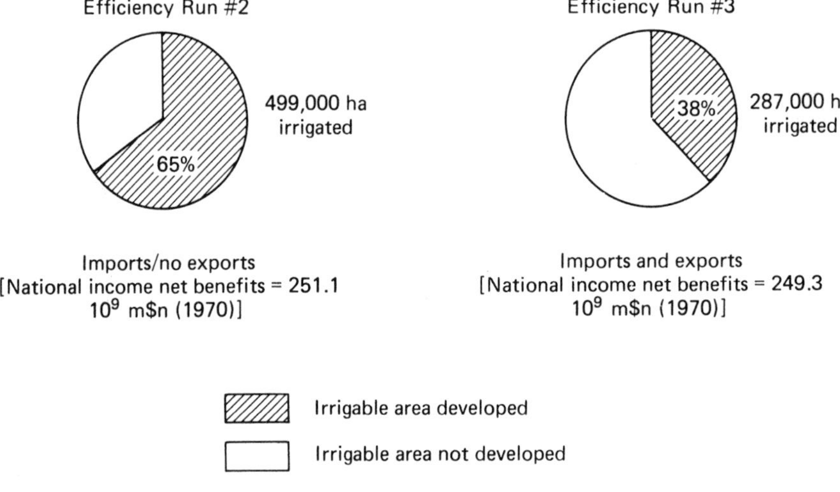

Figure 11-2
Net benefits obtained from different configurations. Note that the difference in net benefits between Efficiency Runs Nos. 2 and 3 is less than one percent.

IRRIGATION/POWER RUNS

The runs in this group examine the possible conflict between using the river for energy production and irrigation and for irrigation alone, a primary issue in the study of the Río Colorado. The runs are designed to explore the degree of complementarity between these two purposes. The objective function includes only national income, and irrigation is designated as the primary purpose in accordance with the interprovincial treaty described in Chapter 1. The runs were made in two stages: first, the optimum irrigation pattern was obtained by running the model with a constraint prohibiting the construction of power plants; and second, the optimum set of complementary power projects was obtained by running the model without any constraints on power but with new constraints setting each irrigation area equal to its size in the first stage. Three sets of runs using different export/import constraints (Table 11-3) were made. The results of the Irrigation/Power runs are shown in Tables 11A-7 to 11A-11.

Table 11-3 Export/Import Constraints for Irrigation/Power Runs*

	Exports	*Imports*
Irrigation/Power Runs #1	None	None
Irrigation/Power Runs #2	Unrestricted	None
Irrigation/Power Runs #3	Unrestricted	Unrestricted

*Each set of two runs is designed to give irrigation priority over power production. In the first run in each set, no energy production is permitted. In the second run, energy production is unconstrained, but the irrigation development pattern is set equal to that in the corresponding irrigation-only run.

In Irrigation/Power Runs #1, irrigation was developed to the maximum possible extent given the flow available. Without interfering with irrigation, complementary power production increased net national income benefits by 35%. In the other two sets of runs, less land was irrigated than in the first as a consequence of export demands, and the introduction of power generated a smaller increase in net benefits. Figure 11-3 shows these results.

Each of the irrigation/power runs with complementary power should be compared to the efficiency run corresponding to it in terms of import/export assumptions in order to ascertain the national income costs of implementing the regional objective of favoring irrigation. These trade-offs are shown in Table 11-4.

In comparing the two stages of each of the irrigation/power runs, it is interesting to note that the decision to add complementary power results in a restructuring of the scheme for water storage as compared to the storage configuration for the first stage (see Table 11A-8). In the first stage of each series, Casa de Piedra supplies all or a substantial share of storage. It is the reservoir in the system with the lowest unit storage cost of water and is thus favorable for irrigation. However, Casa de Piedra is also one of the shallower reservoirs in the system and thus is relatively unfavorable for power production. When complementary power production is permitted, Casa de Piedra appears in the solutions at a much reduced size.

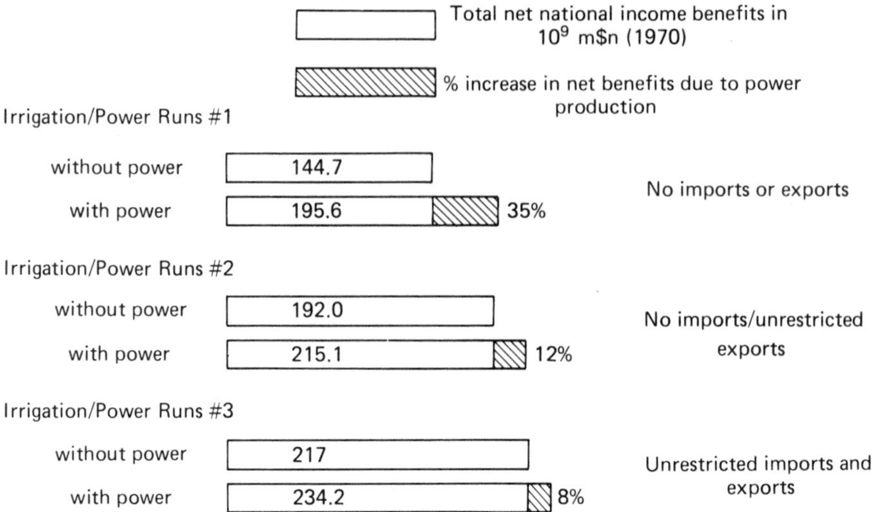

Figure 11-3
The effect of complementary power production on overall net benefits.

Table 11-4 Reduction in National Income Net Benefits when the Regional Objective of Giving Irrigation Priority Over Power Is Considered

Run	*National Income Net Benefits* [10^9 m$n (1970)]	*% Decrease in National Income Net Benefits*	*Irrigated Area* (ha)	*Annual Energy Generation* (GWh)
Efficiency #4*	242.3		291,000	2813
		19%		
Irrigation/Power #1 (with power)	195.6		341,000	1711
Efficiency #6*	227.2		216,000	1701
		6%		
Irrigation/Power #2 (with power)	215.1		233,000	1470
Efficiency #3*	249.3		287,000	1183
		6%		
Irrigation/Power #3 (with power)	234.2		289,000	999

*Efficiency Runs #4, #6, and #3, respectively, are used as base runs because they have the same import and export constraints as their associated irrigation/power runs.

REGIONAL INCOME RUNS

The three runs in this group are multiobjective runs with six terms in the objective function: national income and regional income to each of the five riverine provinces (see Chapter 9). To reflect the regional nature of these runs, no energy production was permitted; both imports and exports were, however, unrestricted.

Three sets of weights were used, one for each of the runs. These are shown in Table 11-5. In the first run, Regional Run #1, only national income was

Table 11-5 Multiobjective Weights Assigned for Regional Income Runs

		Regional Income Weights				
	National Income Weights	*Mendoza*	*Buenos Aires*	*Neuquén*	*Río Negro*	*La Pampa*
Regional Run #1 (base run)	1	0	0	0	0	0
Regional Run #2	1	1	1	1	1	1
Regional Run #3	1	1	1	10	10	10

assigned a positive weight of 1, and regional income to each of the five provinces was assigned a weight of zero. This run thus served as a base run and is identical to the first run in the pair of runs labeled Irrigation/Power Run #3. In the second run, labeled Regional Run #2, the weights were set at 1 for regional income to each of the five provinces, as well as national income; and in Regional Run #3, the third of this series, the weights on the poorer provinces of La Pampa, Río Negro, and Neuquén were changed to 10. A high weight on regional income to a particular province increases the weighted benefit coefficient of that province's regional income in the objective function and thus brings about higher irrigation development in that province as compared to runs in which that province's regional income has a lower weight. The results of the regional runs are summarized in Tables 11A-12 through 11A-17.

Regional Income Run #2, with equal weights on all objectives, produced a configuration nearly identical to that of Regional Run #1. As a result, it was decided to investigate the effects of placing substantially heavier weights on regional income to the three middle (and poorer) provinces of La Pampa, Neuquén, and Río Negro than on income to the nation and to Mendoza and Buenos Aires provinces. This change of weights approximately doubled provincial income benefits to Neuquén and Río Negro and tripled provincial income benefits to La Pampa. All of this was accomplished at the expense of Buenos Aires, whose provincial income benefits decreased by 24%. Table 11-6 summarizes these results. Figure 11-4 shows the shift in regional income benefits between Regional Runs #2 and #3 by grouping Mendoza and Buenos Aires as the wealthier provinces and La Pampa, Neuquén, and Río Negro as the poorer provinces.

The way in which the regional income shift between Runs #2 and #3 is reflected in the development configurations of the two runs is of interest. In Run #3, there are increases in the irrigation areas in the three provinces, as

Table 11-6 Shifts in Provincial Income Net Benefits, 10^9 m$n (1970)

	Mendoza	*Buenos Aires*	*Neuquén*	*Río Negro*	*La Pampa*
Regional Run #2	195.9	9.1	0.05	2.0	0.7
Regional Run #3	195.9	6.9	0.12	4.4	2.1
Net change	0%	−24%	+140%	+120%	+200%

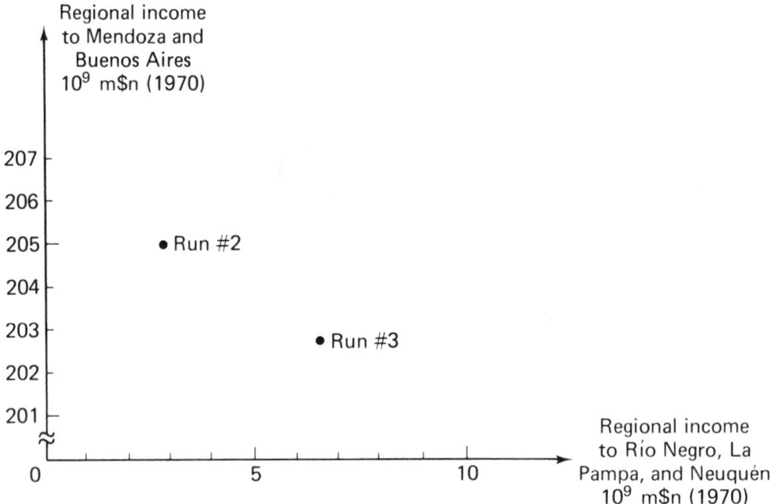

Figure 11-4
Regional income shift with change in regional income weights.

compared to Run #2, and in addition, Agua del Piche, which did not appear in either of the first two regional runs, was included when the middle province weights were increased in Regional Run #3. Agua del Piche provides regulation upstream of the import from the Río Neuquén, thus benefiting the middle provinces of Neuquén, Río Negro, and La Pampa. These configuration changes, emphasizing development in the relatively undeveloped middle reach of the river, represent progress toward the territorial integration objective.

Note also in Table 11-6 that the absolute amounts of regional income generated in these runs are small relative to national income benefits, except for benefits from exports to Mendoza, because of the netting effect of our accounting both for income flows into the region from irrigation development and income flows out of the region to finance the irrigation schemes (see Chapter 9).

An additional way of capturing trade-offs between national and regional objectives was undertaken in our study by using the alternative formulation of the screening model—Eqs. (5.40) to (5.46)—in which the regional objective is to minimize the total deviations of provincial water use from average provincial water use. A transformation curve between the national income objective and the water allocation objective, determined by the constraint method (see Chapters 2 and 5) was obtained early in the project and is shown in Figure 11-5. In the figure, water is equally distributed among the provinces at A on the horizontal axis; movement leftward from this point increases the inequality of water distribution among the provinces and increases national income benefits. (Because the benefit, cost, and engineering parameter values used in these runs were preliminary estimates, the numerical values indicated in Figure 11-5 are not comparable with those in the rest of this chapter.)

ECONOMIC PARAMETER SENSITIVITY RUNS

The screening model results described thus far were all done with the values of the economic parameters that seemed most reasonable given the information at hand. (Alternative approaches to screening are possible: for example, using artificially high benefit estimates and low cost estimates to screen out only the very worst projects, or using artificially low benefit estimates and high cost estimates to isolate only the very best projects.) However, in view of the importance of three economic parameters in particular—the interest rate, the foreign exchange premium, and the energy benefit coefficients—a study of the sensitivity of the model's results to changes in the values of these parameters was made. The results of the sensitivity runs are given in Tables 11A-18 to 11A-22.

Seven sensitivity runs are described here; the changes made in the economic data are summarized in Table 11-7. All other data (including the use of the efficiency objective and interbasin transfer characteristics) remained the same as in Efficiency Run #1, which is the base run for this series.

Sensitivity Runs #1 and #2 explore the effects of changing the interest rate on system configurations (Figure 11-6). In Run #1, a relatively low interest rate of 4% is used. In this run, there is essentially full development of the river, given the import/export assumptions. Irrigation development

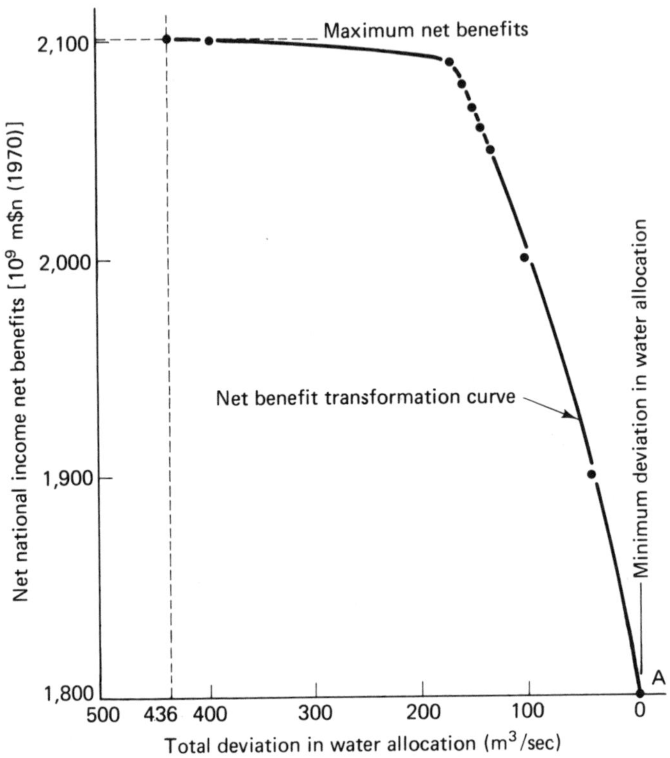

Figure 11-5
Transformation curve between the national income and equal water allocation objectives.

Table 11-7 Summary of Economic Sensitivity Runs

	Interest Rate	*Foreign Exchange Premium*	*Energy Benefit Coefficient* [m$n (1970)/kWh]	*Location of Increased Energy Benefit Coefficient*
Sensitivity Run #1	4%	150%	8.6	
Sensitivity Run #2	16%	150%	8.6	
Sensitivity Run #3	8%	100%	8.6	
Sensitivity Run #4	8%	300%	8.6	
Sensitivity Run #5	8%	150%	24	Río Colorado basin
Sensitivity Run #6	8%	150%	12	Río Colorado basin
Sensitivity Run #7	8%	150%	12	Atuel and Río Colorado basins
Efficiency Run #1 (base run)	8%	150%	8.6	

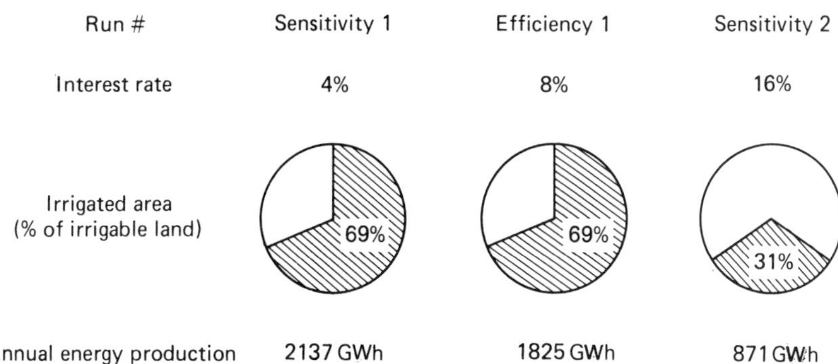

Figure 11-6
The effects of the interest rate on irrigation and power development.

in this run did not vary appreciably from that of Efficiency Run #1; power development, however, increased from an installed capacity of 604 MW to a capacity of 781 MW.

In Sensitivity Run #2, a relatively high interest rate of 16% was used. In this run, few projects appear in the solution, indicating that with high interest rates regional objectives, including the territorial integration objective, are not achieved.

Sensitivity Runs #3 and #4 were used to explore the effects of changing the premium on foreign exchange earnings and expenditures. A lower foreign exchange premium as in Sensitivity Run #3 (100% premium) implies lower national income benefits for irrigation output. The results of Sensitivity Run #3 show a reduction of irrigation development, from 69% of the irrigable area to 44% (Table 11-8). However, increasing the foreign exchange premium

Table 11-8 The Effect of the Foreign Exchange Premium on Development

	Sensitivity Run #3	*Efficiency Run #1*	*Sensitivity Run #4*
Foreign exchange premium	100%	150%	300%
Irrigated area	337,000 ha	524,000 ha	535,000 ha
Annual energy generation	2,229 GWh	1,825 GWh	1,788 GWh

as in Sensitivity Run #4 (300% premium) does not result in a significant increase in irrigation development as compared to Efficiency Run #1. Irrigation development is constrained by water availability in the Sensitivity Run #4 configuration and cannot be increased substantially.

Sensitivity Runs #5, #6, and #7 were made to test the impact on the system configuration of higher power benefits, both in the Río Colorado basin alone and in the Río Colorado and Atuel basins. The benefit coefficient of 24 m$n (1970)/kWh used in Run #5 would reflect an alternative cost situation in Buenos Aires in which the power made available as a result of Río Colorado basin development would be used entirely as peaking power (Chapter 9). The value of 12 m$n (1970)/kWh, in both the Río Colorado and Atuel basins, represents an intermediate assumption as to power values.

Both runs that incorporated higher power coefficients only in the Río Colorado basin, Runs #5 and #6, resulted in configurations that emphasized Río Colorado basin development. In Run #5, where an assumption corresponding to peaking power is used, the export to the Atuel basin is eliminated, and many of the upstream irrigation areas are eliminated or substantially reduced in size. This indicates that should the power dispatching system in Buenos Aires change substantially, changes in the Río Colorado development configuration would be indicated on national income grounds, although not necessarily or probably on regional grounds.

Increasing benefits in both the Río Colorado and Atuel basins to 12 m$n (1970)/kWh resulted in a configuration nearly identical to that of the base run.

A principal reason for undertaking sensitivity analysis as in the runs discussed here is that, with an uncertain future, a single output is unlikely to reveal the "best" investment strategy, because only a single set of input parameter values and weights is considered in obtaining a single solution. To be the best investment strategy, a development configuration probably should be a fairly reliable, fairly good investment over a wide range of parameter and objective values, thus giving the planner some assurance that, in an uncertain world, the investments he suggests are likely to pay off.

Several of the projects in the basin appear to be quite good by this criterion, at least in national income terms and given the import/export assumptions of the sensitivity runs. These projects appear in the solution under a wide range of sensitivity parameter values (Table 11-9). Table 11-9 also shows those projects that did not appear in the solution of any sensitivity run; using the same criterion, such projects can be rated as poor.

SIMULATION MODEL OUTPUTS

The second step in the planning methodology was to use the basic simulation model to analyze the hydrologic reliability of the "best" configurations derived from the screening model—"best" in the sense of most responsive to Argentine objectives. The simulation model analysis was carried out in terms of both hydrologic reliability and net national income benefits. The reliability of a development configuration is taken to be the frequency with which the system meets irrigation, power, and export targets. Regional and other aspects of the runs were captured in the choice of the initial runs to be analyzed.

Four runs chosen for analysis by simulation are described here: These

Table 11-9 Projects Appearing or Not Appearing in All Sensitivity Run Results

	Projects That Appeared in the Solutions of **All** *Sensitivity Runs*	*Projects that Did* **Not** *Appear in the Solution of Any Sensitivity Run*
Reservoirs	Portezuelo del Viento* Las Torrecillas Huelches*	Bardas Blancas
Irrigation areas	Buta Ranquil y Rincón de los Sauces* Mendoza Zone I, II Peñas Blancas y Valle Verde* El Sauzal* Colonia Catriel Río Colorado y Eugenio del Busto* Pedro Luro*	Valle Interior†
Power plants	Portezuelo del Viento* Las Torrecillas	Las Chacras Loma Redonda
Imports and exports	—	Bardas Blancas export Río Negro import

*Also appeared in all efficiency run solutions.
†Also did not appear in any efficiency run solution.

are Irrigation/Power Run #1, including both the irrigation-only and the complementary power versions; and Irrigation/Power Run #2, again including both versions. (The straightforward results of a fifth screening model run chosen for simulation, Efficiency Run #1, are not described here.) These four irrigation/power runs were thought to represent the most feasible solutions given Argentine preferences toward regional objectives. The Irrigation/Power Run #1 series permitted neither imports nor exports of water; the #2 series permitted exports but no imports. A summary of the screening model results for these runs is given in Table 11-10.

Table 11-10 A Summary of the Screening Model Results for Runs Chosen for Simulation

Run	*Net National Income Benefits* [10^9 m$n (1970)]	*Installed Capacity* (MW)	*Irrigated Area* (ha)	*Reservoir Storage Capacity* (MCM)	*Export Capacity** (m^3/sec)
Irrigation/Power #1					
without power	144.7	0	341,000	1,630	0
with complementary power	195.6	766	341,000	4,650	0
Irrigation/Power #2					
without power	192.0	52**	233,000	2,050	43
with complementary power	215.1	541	233,000	4,620	43

*No imports were permitted in these runs.
**On the export to Atuel basin.

In the simulation analysis, the search for system configurations with high net benefits and high reliability is carried out by the analyst rather than by an algorithm such as that embodied in the optimizing models. We performed the simulation analyses of each of the four screening model runs in the following way. First, the configuration given by the screening model was simulated in order to evaluate its performance given hydrologic variability. All run-dependent constraints (such as import/export constraints) in the screening model run were maintained in the associated simulation run. The results were then analyzed, and various modifications to the initial development configuration were proposed. New configurations resulting from these proposals were simulated in order to determine which of these performed best with respect to net benefits and reliability.

In general, two types of modifications can be effective in developing configurations that achieve high net benefits and reliability. These are: (1) increases in reservoir storage, which increase streamflow regulation and thus reduce short-term irrigation losses (but at the expense of higher reservoir costs); and (2) decreases in irrigation acreage, which decrease short-term irrigation losses at the expense of reduced long-term irrigation benefits.

Because in the simulation model the configuration is chosen as a model input rather than obtained as a model output as in the screening model, we present the results in a format that emphasizes overall system performance rather than the detailed system configuration itself. System performance in the tables of results is expressed in terms of net national income benefits and reliability; reliability is measured as the percentage ratio between the actual net benefits obtained and the long-term net benefits that would have been obtained had there been no deficits in the water supply. (In the case of exports to Mendoza, the ratio has been defined in terms of gross rather than net benefits).

SIMULATION OF IRRIGATION/POWER RUN #1 (FOR IRRIGATION ONLY)

Irrigation/Power Run #1, without complementary power, is the screening model run in which irrigation within the basin was given absolute priority for water use by assuming no imports, exports, or power production. The run configurations and results are shown in Tables 11A-23 and 11A-24.

The results of simulating this configuration showed that the storage capacity (1,630 MCM at Casa de Piedra) was not enough to regulate the river and meet the irrigation demands with high reliability. Only about 60% of the long-term no-deficit irrigation net benefits were attained. A proposed improvement to the Irrigation/Power Run #1 configuration was to increase storage capacity at Casa de Piedra to 5,000 MCM. The simulation of this modified configuration showed that, although the river was more regulated, the percentage of long term irrigation benefits attained still remained low at

70%. Because of this, a third configuration was proposed and tested in which storage capacity at Casa de Piedra remained at 5,000 MCM, but the total irrigation area was reduced by about 10%. This change produced a more reliable irrigation system with higher net benefits; these benefits were approximately 94% of the long-term no-deficit benefits for the reduced area (85% for the full area).

The fourth configuration that was proposed and tested included an increase of total storage capacity to 9,000 MCM (4,000 MCM at Las Torrecillas), and a readjustment of all but one of the irrigation areas back to their original sizes (Rincón de los Sauces was eliminated because it would be inundated by the Las Torrecillas reservoir—see Chapter 1). The results of the simulation showed that this configuration was not better than the previous one in terms of net benefits. Thus, a new configuration with the location of additional storage changed to Huelches was run in the simulation model; this showed the highest net benefits of the series. A final configuration that was proposed and simulated was one in which the irrigation area was decreased while keeping the storage capacity constant. In this case, the simulation results showed that overall net benefits decreased slightly. Net benefits and reliability in relation to storage capacity and area irrigated for this series of runs are summarized in Table 11-11. An interesting result of this series of runs is that

Table 11-11 Net Benefits and Reliability in Relation to Storage Capacity and Area Irrigated, Irrigation Power Runs #1 (without Power)

	Simulation Runs					
Characteristics	I	II	III	IV	V	VI
Reservoir capacity (MCM)	1,630	5,000	5,000	9,000	9,000	9,000
Irrigated area (ha)	341,000	341,000	307,000	338,000	341,000	307,000
Net irrigation benefits as % of long-term no-deficit benefits	60%	70%	85%	84%	99%	99%
Total net benefits [10^9 m$n (1970)]	84.6	96.8	124.7	110.3	137.7	132.5

the irrigated area from the corresponding screening model run (341,000 ha) can be irrigated with positive net national income benefits and with reasonable reliability as long as storage capacity is increased sufficiently. In these runs the search for higher net benefits tended to lead toward relatively high storage levels (as compared to screening model results) rather than to the alternative adjustment to increase reliability, reducing the irrigated area, because of the relatively low additional costs for storage assumed in the model. In detailed project studies, it would be important to conduct sensitivity analysis of these results with respect to the reservoir cost parameters and their relationship to other benefit and cost parameters, particularly those relating to short-term loss functions.

SIMULATION OF IRRIGATION/POWER RUN #1 (WITH COMPLEMENTARY POWER)

In this series of runs, the analysts were concerned not only with irrigation reliability and net benefits but also with the reliability and net benefits of the complementary power production that was permitted. Configurations and results for these runs are given in Tables 11A-25 and 11A-26.

The initial simulation of Irrigation/Power Run #1 (with complementary power) showed that this configuration contains a very unreliable system that can achieve only about 50% of long-term no-deficit irrigation benefits, and in which power targets are frequently missed. A proposed improvement, tested with a second run, was to increase total storage capacity to 10,000 MCM. The results of the simulation run showed that total net benefits could be more than doubled, with the sharpest increase being in irrigation. However, irrigation benefits were still low in relative terms, and power targets were frequently missed. A further modification to the configuration was thus suggested in which the irrigation area was reduced by 5%. The simulation results from this run showed that net benefits increased. A few other configurations were proposed and tested, but the simulation results showed only marginal changes in the objective function value.

An important observation derived from the results of this set of runs is that power production does not conflict with irrigation supply (i.e., does not reduce irrigation benefits) only if significant additional storage is provided. Moreover, the economic advantages of power generation are not large. In the screening model Irrigation/Power Runs #1, the introduction of power increased net benefits by 35%; the increase estimated by the simulation model is only about 16% because of the unreliability of the power system.

SIMULATION OF IRRIGATION/POWER RUN #2 (FOR IRRIGATION ONLY)

This development configuration contains an export to Mendoza, and so a principal question in the simulation analysis of this configuration is whether to give priority to the export or to the downstream demands under conditions of streamflow variability. The first two configurations tested via simulation (Irrigation/Power Run #2 and a variant with increased storage) assumed priority for downstream irrigation. The results showed that export flows were unreliable, leading to low overall benefits. (Tables 11A-27 and 11A-28 show configurations and results for this set of runs.)

A modification to the configuration was made that included a change in the operating policy at La Estrechura reservoir in order to give priority to exports. Simulation of this new configuration showed that the export benefits could be increased greatly at the cost of a small decrease in the downstream irrigation net benefits. Although export benefits were estimated at only 85% of long-term no-deficit benefits, further improvement in this indicator was prohibited by the impossibility of additional increases in storage at La Estrechura. As was true for the Irrigation/Power #1 Runs (for irrigation only) an interesting result of this series of runs is that the irrigated area from the corresponding screening model run (233,000 ha) can be irrigated with positive net national income benefits and with reasonable reliability as long as storage capacity is increased sufficiently.

SIMULATION OF IRRIGATION/POWER RUN #2 (INCLUDING COMPLEMENTARY POWER)

This configuration includes the irrigation sites and the export to the Atuel basin of the previous configuration and also includes complementary power production. Configurations and results for these runs are given in Tables 11A-29 and 11A-30. Simulation analysis of this configuration and five variants showed that the inclusion of complementary power was just barely a paying proposition. Maximum net benefits from the runs studied were 166.9×10^9 m\$n (1970) as compared to the maximum of 160.9×10^9 m\$n (1970) for the Irrigation/Power Runs #2 without complementary power. Additional storage for power had to be located in the deeper, more costly reservoirs, and the lack of reliability of complementary power does not allow the power benefit to offset these increased costs by a substantial margin.

A comparison between the simulation run in each series with the highest net national income benefits and the associated screening model run is given in Table 11-12. A detailed comparison of simulation results for the best run in each series is given in Table 11A-31.

Table 11-12 Summary Comparison of Simulation Runs (The Best of Each Series) with the Corresponding Screening Runs

Run	*Simulation Model Net Benefits* [10^9 m\$n (1970)]	*Screening Model Net Benefits* [10^9 m\$n (1970)]	*Simulation/ Screening Net Benefits Ratio*
Irrigation/Power #1			
without power	137.7	144.7	0.95
with complementary power	159.6	195.6	0.82
Irrigation/Power #2			
without power	160.9	192.0	0.84
with complementary power	166.9	215.1	0.78

SEQUENCING MODEL OUTPUTS

The third step in our methodology was to analyze the "best" configurations resulting from the simulation analyses by means of the sequencing model; "best" again is used here in the sense of most responsive to Argentine objectives. The results of the sequencing model are designed to be workable development alternatives at the prefeasibility level.

The configurations selected for sequencing that are described here are Irrigation/Power Runs #1, both for irrigation only and with complementary power, and Irrigation/Power Run #2 with complementary power. The particular variant of the simulation model runs that was used for sequencing in each case was selected on the basis of net benefits and reliability. The configuration in each sequencing run is the same as that in the simulation run selected for analysis, except that some small irrigation areas are aggregated to form larger areas, and some larger irrigation areas are disaggregated to permit construction of only part of the area in a given time period.

The sequencing model contains parameters related to flow whose values are project-specific (see Chapter 8); these must be determined prior to each run on the basis of the screening and simulation model results. The majority of these parameters can be determined by checking the simulation model results related to flow decision variables for the critical season to which they refer. An exception is $\bar{c}_s$, the consumptive use at a reservoir due to filling during the critical season of the year. This parameter was obtained from separate simulation analyses of reservoir fill.

A sequencing model run begins with a set of projects whose sizes have already been determined as a result of the screening/simulation process. The questions addressed with the model are whether and when to build each of these projects, taking into account project interrelationships and budget and population constraints where these are applicable. The output of the model is the construction period that, given the model assumptions, is optimal for each of the projects. In our analysis prior to making sequencing runs, we found that budget constraints in the aggregate would probably not be binding for Río Colorado development, (Chapter 9) and so these were not used in the model runs. Population constraints would, however, probably be binding for significant levels of development because of the relatively low current population (and hence low numbers of farmers available to work new irrigation areas) in the Río Colorado basin (Chapter 1). In the model, these population constraints (Chapter 9) were implemented and acted to allocate projects over time in the four construction periods. (In more detailed studies, it would be appropriate to examine the effects on sequencing of other constraints as well, including constraints on governmental capacities to implement projects, constraints on the capacity of the construction industry, and others).

The full results of the sequencing model for the three configurations of Irrigation/Power Run #1 (irrigation only), Irrigation/Power Run #1 (with complementary power), and Irrigation/Power Run #2 (with complementary power) are given in Table 11-13. Figures 11-7-I through 11-7-IV show the different stages suggested for sequencing the configuration of Irrigation/Power Run #1 (irrigation only). In Table 11-13, it will be seen that the population constraints and the project linkages built into the sequencing model result in at least one project being postponed until the fourth construction period in each run. (Existing projects, labeled E in the table, are all implemented in the first period since they are entered into the model with positive benefits and zero costs.)

Table 11-13 Sequencing Model Results*

Project	Type	Irrigation/Power Run #1										Irrigation/Power Run #2				
		Irrigation Only					With Power					With Power				
		Size	1	2	3	4	Size	1	2	3	4	Size	1	2	3	4
La Estrechura	Reservoir	—					—					960 MCM	N			
	Export	—					—					36 m³/sec		N		
Los Morros	Power plant	—					—					51 MW		N		
Portezuelo del Viento	Reservoir	—					3,600 MCM	N				3,600 MCM	N			
	Power plant	—					156 MW	N				78 MW	N			
Buta Ranquil, Rincón de los	Irrigation	500 ha	E				500 ha	E				500 ha	E			
Sauces, and Mendoza Zone I, II	area	4,000 ha			N		3,000 ha		N			1,000 ha		N		
Las Torrecillas	Reservoir	—					6,000 MCM	N				9,000 MCM	N			
	Power plant	—					191 MW	N				100 MW	N			
Peñas Blancas, Valle Verde and	Irrigation	6,400 ha	E				6,400 ha	E				6,400 ha	E			
Rincón Colorado	area	13,600 ha			N		13,600 ha				N	13,600 ha				N
El Sauzal and 25 de Mayo I	Irrigation	1,700 ha	E				1,700 ha	E				1,700 ha	E			
	area	5,200 ha			N		5,200 ha		N			5,200 ha		N		
Los Divisaderos	Power plant	—					11 MW		N			8 MW		N		
Tapera de Avendaño	Power plant	—					144 MW	N				130 MW	N			
25 de Mayo V and Colonia Catriel	Irrigation	1,400 ha	E				1,400 ha	E				1,400 ha	E			
	area	10,600 ha		N			10,600 ha		N			10,600 ha		N		
		17,400 ha			N		17,400 ha				N	13,400 ha			N	
Casa de Piedra	Reservoir	5,000 MCM		N			39 MCM				N	47 MCM				N
Planicie de Curacó	Irrigation	25,600 ha			N		25,600 ha				N	25,600 ha				N
Huelches	Reservoir	4,000 MCM		N			4,000 MCM	N				4,000 MCM	N			
	Power plant	—					75 MW	N				49 MW	N			
Río Colorado and Eugenio del	Irrigation	4,500 ha	E				4,500 ha	E				4,500 ha	E			
Busto	area	12,500 ha		N			12,500 ha		N			12,500 ha			N	
Bajo de los Baguales	Irrigation	18,850 ha			N		18,850 ha				N	—				
Pedro Luro	Irrigation	60,000 ha	E				60,000 ha	E				60,000 ha	E			
	area	75,000 ha		N			75,000 ha		N			76,100 ha		N		
		83,000 ha				N	83,000 ha				N	—				
Net Benefits (Sequencing) 10^9 m$n (1970)		84.0					179.0					204.8				
Net benefits (Simulation) 10^9 m$n (1970)		137.7					159.6					163.2				
Net benefits (Screening) 10^9 m$n (1970)		144.7					195.6					215.1				

**Notation:* E = Existing project
N = New project.

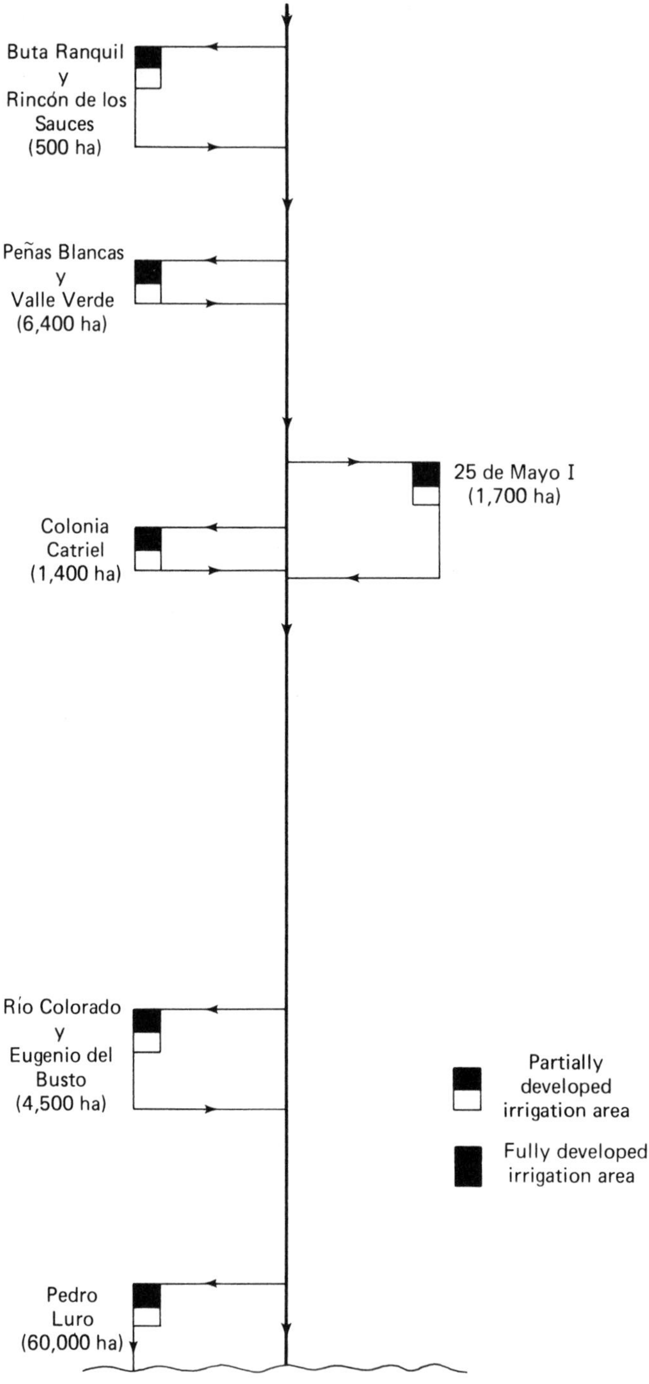

Figure 11-7-I
Sequencing model results for Irrigation/Power Run No. 1 (irrigation only), Period I (existing projects).

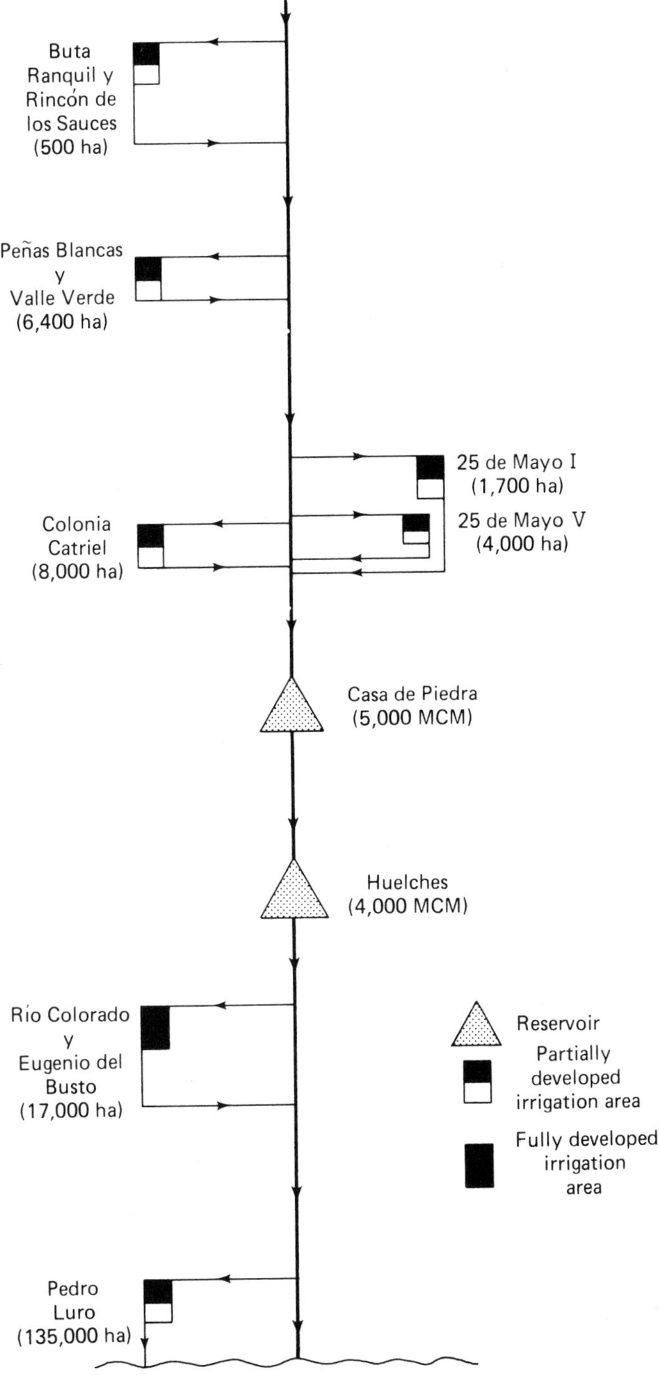

Figure 11-7-II
Sequencing model results for Irrigation/Power Run No. 1 (irrigation only), Period II.

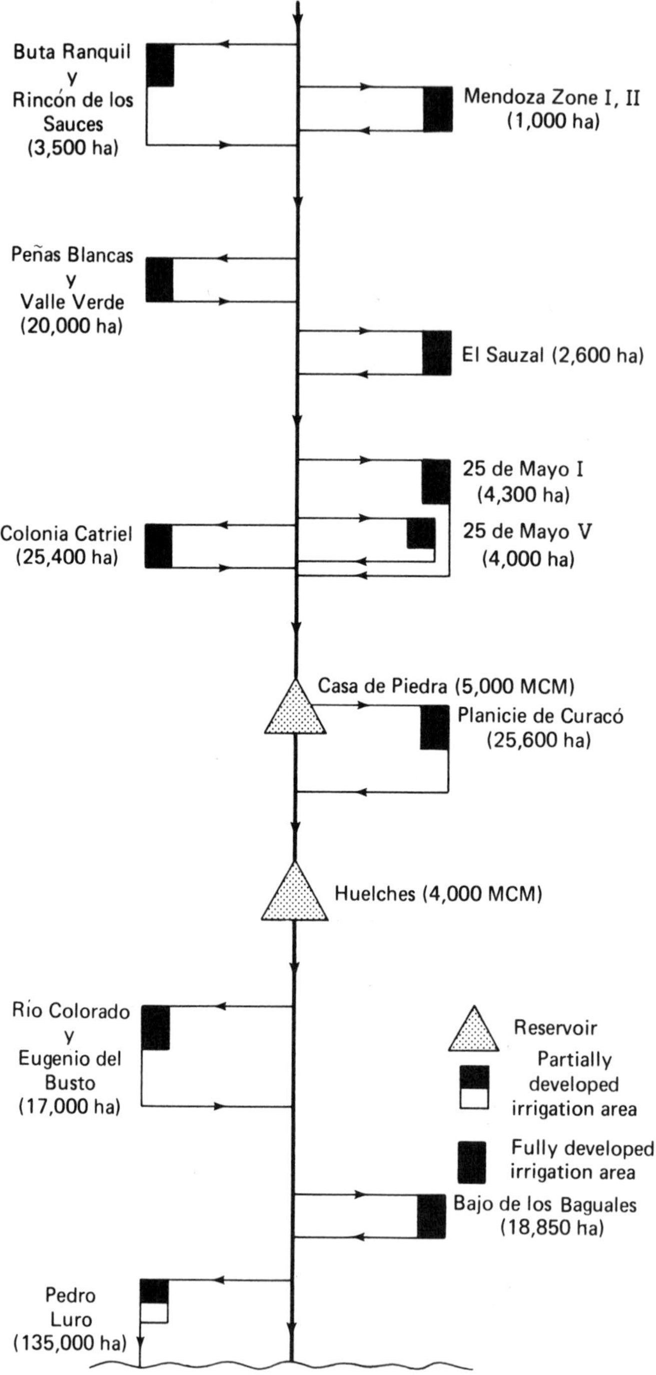

Figure 11-7-III
Sequencing model results for Irrigation/Power Run No. 1 (irrigation only), Period III.

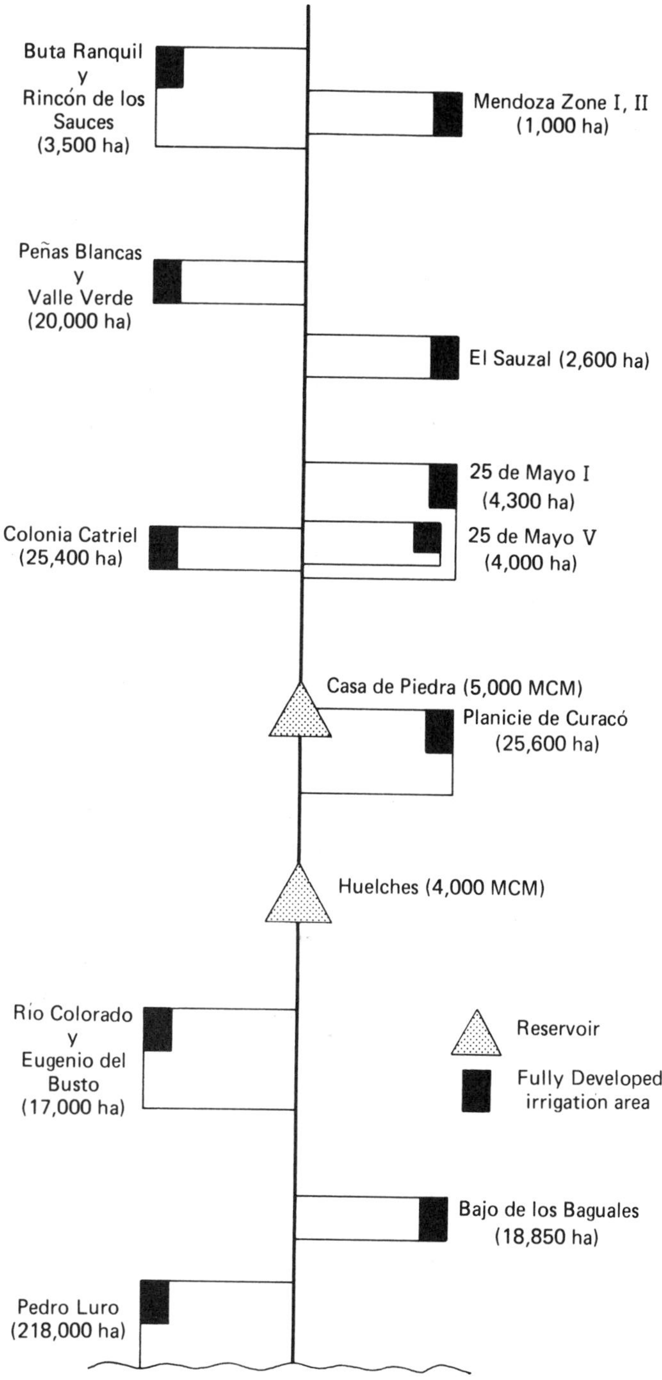

Figure 11-7-IV
Sequencing model results for Irrigation/Power Run No. 1 (irrigation only), Period IV.

APPENDIX 11A TABLES OF MODEL OUTPUT

Table 11A-1 Import/Export Characteristics of Efficiency Runs

Efficiency Run No.	*Characteristics*	*Comments*
1	Imports/Exports	Import restricted to 100 m^3/sec
2	Imports/No exports	Import restricted to 100 m^3/sec
3	Imports/Exports	Import restricted to 100 m^3/sec; export required to be over 100 m^3/sec
4	No imports/No exports	
5	Imports/Exports	Import required to increase during growing seasons to 300 m^3/sec
6	No imports/Exports	Export required to be exactly 43 m^3/sec

Note: Runs are ordered in decreasing value of their resultant objective function.

Table 11A-2 Summary of Efficiency Results

Characteristics	*Upper Bound*	*Run No.* 1	2	3	4	5	6
National income net benefits [10^9 m$n (1970)]		254.2	251.1	249.3	242.3	231.7	227.2
No. of irrigation projects	17	16	15	9	9	16	10
Irrigation area (1,000 ha)	763	524	499	287	291	647	216
% total irrigable area	100%	69%	65%	38%	38%	85%	28%
No. of reservoirs	8	6	5	5	5	5	6
Reservoir capacity (MCM)	33,240	9,950	17,040	4,240	15,600	8,250	8,590
% total storage capacity	100%	30%	51%	13%	47%	25%	26%
No. of power projects	13	8	9	6	7	8	8
Installed capacity (MW)		604	957	349	876	411	537
Annual production (GWh)		1,825	3,161	1,183	2,813	1,382	1,701
Capacity factor		0.34	0.38	0.39	0.37	0.38	0.36
No. of imports	2	1	1	1	0	1	0
Import capacity (m^3/sec)		100	100	100	0	300	0
No. of exports	2	1	0	2	0	1	1
Export capacity (m^3/sec)		43	0	113	0	43	43

Table 11A-3 Efficiency Results: Reservoirs*

Reservoir	*Upper Bound* (MCM)	*Reservoir Capacity* (MCM) *Run No.* 1	2	3	4	5	6	*No. of Times in Solution*
Mendoza Export								
La Estrechura	960	713	0	577	0	713	713	4
Portezuelo del Viento	3,600	1,415	3,600	1,838	3,600	1,415	1,399	All
Bardas Blancas	1,680	0	0	137	0	0	0	1
Central Basin								
Las Torrecillas	13,400	3,022	6,603	0	6,721	3,022	3,121	5
Agua del Piche	4,050	2,030	3,456	0	3,505	0	2,026	4
Lower Basin								
Casa de Piedra	5,000	1,196	2,214	879	778	1,218	830	All
Huelches	4,250	1,575	1,164	813	997	1,883	496	All
Pichi Mahuida	300	0	0	0	0	0	0	0
Total	33,240	9.950	17,040	4,240	15,600	8,250	8,590	

**Note:* Column figures in the output tables do not necessarily add to totals because of rounding.

Table 11A-4 Efficiency Results: Irrigation Areas

Irrigation Area	Irrigable Area (ha)	Area (ha) Run No. 1	2	3	4	5	6	No. of Times in Solution
Buta Ranquil y Rincón de los Sauces	3,500	3,500	3,500	500	500	3,500	500	All
Mendoza Zone I, II	5,020	4,460	4,460	1,000	1,000	4,460	1,000	All
Rincón Colorado	500	500	500	0	0	500	0	3
Peñas Blancas y Valle Verde	20,000	20,000	20,000	6,400	6,400	20,000	20,000	All
El Sauzal	2,600	2,600	2,600	2,600	2,600	2,600	2,600	All
25 de Mayo I	4,300	4,300	4,300	0	0	4,300	800	4
25 de Mayo V	4,000	4,000	4,000	4,000	4,000	4,000	4,000	All
Colonia Catriel	25,400	25,400	25,400	21,400	21,400	25,400	21,400	All
25 de Mayo II, III, IV	54,720	54,720	54,720	0	0	54,720	0	3
Casa de Piedra	78,000	78,000	78,000	0	0	78,000	0	3
Planicie de Curacó	25,600	25,600	25,600	25,600	25,600	25,600	25,600	All
Huelches	150,000	23,100	0	0	0	14,570	0	2
Río Colorado y Eugenio del Busto	17,000	17,000	17,000	17,000	17,000	17,000	17,000	All
Valle Interior	110,000	0	0	0	0	0	0	0
Valles Marginales y Valle del Prado	4,040	3,040	1,040	0	0	3,040	0	3
Bajo de los Baguales	40,000	40,000	40,000	0	0	40,000	0	3
Pedro Luro	218,000	218,000	218,000	20,830	21,210	218,000	12,320	All
Total	763,000	524,000	499,000	287,000	291,000	647,000	216,000	

Table 11A-5 Efficiency Results: Hydroelectric Power Plants

Power Plant	Capacity or Production	Installed Capacity (MW) and Annual Production (GWh)						No. of Times in Solution
		Run No.						
		1	2	3	4	5	6	
Los Morros	Cap	52	0	30	0	52	52	4
	Prod	264	0	156	0	264	264	
Portezuelo del Viento	Cap	72	168	99	168	72	74	All
	Prod	306	841	419	841	306	322	
Las Chacras	Cap	0	0	58	0	0	0	1
	Prod	0	0	297	0	0	0	
Las Torrecillas	Cap	129	249	0	250	129	138	5
	Prod	395	753	0	757	395	423	
Agua del Piche	Cap	91	180	0	180	0	97	4
	Prod	276	539	0	544	0	290	
Los Divisaderos	Cap	10	10	9	10	11	10	All
	Prod	30	30	26	30	33	30	
Tapera de Avendaño	Cap	80	101	0	120	0	80	4
	Prod	205	337	0	361	0	215	
Loma Redonda	Cap	0	0	0	0	0	0	0
	Prod	0	0	0	0	0	0	
Casa de Piedra	Cap	54	83	50	46	6	28	All
	Prod	157	241	120	115	18	64	
Huelches	Cap	116	112	103	102	91	58	All
	Prod	192	258	165	165	231	93	
El Chivero	Cap	0	37	0	0	39	0	2
	Prod	0	108	0	0	102	0	
Pichi Mahuida	Cap	0	0	0	0	0	0	0
	Prod	0	0	0	0	0	0	
Saltos Andersen	Cap	0	17	0	0	11	0	2
	Prod	0	54	0	0	33	0	
Total	Cap	604	957	349	876	411	537	
	Prod	1,825	3,161	1,183	2,813	1,382	1,701	

Table 11A-6 Efficiency Results: Interbasin Transfers

Interbasin Transfer	Diversion Capacity (m^3/sec)					
	Run No.					
	1	2	3	4	5	6
La Estrechura export	43	0	25	0	43	43
Bardas Blancas export	0	0	88	0	0	0
Río Neuquén import	100	100	100	0	0	0
Río Negro import	0	0	0	0	300	0
Total imports	100	100	100	0	300	0
Total exports	43	0	113	0	43	43

Table 11A-7 Summary of Irrigation/Power Results

		Run Number					
		1		2		3	
Characteristics	Upper Bound	*Irr. Only*	*With Power*	*Irr. Only*	*With Power*	*Irr. Only*	*With Power*
National income net benefits 10^9 m$n (1970)		144.7	195.6	192.0	215.1	217	234.2
No. of irrigation projects	17	12	12	10	10	9	9
Irrigation area (1,000 ha)	763	341	341	233	233	289	289
% Total irrigable area	100%	45%	45%	30%	30%	38%	38%
No. of reservoirs	8	1	5	2	6	4	5
Reservoir capacity (MCM)	33,240	1,630	4,650	2,050	4,620	3,570	3,420
% Total storage capacity	100%	5%	14%	6%	14%	11%	10%
No. of power projects	13		6	1*	8	2*	6
Installed capacity (MW)			766	52*	541	99*	309
Annual production (GWh)			1,711	264*	1,470	504*	999
Capacity factor			0.25	0.58	0.31	0.58	0.37
No. of imports	2	0	0	0	0	1	1
Import capacity (m^3/sec)		0	0	0	0	100	100
No. of exports	2	0	0	1	1	2	2
Export capacity (m^3/sec)		0	0	43	43	115	115
Increase in net benefits due to power (%)			35%		12%		8%

*On export to Atuel Basin.

Table 11A-8 Irrigation/Power Results: Reservoirs

		Reservoir Capacity (MCM)					
		Run No.					
		1		2		3	
Reservoir	*Upper Bound* (MCM)	*Irr. Only*	*With Power*	*Irr. Only*	*With Power*	*Irr. Only*	*With Power*
Mendoza Export							
La Estrechura	960	0	0	713	713	713	713
Portezuelo del Viento	3,600	0	1,440	0	1,394	1,140	1,140
Bardas Blancas	1,680	0	0	0	0	105	105
Central Basin							
Las Torrecillas	13,400	0	1,584	0	908	0	0
Agua del Piche	4,050	0	1,076	0	1,096	0	0
Lower Basin							
Casa de Piedra	5,000	1,630	39	1,334	47	1,613	31
Huelches	4,250	0	508	0	463	0	1,427
Pichi Mahuida	300	0	0	0	0	0	0
Total	33,240	1,630	4,650	2,050	4,620	3,570	3,420

Table 11A-9 Irrigation/Power Results: Irrigation Areas

		Run No.					
		1		2		3	
Irrigation Area	*Irrigable Area*	*Irr. Only*	*With Power*	*Irr. Only*	*With Power*	*Irr. Only*	*With Power*
Buta Ranquil y Rincón de los Sauces	3,500	3,500	3,500	500	500	500	500
Mendoza Zone I, II	5,020	1,000	1,000	1,000	1,000	1,000	1,000
Rincón Colorado	500	0	0	0	0	0	0
Peñas Blancas y Valle Verde	20,000	20,000	20,000	20,000	20,000	12,900	12,900
El Sauzal	2,600	2,600	2,600	2,600	2,600	2,600	2,600
25 de Mayo I	4,300	4,300	4,300	4,300	4,300	0	0
25 de Mayo V	4,000	4,000	4,000	4,000	4,000	4,000	4,000
Colonia Catriel	25,400	25,400	25,400	21,400	21,400	21,400	21,400
25 de Mayo II, III, IV	54,720	0	0	0	0	0	0
Casa de Piedra	78,000	0	0	0	0	0	0
Planicie de Curacó	25,600	25,600	25,600	25,600	25,600	25,600	25,600
Huelches	150,000	0	0	0	0	0	0
Río Colorado y Eugenio del Busto	17,000	17,000	17,000	17,000	17,000	17,000	17,000
Valle Interior	110,000	0	0	0	0	0	0
Valles Marginales y Valle del Prado	4,040	0	0	0	0	0	0
Bajo de los Baguales	40,000	18,850	18,850	0	0	0	0
Pedro Luro	218,000	218,000	218,000	136,100	136,100	215,100	215,100
Total	763,000	341,000	341,000	233,000	233,000	289,000	289,000

Table 11A-10 Irrigation/Power Results: Hydroelectric Power Plants

		Installed Capacity (MW) *and Annual Production* (GWh)					
		Run No.					
	Capacity	1		2		3	
Power Plant	*Produc-tion*	*Irr. Only*	*With Power*	*Irr. Only*	*With Power*	*Irr. Only*	*With Power*
Los Morros	Cap	0	0	52	51	52	52
	Prod	0	0	264	258	264	264
Portezuelo del Viento	Cap	0	156	0	78	0	69
	Prod	0	597	0	309	0	247
Las Chacras	Cap	0	0	0	0	47	47
	Prod	0	0	0	0	240	240
Las Torrecillas	Cap	0	191	0	100	0	0
	Prod	0	394	0	281	0	0
Agua del Piche	Cap	0	189	0	105	0	0
	Prod	0	299	0	198	0	0
Los Divisaderos	Cap	0	11	0	8	0	10
	Prod	0	33	0	13	0	26
Tapera de Avendaño	Cap	0	144	0	130	0	0
	Prod	0	259	0	287	0	0
Loma Redonda	Cap	0	0	0	0	0	0
	Prod	0	0	0	0	0	0
Casa de Piedra	Cap	0	0	0	0	0	0
	Prod	0	0	0	0	0	0
Huelches	Cap	0	75	0	49	0	102
	Prod	0	129	0	82	0	162
El Chivero	Cap	0	0	0	20	0	29
	Prod	0	0	0	42	0	60
Pichi Mahuida	Cap	0	0	0	0	0	0
	Prod	0	0	0	0	0	0
Saltos Andersen	Cap	0	0	0	0	0	0
	Prod	0	0	0	0	0	0
Total	Cap	0	766	52	541	99	309
	Prod	0	1,711	264	1,470	504	999

Table 11A-11 Irrigation/Power Results: Interbasin Transfers

	Diversion Capacity (m^3/sec)					
	Run No.					
	1		2		3	
Interbasin Transfer	*Irr. Only*	*With Power*	*Irr. Only*	*With Power*	*Irr. Only*	*With Power*
La Estrechura export	0	0	43	43	43	43
Bardas Blancas export	0	0	0	0	72	72
Río Neuquén import	0	0	0	0	100	100
Río Negro import	0	0	0	0	0	0
Total imports	0	0	0	0	100	100
Total exports	0	0	43	43	115	115

Table 11A-12 Summary of Regional Income Results

Characteristics	*Upper Bound*	*Run No.* 1	2	3
National income net benefits 10^9 m$n (1970)		217	220.5	199.8
No. of irrigation projects	17	9	9	16
Irrigation area (1,000 ha)	763	289	289	387
% Total irrigable area	100%	38%	38%	51%
No. of reservoirs	8			
Reservoir capacity (MCM)	33,240	3,570	3,570	4,080
% Total storage capacity	100%	11%	11%	12%
No. of power projects	13	2*	2*	2*
Installed capacity (MW)		99*	99*	99*
Annual production (GWh)		504*	504*	504*
Capacity factor		0.58	0.58	0.58
No. of exports	2	1	1	1
Export capacity (m^3/sec)		100	100	100
No. of exports	2	2	2	2
Export capacity (m^3/sec)		115	115	115

*On export to Atuel basin.

Table 11A-13 Net Provincial Income Benefits*

Province	*Run No.* 2	3	1
Mendoza	195.9	195.9	—
Neuquén	0.05	0.12	—
Río Negro	2.0	4.4	—
La Pampa	0.7	2.1	—
Buenos Aires	9.1	6.9	—
National income	220.5	199.8	217

*Benefits are given in 10^9 m$n (1970).

Table 11A-14 Regional Income Results: Reservoirs

Reservoir	Upper Bound (MCM)	*Reservoir Capacity* (MCM) *Run No.* 2	3	1
Mendoza Export				
La Estrechura	960	713	713	713
Portezuelo del Viento	3,600	1,140	1,140	1,140
Bardas Blancas	1,680	105	105	105
Central Basin				
Las Torrecillas	13,400	0	0	0
Agua del Piche	4,050	0	291	0
Lower Basin				
Casa de Piedra	5,000	1,613	1,599	1,613
Huelches	4,250	0	228	0
Pichi Mahuida	300	0	0	0
Total	33,240	3,570	4,080	3,570

Table 11A-15 Regional Income Results: Irrigation Areas

Irrigation Area	*Irrigable Area* (ha)	*Area* (ha) *Run No.* 2	3	1
Buta Ranquil y Rincón de los Sauces	3,500	500	3,500	500
Mendoza Zone I, II	5,020	1,000	1,000	1,000
Rincón Colorado	500	0	500	0
Peñas Blancas y Valle Verde	20,000	12,900	20,000	12,900
El Sauzal	2,600	2,600	2,600	2,600
25 de Mayo I	4,300	0	4,300	0
25 de Mayo V	4,000	4,000	4,000	4,000
Colonia Catriel	25,400	21,400	25,400	21,400
25 de Mayo II, III, IV	54,720	0	54,720	0
Casa de Piedra	78,000	0	78,000	0
Planicie de Curacó	25,600	25,600	25,600	25,600
Huelches	150,000	0	48,800	0
Río Colorado y Eugenio del Busto	17,000	17,000	17,000	17,000
Valle Interior	110,000	0	0	0
Valles Marginales y Valle del Prado	4,040	0	1,040	0
Bajo de los Baguales	40,000	0	40,000	0
Pedro Luro	218,000	20,440	60,000	204,000
Total	763,000	289,000	387,000	289,000

Table 11A-16 Regional Income Results: Hydroelectric Power Plants

Power Plant	Capacity or Production	*Installed Capacity* (MW) *and Annual Production* (GWh) *Run No.* 2	3	1
Los Morros	Cap	52	52	52
	Prod	264	264	264
Portezuelo del Viento	Cap	0	0	0
	Prod	0	0	0
Las Chacras	Cap	47	47	47
	Prod	240	240	240
Las Torrecillas	Cap	0	0	0
	Prod	0	0	0
Agua del Piche	Cap	0	0	0
	Prod	0	0	0
Los Divisaderos	Cap	0	0	0
	Prod	0	0	0
Tapera de Avendaño	Cap	0	0	0
	Prod	0	0	0
Loma Redonda	Cap	0	0	0
	Prod	0	0	0
Casa de Piedra	Cap	0	0	0
	Prod	0	0	0
Huelches	Cap	0	0	0
	Prod	0	0	0
El Chivero	Cap	0	0	0
	Prod	0	0	0
Pichi Mahuida	Cap	0	0	0
	Prod	0	0	0
Saltos Andersen	Cap	0	0	0
	Prod	0	0	0
Total	Cap	99	99	99
	Prod	504	504	504

Table 11A-17 Regional Income Results: Interbasin Transfers

Interbasin Transfer	*Diversion Capacity* (m^3/sec) *Run No.* 2	3	1
La Estrechura export	43	43	43
Bardas Blancas export	72	72	72
Río Neuquén import	100	100	100
Río Negro import	0	0	0
Total imports	100	100	100
Total exports	115	115	115

Table 11A-18 Summary of Sensitivity Results

Characteristics	*Upper Bound*	*Discount Rate*		*Foreign Exchange Premium*		*Energy Benefits*			*(Efficiency Run #1)*
		$r = 4\%$	$r = 16\%$	$p = 100\%$	$p = 300\%$	24 m$n (1970)/kWh*	12 m$n (1970)/kWh*	12 m$n (1970)/kWh†	
	Sensitivity Run No.:	1	2	3	4	5	6	7	
No. of irrigation projects	17	15	7	10	16	10	14	13	16
Irrigation area (1,000 ha)	763	525	239	337	535	315	414	403	524
% total irrigable area	100%	69%	31%	44%	69%	41%	54%	53%	69%
No. of reservoirs	8								
Reservoir capacity (MCM)	33,240	10,320	3,670	10,840	9,080	20,320	10,330	10,360	9,950
% total storage capacity	100%	31%	11%	33%	27%	61%	31%	31%	30%
No. of power projects	13	11	4	10	8	9	11	11	8
Installed capacity (MW)		781	222	718	616	1,271	776	784	604
Annual production (Gwh)		2,137	871	2,229	1,788	3,746	2,259	2,281	1,825
Capacity factor		0.31	0.45	0.35	0.15	0.34	0.33	0.33	0.35
No. of imports	2	1	0	1	1	1	1	1	1
Import capacity (m^3/sec)		100	0	100	100	100	100	100	100
No. of exports	2	1	1	1	1	0	1	1	1
Export capacity (m^3/sec)		43	25	43	43	0	43	43	43

*Río Colorado basin only.
†Río Colorado and Atuel basins.

Table 11A-19 Sensitivity Results: Reservoirs

Reservoir	Upper Bound (MCM)	*Reservoir Capacity* (MCM)							Efficiency Run #1	No. of Times in Solution
		Discount Rate		*Foreign Exchange Premium*		*Energy Benefits*				
		$r = 4\%$	$r = 16\%$	$p = 100\%$	$p = 300\%$	24 m$n (1970)/kwh*	12 m$n (1970)/kwh*	12 m$n (1970)/kwh†		
	Sensitivity Run No.:	1	2	3	4	5	6	7		
Mendoza Export										
La Estrechura	960	713	372	713	713	0	713	713	713	7
Portezuelo del Viento	3,600	1,513	1,200	1,412	1,484	3,600	1,398	1,398	1,415	All
Bardas Blancas	1,680	0	0	0	0	0	0	0	0	0
Central Basin										
Las Torrecillas	13,400	3,387	1,369	3,042	3,122	7,107	3,064	3,064	3,022	All
Agua del Piche	4,050	2,223	0	2,066	1,294	3,605	2,107	2,130	2,030	7
Lower Basin										
Casa de Piedra	5,000	1,143	0	1,097	1,218	1,584	1,198	1,198	1,196	7
Huelches	4,250	1,113	728	2,511	1,253	4,127	1,554	1,554	1,575	All
Pichi Mahuida	300	225	0	0	0	300	300	300	0	4
Total	33,240	10,320	3,670	10,840	9,080	20,320	10,330	10,360	9,950	

*Río Colorado basin only.

†Río Colorado and Atuel basins.

Table 11A-20 Sensitivity Results: Irrigation Areas

Irrigation Area	Irrigable Area (ha)	Area (ha): Discount Rate r = 4%	r = 16%	Foreign Exchange Premium p = 100%	p = 300%	Energy Benefits 24 m$n (1970)/kwh*	12 m$n (1970)/kwh*	12 m$n (1970)/kwh†	Efficiency Run #1	No. of Times in Solution
Sensitivity Run No.:		1	2	3	4	5	6	7		
Buta Ranquil y Rincón de los Sauces	3,500	500	500	500	3,500	500	500	500	3,500	All
Mendoza Zone I, II	5,020	1,000	1,000	1,000	4,820	1,000	1,000	1,000	4,460	All
Rincón Colorado	500	500	0	0	500	0	500	0	500	4
Peñas Blancas y Valle Verde	20,000	20,000	6,400	6,400	20,000	6,400	20,000	20,000	20,000	All
El Sauzal	2,600	2,600	2,600	2,600	2,600	1,700	2,600	2,600	2,600	All
25 de Mayo I	4,300	0	0	0	4,300	0	4,300	4,300	4,300	4
25 de Mayo V	4,000	4,000	0	4,000	4,000	0	4.000	4,000	4,000	6
Colonia Catriel	25,400	25,400	1,400	21,400	25,400	1,400	25,400	25,400	25,400	All
25 de Mayo II, III, IV	54,720	54,720	0	0	54,720	0	54,390	43,920	54,720	5
Casa de Piedra	78,000	78,000	0	0	78,000	0	0	0	78,000	3
Planicie de Curacó	25,600	25,600	0	25,600	25,600	25,600	25,600	25,600	25,600	7
Huelches	150,000	34,800	0	0	35,700	0	0	0	23,100	3
Río Colorado y Eugenio del Busto	17,000	17,000	9,300	17,000	17,000	17,000	17,000	17,000	17,000	All
Valle Interior	110,000	0	0	0	0	0	0	0	0	0
Valles Marginales y Valle del Prado	4,040	3,040	0	0	1,040	2,040	1,040	1,040	3,040	6
Bajo de los Baguales	40,000	0	0	40,000	40,000	40,000	40,000	40,000	40,000	7
Pedro Luro	218,000	218,000	218,000	218,000	218,000	218,000	218,000	218,000	218,000	All
Total	763,000	525,000	239,000	337,000	535,000	315,000	414,000	403,000	524,000	

*Río Colorado basin only.

†Río Colorado and Atuel basins.

Table 11A-21 Sensitivity Results: Hydroelectric Power Plants

Power Plant	Capacity or Production	Discount Rate *r* = 4%	*r* = 16%	Foreign Exchange Premium *p* = 100%	*p* = 300%	Energy Benefits 24 m$n (1970)/ kwh*	12 m$n (1970)/ kwh*	12 m$n (1970)/ kwh†	Efficiency Run #1	No. of Times in Solution
	Sensitivity Run No.:	1	2	3	4	5	6	7		
Los Morros	Cap	52	31	52	52	0	52	52	52	7
	Prod	264	156	264	264	0	264	264	264	
Portezuelo del Viento	Cap	75	75	72	80	189	72	72	72	All
	Prod	320	373	307	321	870	309	309	306	
Las Chacras	Cap	0	0	0	0	0	0	0	0	0
	Prod	0	0	0	0	0	0	0	0	
Las Torrecillas	Cap	138	106	131	133	246	133	133	249	All
	Prod	420	312	402	404	698	405	405	395	
Agua del Piche	Cap	96	0	93	85	178	95	103	91	7
	Prod	294	0	282	231	544	288	310	276	
Los Divisaderos	Cap	9	10	10	10	0	10	10	10	7
	Prod	14	30	30	30	0	30	30	30	
Tapera de Avendaño	Cap	115	0	79	84	156	82	82	80	7
	Prod	269	0	230	206	461	209	209	205	
Loma Redonda	Cap	0	0	0	0	0	0	0	0	0
	Prod	0	0	0	0	0	0	0	0	
Casa de Piedra	Cap	64	0	89	61	120	79	79	54	7
	Prod	160	0	240	150	328	208	208	157	
Huelches	Cap	101	0	130	111	186	112	112	116	7
	Prod	175	0	312	182	423	251	251	192	
El Chivero	Cap	54	0	50	0	70	53	53	0	5
	Prod	93	0	126	0	159	120	120	0	
Pichi Mahuida	Cap	61	0	0	0	92	61	61	0	4
	Prod	96	0	0	0	186	117	117	0	
Saltos Andersen	Cap	16	0	12	0	34	27	27	0	5
	Prod	32	0	36	0	77	58	58	0	
Total	Cap	781	222	718	616	1,271	776	784	604	
	Prod	2,137	871	2,229	1,788	3,746	2,259	2,281	1,825	

Installed Capacity (MW) and Annual Production (Gwh)

*Río Colorado basin only.
†Río Colorado and Atuel basins.

Table 11A-22 Sensitivity Results: Interbasin Transfers

	Diversion Capacity (m³/sec)								
	Discount Rate		*Foreign Exchange Premium*		*Energy Benefits*				
Interbasin Transfer	$r = 4\%$	$r = 16\%$	$p = 100\%$	$p = 300\%$	24 m$n (1970)/ kwh*	12 m$n (1970)/ kwh*	12 m$n (1970)/ kwh†	*Effi-ciency Run #1*	*No. of Times in Solution*
Sensitivity Run No.:	1	2	3	4	5	6	7		
La Estrechura export	43	25	43	43	0	43	43	43	7
Bardas Blancas export	0	0	0	0	0	0	0	0	0
Río Neuquén import	100	0	100	100	100	100	100	100	7
Río Negro import	0	0	0	0	0	0	0	0	0
Total imports	100	0	100	100	100	100	100	100	
Total exports	43	25	43	43	0	43	43	43	

*Río Colorado basin only.
†Río Colorado and Atuel basins.

Table 11A-23 Results of Simulation Runs, Irrigation/Power #1 (Irrigation Only)*

Characteristics	Run No. I	II	III	IV	V†	VI
Model Input Values						
Total reservoir capacity (MCM)	1,630	5,000	5,000	9,000	9,000	9,000
Total reservoir costs	2.8	5.1	5.1	12.4	9.2	12.4
Total irrigation area (1,000 ha)	341	341	307	338	341	307
Total irrigation costs	246.7	246.7	224.8	244.2	246.7	218.7
Total costs	249.5	251.8	229.9	256.6	255.9	231.1
Model Results						
Gross irrigation benefits	334.1	348.6	354.5	366.9	393.6	363.6
Net irrigation benefits as % of long-term no-deficit net benefits	60%	70%	85%	84%	99%	99%
Total net benefits	84.6	96.8	124.7	110.3	137.7	132.5

*All benefits and costs are given in 10^9 m$n (1970).

†Run selected for sequencing.

Table 11A-24 Reservoir Storage Capacities in Simulation Runs, Irrigation/Power #1 (Irrigation Only)

Reservoir	Storage Capacity (MCM), Run No. I	II	III	IV	V	VI
Casa de Piedra	1,630	5,000	5,000	5,000	5,000	5,000
Las Torrecillas	—	—	—	4,000	—	4,000
Huelches	—	—	—	—	4,000	—
Total	1,630	5,000	5,000	9,000	9,000	9,000

Table 11A-25 Results of Simulation Runs, Irrigation/Power #1 (With Power)*

Characteristics	Run No.						
	I	II	III	IV†	V	VI	VII
Model Input Values							
Total reservoir capacity (MCM)	4,647	10,000	10,000	13,639	13,639	13,639	13,600
Total reservoir costs	25.7	38.2	38.2	37.1	37.1	37.1	35.6
Total irrigation area (1,000 ha)	341	341	323	341	339	339	339
Total irrigation costs	246.7	246.7	235.1	246.7	245.5	245.5	245.5
Total installed power capacity (MW)	622	622	622	433	467	462	462
Total power costs	41.3	41.3	41.3	27.7	34.7	34.4	34.4
Total costs	313.7	326.2	314.6	311.5	317.3	317	315.5
Model Results							
Gross irrigation benefits	321.3	367	374.2	389.5	388.1	388.1	392.1
Net irrigation benefits as % of long-term no-deficit net benefits	51%	82%	99%	98%	98%	98%	100%
Average firm energy production (GWh/yr)	498	828	981	891	842	833	697
Gross firm energy benefits	45.6	75.8	89.8	81.6	77.1	76.3	63.8
Total gross benefits	366.9	442.8	464	471.1	465.2	464.4	455.9
Total net benefits	53.2	116.6	149.4	159.6	147.9	147.4	140.4

*All benefits and costs are given in 10^9 m$n (1970).

†Run selected for sequencing.

Table 11A-26 Reservoir Storage Capacities in Simulation Runs, Irrigation/Power #1 (With Power)

	Storage Capacity (MCM)						
	Run No.						
Reservoir	I	II	III	IV	V	VI	VII
Portezuelo del Viento	1,440	3,600	3,600	3,600	3,600	3,600	3,600
Las Torrecillas	1,584	4,777	4,777	6,000	6,000	6,000	6,000
Agua del Piche	1,076	1,076	1,076	0	0	0	0
Casa de Piedra	39	39	39	39	39	39	4,000
Huelches	508	508	508	4,000	13,639	4,000	0
Total	4,647	10,000	10,000	13,639	13,639	13,639	13,600

Table 11A-27 Results of Simulation Runs, Irrigation/Power #2 (Irrigation Only)*

	Run No.		
Characteristics	I	II	III
Model Input Values			
Total reservoir capacity (MCM)	2,049	10,460	10,460
Total reservoir costs	7.5	19.1	19.1
Total irrigation area (1,000 ha)	233	233	233
Total irrigation costs	171.7	171.7	171.7
Total installed power capacity (MW)	52†	52†	52†
Total power costs	0.5	0.5	0.5
Total export capacity (m^3/sec)	43	43	43
Total export costs	48.3	48.3	48.3
Total costs	228	239.6	240
Model Results			
Gross irrigation benefits	266.4	285.5	285.4
Net irrigation benefits as % of long-term no-deficit net benefits	83%	99%	99%
Average firm energy production (GWh/yr)	146	166	189
Gross firm energy benefits	13.4	15.2	17.3
Average export (m^3/sec)	28.3	32.1	36.5
Gross export benefits	76.1	86.1	98.2
Gross export benefits as % of long-term no-deficit benefits	66%	75%	85%
Total gross benefits	355.9	386.8	400.9
Total net benefits	127.9	147.2	160.9

*All benefits and costs are given in 10^9 m$n (1970).
†On export to Atuel basin.

Table 11A-28 Reservoir Storage Capacities in Simulation Runs, Irrigation/Power #2 (Irrigation Only)

	Storage Capacity (MCM)		
	Run No.		
Reservoir	I	II	III
La Estrechura	715	960	960
Las Torrecillas	—	5,000	5,000
Casa de Piedra	1,334	4,500	4,500
Total	2,049	10,460	10,460

Table 11A-29 Results of Simulation Runs, Irrigation/Power #2 (With Power)*

	Run No.					
Characteristics	I	II	III	IV	V†	VI
Model Input Values						
Total reservoir capacity (MCM)	4,612	4,612	14,607	16,607	17,607	17,607
Total reservoir costs	29.9	29.9	43.4	44.8	45.4	45.4
Total irrigation area (1,000 ha)	233	233	233	233	233	233
Total irrigation costs	171.7	171.7	171.7	171.7	171.7	171.7
Total installed power capacity (MW)	544	544	436	487	437	437
Total power costs	44.5	44.5	35.2	38.4	35.3	35.3
Total export capacity (m^3/sec)	42	42	42	42	42	42
Total export costs	47.2	47.2	47.2	47.2	47.2	47.2
Total costs	293.3	293.3	297.5	302.1	299.6	299.6
Operating policy at export reservoir	IRR	EXP	EXP	EXP	EXP	EXP
Model Results						
Gross irrigation benefits	269.1	243	282.4	283.7	282.7	284.4
Net irrigation benefits as % of long-term no-deficit benefits	80%	63%	97%	99%	98%	99%
Average firm energy production (GWh/yr)	833	827	915	952	895	856
Gross firm energy benefits	76.3	75.7	83.8	87.2	82.0	78.4
Average export (m^3/sec)	30.1	35.3	36.6	36.6	36.6	36.6
Gross export benefits	81.2	94.6	98.1	98.1	98.1	98.1
Gross export benefits as % of long-term no-deficit benefits	72%	84%	87%	87%	87%	87%
Total gross benefits	419.4	413.3	464.3	469	462.8	460.9
Total net benefits	126.1	120.0	166.8	166.9	163.2	161.3

*All benefits and costs are given in 10^9 m$n (1970).

†Run selected for sequencing.

Table 11A-30 Reservoir Storage Capacities in Simulation Runs, Irrigation/Power #2 (With Power)

	Storage Capacity (MCM)					
	Run No.					
Reservoir	I	II	III	IV	V	VI
La Estrechura	704	704	960	960	960	960
Portezuelo del Viento	1,394	1,394	3,600	3,600	3,600	3,600
Las Torrecillas	908	908	6,000	8,000	9,000	9,000
Agua del Piche	1,096	1,096	—	—	—	—
Casa de Piedra	47	47	47	47	47	47
Huelches	463	463	4,000	4,000	4,000	4,000
Total	4,612	4,612	14,607	16,607	17,607	17,607

Table 11A-31 Comparison of Simulation Run Results (the Highest Net Benefits in Each Series)*

	Run No.			
	Irrigation/Power #1		*Irrigation/Power #2*	
Characteristics	*Irr. Only*	*With Power*	*Irr. Only*	*With Power*
Model Input Values				
Total reservoir capacity (MCM)	9,000	13,639	10,460	16,607
Total reservoir costs	9.2	37.1	19.1	44.8
Total irrigation area (1,000 ha)	341	341	233	233
Total irrigation costs	246.7	246.7	171.7	171.7
Total installed power capacity (MW)	—	433	52†	487
Total power costs	—	27.7	0.5†	38.4
Total import capacity (m^3/sec)	—	—	—	—
Total import costs	—	—	—	—
Total export capacity (m^3/sec)	—	—	43	42
Total export costs	—	—	48.3	47.2
Total costs	255.9	311.5	240	302.1
Model Results				
Gross irrigation benefits	393.6	389.5	285.4	283.7
Net irrigation benefits as % of long-term no-deficit benefits	99%	98%	99%	99%
Average firm energy production (GWh/yr)	—	891	189	952
Gross firm energy benefits	—	81.6	17.3†	87.2
Average export (m^3/sec)	—	—	36.5	36.6
Gross export benefits as % of long-term no-deficit benefits	—	—	98.2	98.1
Total gross benefits	393.6	471.1	400.9	469
Total net benefits	137.7	159.6	160.9	166.9
Screening model total net benefits	144.7	195.6	192.0	215.1
Simulation/screening net benefit ratio	0.95	0.82	0.84	0.78

*All benefits and costs are given in 10^9 m$n (1970).

†On export to Atuel basin.

Table 11A-32 Rio Colorado Site Names and English Translations

La Estrechura	The Narrows
Los Morros	The Bluffs
Portezuelo del Viento	Pass of the Winds
Bardas Blancas	White Slopes
Las Chacras	The Farms
Buta Ranquil	(possibly, Shelter of the Ranqueles, an Indian Tribe)
Rincón de los Sauces	Willow Corner
Mendoza Zona 1, 2	Mendoza Zone 1, 2
Las Torrecillas	The Little Towers
Rincón Colorado	Colorado Corner
Agua del Piche	Water of the Armadillo
Peñas Blancas	White Rocks
Valle Verde	Green Valley
El Sauzal	Willow Grove
25 de Mayo	25th of May (Argentine National Holiday)
Los Divisaderos	The Lookouts
Colonia Catriel	Catriel Settlement
Loma Redonda	Round Hill
Tapera de Avendaño	Ruins of Avendaño
Planicie de Curacó	Plain of Curaco
Casa de Piedra	Stone House
Río Negro	Black River
Huelches	(possibly, Indian Warriors, or, the Name of an Indian Tribe)
El Chivero	Place of Goats
Pichi Mahuida	Little Hill (or, Hill of Herbs)
Río Colorado	Colorado River
Eugenio del Busto	(A proper name)
Saltos Andersen	Andersen Rapids
Valles Marginales	Marginal Valleys
Valle del Prado	Valley of Pasture
Valle Interior	Interior Valley
Bajo de los Baguales	Wild Horse Gulch
Pedro Luro	(A proper name)

CHAPTER TWELVE — PERSPECTIVES ON THE CASE STUDY

The purposes of the planning study described in this book were (1) to illustrate the use of modern water resources planning methods by an application and (2) to demonstrate the choices available for the development of the Río Colorado and thereby to facilitate the process of choice. The results presented were those, with minor exceptions and additions, that were described in Chapter 11.

OUTCOME OF THE STUDY

The first important activity that took place in Argentina following the completion of the final report of the project was the presentation of two reports by the Subsecretaría de Estado de Recursos Hídricos (State Subsecretariat for Water Resources, SSRH) (SSRH, 1973, 1974). These reports, prepared by the MIT-trained group of Argentine professionals, were submitted to the members of the Comisión Técnica Interprovincial del Río Colorado (Interprovincial Technical Commission of the Río Colorado, COTIRC) for their consideration. The reports represent an important continuation of the project effort in that they contain specific (though preliminary) recommendations for allocating water among the provinces based on the results derived at MIT.

In the reports it is proposed to begin the development of the basin with projects in Irrigation/Power Run #2 (without power); then to add projects from Irrigation/Power Run #2 (with complementary power); and to reach a final development of the basin based on projects in Efficiency Run #1. It is suggested in the reports that for planning and decision purposes projects can be aggregated within subregions of the basin in order to provide the provinces with some choice of projects within the general framework of water allocation implied by the configurations chosen.

Modified proposals based on those of the Subsecretariat's reports were accepted by the provincial authorities in October 1976 as part of an agreement drawn up during a sixth conference of the riverine provinces. (For an account of earlier provincial conferences, see Chapter 1). This agreement was then approved by the Federal Government (República Argentina, 1977) and has become the basis for the development of the Río Colorado.

MATHEMATICAL MODELING

The modeling technique used in our study, which was described in Chapter 4 and later chapters, consisted primarily of three large models that were used sequentially to develop design alternatives. The screening model provided a starting point for simulation analyses, the outputs of which were then used as the input for the sequencing model. There are several perspectives on our use of models that might suggest somewhat different approaches to the problem than the one that we chose.

The screening model and the simulation model used in our study are complex. Complex models are more difficult to interpret than simple models because of the number and subtlety of the interactions in the models that are manifested in the results. (See the discussion in Appendix A of the local optima in the screening model that resulted from a subtle interaction among several nonlinear functions.) Simpler models are more manageable than complex ones; they permit the analyst to trace out interactions among system components more readily. We think that the question of the appropriate level of complexity of models is an important new field for research [for one of the few examples of studies of this question, see Rogers (1978)]. It would be helpful if rules of thumb could be developed to guide field-level planners in the choice of models, not only in terms of type but in terms of the appropriate level of complexity of each model for different types of water resource planning problems. This is part of a more general question, about which little is known, of the net benefits of using models as compared to using more traditional methods [one example of an attempt to compare the effects of employing models and traditional techniques is found in Hufschmidt and Fiering (1966)].

An approach to modeling alternative to the one that we used (and to the variants that we describe in Appendix A) is suggested by the view in the reports of the Subsecretariat (SSRH, 1973, 1974) that for planning and decision purposes projects can be aggregated within subregions of the basin in order to provide the provinces with some choice of projects within a general framework of water allocation.

Had we considered the Río Colorado from this perspective, a decentralized modeling approach might have seemed appropriate. A set of five simple screening models, one for each province, could have been built, and these could have been linked through a central coordinating model. This would have permitted an iterative determination of how plans optimal for each province, obtained from the provincial screening models, could have been integrated into an overall plan reflecting national as well as provincial preferences among objectives. [Decentralized modeling systems have been explored by Haimes (1977).]

A further perspective on our modeling work relates to the proper allocation of time to model development during a study. One can think of a study such as ours as divided into three stages (which, of course, overlap): thinking about the problem and deciding on the models that seem most appropriate for addressing it; developing these models; and running the models and analyzing the results. In our study, most of our time was devoted to the middle stage—model development. In retrospect, we would have liked to have had more time than we had both to consider the choice of models, and to generate and analyze alternative configurations for the river and to perform sensitivity analyses on them.

An institutional consideration relating to modeling as well as to the study more generally was the loss of contact between MIT and the Argentines after the termination of the contract, a loss that was not helpful. A period of interaction should have been scheduled, at a fairly low budget, for 1 to 2 years after the termination of the main contract. This would have permitted further development of, and advice on, the models set up for the Río Colorado; assistance in bringing the models on line in Buenos Aires; and also a locus of interest to which those Argentine officials most concerned to continue the work, and perhaps to extend it to other Argentine river basins, could have turned for support and encouragement. As it was, once the contract terminated, there was no such locus of interest, which certainly made the task of those Argentines interested in continuing the work more difficult. [Recent Argentine contributions to water resources systems analysis are summarized in Dalbagni, Aisiks, Velez, Elinger, Karacsonyi, and Devoto (1977).] Had there been an international panel of experts to review and evaluate the work, this might have provided another mechanism to maintain continuity and contact among the study participants after the project had formally ended. [For a description of the role of an expert board of consultants in the context of a United States water resources planning study, see Schwarz, Major, and Frost (1975).]

MULTIOBJECTIVES

Regarding the use of multiobjectives, we think that the set of objectives that we used defined the choice problem for the Río Colorado correctly. However, we would have liked to have communicated more fully and frequently with Argentine decision-makers than we did with respect to three aspects of our work with multiobjectives. [On the importance of communications in multiobjective planning, see Major (1977, chap. 4).] First, we would have liked to have been able to ensure more completely that the ways in which we embodied Argentine objectives in the equations of our models reflected precisely the meanings of these objectives to the Argentines, a task that is not simple. Second, we would have benefited from more information than we had about the relative weights of the Argentines on various objectives; this information would have enabled us to allocate our planning resources so as to better explore those parts of net benefit space that were most likely to be relevant to Argentine decision-making. Third, we would have liked to have devoted additional time to exploring and testing means of presenting multiobjective results, such as graphs versus tables, and complete listings of impacts on objectives versus the presentation of selected key impacts.

THE SCOPE OF THE STUDY

A fundamental question in a planning study is what to include within the scope of the analysis. One way in which we probably would have shifted our resources (or used a larger budget) had we the opportunity to do the study over again, would be to move toward a fuller consideration of the overall behavioral relationships governing the system. These include government decision-making patterns, farm management procedures, farmer migration behavior, and indeed, the entire sociology of rural areas. The success of any development in the Río Colorado will be heavily dependent on all of these things; it is not merely a function of the physical relationships in the system that were at the heart of our study (although we spent substantial effort on cost and benefit estimation). The multidisciplinary range of the study team ought to have been expanded at least to include a professional with skills relevant to rural sociology in Argentina.

A second reallocation of resources would be to attempt to link the Río Colorado plans more firmly to national planning policies and parameters. We linked our work to larger parameters through our estimation of benefits from production of beef, through our treatment of electricity benefits, through the use of shadow prices on foreign exchange earnings through beef sales, and in other ways; but, nonetheless, we feel that further effort in this direction would have been helpful and would be justified in future studies. This and the previous point might be summarized by saying that our multidisciplinary team was perhaps weighted too heavily toward engineers and mathematical modelers and not sufficiently weighted toward the social and policy sciences.

REFERENCES

DALBAGNI, JUAN, ENRIQUE G. AISIKS, OSCAR G. VELEZ, MARCOS M. ELINGER, JORGE KARACSONYI, and GUSTAVO A. DEVOTO. "Actividades de Análisis de Sistemas Aplicados al Desarrollo Hídrico en la Argentina." Papers presented at the International Symposium on Systems Analysis Applied to Water Resources Development, Mar del Plata, Argentina, 1977.

HAIMES, YACOV Y. *Hierarchical Analyses of Water Resources Systems: Modeling and Optimization of Large-Scale Systems.* New York: McGraw-Hill, 1977.

HUFSCHMIDT, MAYNARD M., and MYRON B FIERING. *Simulation Techniques for Water Resource Systems.* Cambridge, Mass.: Harvard University Press, 1966.

MAJOR, DAVID C. *Multiobjective Water Resource Planning.* American Geophysical Union, Water Resources Monograph 4, Washington, D.C., 1977.

REPÚBLICA ARGENTINA. Ley No. 21.611. *Boletín Oficial de la República Argentina.* No. 23.725, 18 August, 1977.

ROGERS, PETER. "On the Choice of the 'Appropriate Model' for Water Resources Planning and Management." *Water Resources Research,* **14(6)**, December, 1978.

SCHWARZ, HARRY E., DAVID C. MAJOR, and JOHN E. FROST, JR. "The North Atlantic Regional Water Resources Study." In *Proceedings of the Conference on Interdisciplinary Analysis of Water Resource Systems,* edited by J. Ernest Flack. New York: American Society of Civil Engineers, 1975.

SSRH (Subsecretaría de Estado de Recursos Hídricos). "Programa Unico de Habilitación de Areas de Riego y Distribución de Caudales: Versión Preliminar." Buenos Aires, August, 1973.

SSRH (Subsecretaría de Estado de Recursos Hídricos). "Consideraciones sobre Alternativas del Programa Unico." Buenos Aires, February, 1974.

APPENDIX A — MODEL CHOICE AND DEVELOPMENT

This appendix describes the general pattern of development of the models used in the study and the principal changes that took place in each model as the study proceeded.

The general line of development of the models was as follows. In the early stages of the work it was thought that a suitable approach would be to use a relatively simple screening model together with a relatively detailed simulation model. The function of the screening model would be to rule out obviously poor projects. The function of the simulation model would be to provide detailed analyses of various combinations of projects from among those that passed muster in the screening model. It was thought also that questions of stochasticity and scheduling could be dealt with in the context of these two models—that stochasticity could be dealt with in the simulation model, and that scheduling could be done by hand, without the use of an explicit model, either before or after simulation.

During the first year of the project, as variants of the screening and simulation models were explored, it was seen that, given the number of reasonably good sites on the Río Colorado, the screening model would have to be used to make more refined choices than had originally been thought necessary. The alternative would have been a tedious and largely random selection of projects by hand from among those that passed a crude screening test. At the same time, it became clear that the detailed simulation model would be too large and too expensive to operate for it to be used on a routine basis to evaluate large numbers of alternative configurations. Hence, the screening model became more detailed, and, instead of using the detailed simulation model described in Chapter 7 for routine evaluation of basin configurations, the simpler basic simulation model described in Chapter 6 was developed for that purpose.

The question of scheduling was also reassessed. As the screening model became more detailed, a version of this model was considered that would have both screened and scheduled projects. It would have been possible, although expensive, to run such screened and scheduled configurations in a simulation model. The alternative of scheduling projects by hand either before or after simulation also remained. It was finally decided that scheduling should be done after simulation and that the scheduling should be done in a mixed-integer programming model that we called the *sequencing model*, as described in Chapter 8. With the choice of this model, the final set of three models was completed, and it was this set that was used to generate program alternatives. Other models were also considered and in some cases formulated. Two of these—an operating policy model and a systems dynamics model—are discussed later, following the discussions of the development of the three basic models.

THE SCREENING MODEL

The development of the screening model is described in this section. [See also Cohon, Facet, Haan, and Marks (1973).]

The first version of the screening model that was formulated was a linear programming model with deterministic hydrologic inputs. The model embodied a simplified configuration of the river basin with 13 sites. The model was constructed as a steady-state representation of the system. All selected projects were assumed to come "on line" simultaneously and to operate for a 50-year period, every year of which was the same hydrologically. The one year considered in the model was divided into two seasons of equal length. In addition to being a "one-year-every-year-is-the-same" model, the objective function was unidimensional (the maximization of net present value of national income benefits). A substantial effort was made to obtain reasonable results from this simple model, prior to attempting changes in it.

The first change in the model was the use of three modeling seasons rather than two. The reason for this was that monthly irrigation water demands could be conveniently aggregated into 4-month seasons—one when demands were essentially zero, and two seasons of high demand. Although the change created no conceptual difficulties, the amount of labor required to keypunch the input data and obtain the first results for the new, larger model was significant. This was complicated by the incorporation of new sites into the configuration, which increased the total number of sites to 18. Because of this, it was decided to write a program to generate the linear programming input data from raw data.

The three-season, 18-site model proved to be quite useful for the generation of results suitable for review by Argentine decision-makers. Although they were satisfied with the three-season representation in this model, they felt that more site disaggregation would be advisable. The resulting changes in the model yielded a 28-site configuration. Another iteration with the decision-makers resulted in the 38-site configuration used in the final model.

It is interesting to note that relatively straightforward changes such as the changes from two to three seasons, and from 13 to 38 sites, can result in substantially increased computational complexity. The increase in the number of seasons increased the number of constraints (the important factor in costs in mathematical programming) by about 50%, increasing computer time by about 100%. Increasing the number of sites resulted in somewhat more than doubling the number of constraints, from 196 to 435, requiring a sixfold increase in computer time.

Other differences between the original two-season, 13-site model and the final three-season, 38-site model resulted from formulation changes designed to represent adequately the technological and economic characteristics of the problem. Two changes that were relatively simple from the computational point of view were the consideration of reservoir evaporation losses and natural stream losses in the continuity constraints, and the inclusion of overseason effects in irrigation return flow. These changes introduced little computational complexity, and although the effect of these modifications on the screening model results was expected to be significant, the results showed this expectation to be incorrect. Reservoir and stream losses amounted to at most 6-7% of the storage volumes and streamflows. The redistribution of irrigation return flows from one season over all of the seasons was basically the same for all irrigation sites. Although these effects may be important in detailed simulation analyses of the system's operation, they are relatively less important in a screening process, in which rather gross overall assumptions are made about the hydrologic aspects of the system.

Nonetheless, modifications in the model such as these, which turned out to have little impact on results, were still felt to be useful. If the realism of a model can be enhanced with little computational complexity, then making the required changes may be worthwhile from the standpoint of communication with decision-makers.

Other changes in the screening model were investigated that would have had more substantial computational consequences. One such change that was not undertaken was to incorporate the effects of overyear streamflow variability in the screening model. The reason for rejecting this change in the model was the large increase in computational requirements that it would have entailed (Haan, 1972). A preliminary analysis indicated that a stochastic linear programming model would require four to five times as many constraints as a corresponding deterministic formulation. Thus, the screening model remained deterministic, and stochasticity was dealt with only in the simulation models. [An alternative possibility for incorporating streamflow variability into the screening model was the utilization of a multiyear (deterministic) approach (see Cohon et al., 1973). This approach, which involves relaxing the assumption made in the screening model that every year is the same, was not considered in detail for the project.]

A second change that was considered in the screening model, and also not undertaken for computational reasons, was the incorporation of scheduling considerations. A scheduling model was formulated (Hammond, 1972) for many years or periods of years, with the objective of allowing the model to select at the same time not only project locations and sizes but also dates of implementation. The scheduling model, had it been used, would thus have replaced the steady-state screening model in the methodology, providing an initial scheduled configuration for further analysis by simulation. The result of the simulation analysis would then have been a hydrologically reliable scheduled configuration.

However, the size of the scheduling model at the level of detail that seemed appropriate after iterations with decision-makers would have been computationally impractical for the Río Colorado problem. An alternative, to decrease the size of the model by spatial and temporal aggregation, was explored. This approach resulted in a large although solvable model that was, however, inadequate because the level of aggregation required made it difficult to relate to the hydrologic and physical system of the Río Colorado. [The conversion of the screening model to a scheduling model would also have made the simulation process significantly more complex and time-consuming, because the approach used in simulation (that is, to assume that the capacities and structures in the system all existed at the beginning of the simulation period) would no longer have been adequate.]

A substantial modification in the form of the screening model that was undertaken was the incorporation of integer variables into what had been a purely linear programming model. The model thus became a mixed-integer programming model. (See Chapter 3.) This change was undertaken in order to permit the model to better represent the fixed costs of reservoirs and complementarities between projects, as explained in Chapter 5. During the initial phases of this change, experimentation with integer variables indicated that computer time would not increase greatly as compared to the strictly linear model. But once the model was converted to mixed-integer form and production runs were begun, a variety of software and other problems that resulted in increasing average run time by a factor of two were encountered.

Another substantial modification to the screening model that was incorporated during the course of the project was the use of "separable" programming. When nonlinear functions are used to represent variables such as the cost of dams, these must be represented by piece-wise linear approximations in the programming model, which cannot utilize nonlinear functions. This approximation does not cause difficulties in a programming model provided that when costs are being minimized, for example, costs per unit increase with the size of a project. In such a case, the piece-wise linear approximation for the first part of the project—say the base of a dam—enters the solution first, because it is the cheapest per physical unit (say height measured in meters). However, when costs decrease per unit, a special set of procedures in the solution algorithm must be utilized to ensure that the piece-wise linear functions enter the solution in the right order to ensure, for example, that the model does not build the crest of a dam before building the base. The set of procedures that governs the piece-wise linear approximations and their entry into the solution is called *separable* programming. As the screening model developed, a decision was made to use separable programming to model nonlinear storage-head functions and nonlinear cost functions; many of the latter displayed decreasing unit costs. (The approach used in the initial version of the model was to approximate each such function by a single linear relationship.)

This modification of the model had a cost. The use of separable programming, which permits the use of decreasing cost functions (more generally, convex benefit functions or concave cost functions when maximizing), opens the possibility of model solutions that are local rather than global optima. There is no way to tell directly from the computer output, in general, when a solution is a local rather than a global optimum; so the use of separable programming required us to test continuously for local optima when these were suspected from our knowledge of the system. When a local optimum was suspected, the variable or variables in question were forced into a new solution, and if the net benefits of the new solution were higher than those of the first, a local optimum in the first had been found. However, the new solution was merely a better solution and not in general a global optimum. Substantial time was spent in dealing with the problems posed by the existence of local optima. The experience of the planners using the screening model that was modified to include separable programming led them to the conclusion that the use of this technique should be very carefully weighed in terms of its advantages and disadvantages before it is adopted for a model. In some cases, the alternative of using linear cost and benefit functions with extensive sensitivity analysis might be a superior one.

THE SIMULATION MODEL

The most important change in the use of simulation modeling during the project was the change from complete reliance on the detailed simulation model, the first model built, to the use of the basic simulation model for the evaluation of program alternatives and the use of the detailed model for special purpose tasks. This change was the result of the perception that the detailed simulation model, designed to evaluate in substantial physical detail the performance of program alternatives, was too large for routine use for that purpose. The recognition of this fact occurred gradually to the planners as the detailed model grew more complex, and toward the end of the first year of the project, work was begun on the basic simulation model. Its operations were directed toward providing estimates of system net benefits and reliability, permitting rapid evaluation of alternatives and thus expanding the ability of the analysts effectively to suggest system changes.

The detailed simulation model was then used for the purposes of generating streamflow data, providing parameter inputs for the other models, and verifying the results of other models. The contrasts between these two models are described in Chapter 7.

Each of the two simulation models underwent developmental changes in the course of the project. The detailed simulation model's structure was designed precisely so that many changes could be made by simply adding or eliminating modules, and during the course of the project, many such changes were made. Initially, for example, a snowmelt module was developed and included in the model; in later runs, however, this module was not used because more realistic results could be obtained through direct use of the available streamflow data. Conversely, some other modules, such as those for detailed reservoir simulation, were not included in the original model but were added later.

The basic model initially was developed along the lines of previous simulation models and contained relatively few subroutines. As the project developed, two major changes were made: the consideration of temporal relationships in determining irrigation crop yield was added, and the spatial water allocation rule was modified in order to share proportionally the effects of drought among the irrigation areas. Both these changes added considerable complexity to the model. Together with a number of modifications required to simulate complex basin configurations, they led to the final form of the basic model with its 55 subroutines and approximately 5,000 cards.

Developing and changing models in the course of the project has costs as well as benefits. In the case of the simulation models, these costs included our inability to exploit fully the strengths of either model because of time constraints resulting from the shift in modeling strategy.

THE SEQUENCING MODEL

This model was developed during the second year of the project as a result of the decision to reject a combined screening/scheduling approach in the screening model itself. The sequencing model is a model that sequences previously sized projects optimally in time according to net benefits, budget and population constraints, and constraints on project interrelationships. The choice of mixed-integer programming in the form described in Chapter 8 was a relatively straightforward choice for the model, and the sequencing model did not undergo substantial evolution once its formulation had been agreed upon.

OTHER MODELS

In addition to the three models that constituted the series of models for developing program alternatives, and the variants of these models that were explored, other models were also considered and in some cases constructed. These were designed to evaluate additional aspects of the Río Colorado planning problem. Two of these models are described here.

The first model was a proposed linear programming model for obtaining optimal reservoir operating rules. It was thought that these should be explored because simulation models, on the one hand, cannot be used efficiently to determine optimal operating rules, and, on the other hand, the screening model yields operating rules for the river only for an average year, from season to season, for the assumed mean flows.

The approach considered was to fix project sizes and targets (as with the sequencing model) on the basis of screening model output and then to use mathematical programming for several years of varying hydrology to determine optimal operating rules for these projects and targets. The objective function would have been the minimization of short-run losses resulting from deviations from target allocations.

However, after tentative formulations of the model were undertaken and reviewed, it was decided not to implement the model. First, it appeared that the approach of using fixed project sizes and targets (necessary to maintain computational feasibility) would have required a substantial number of iterations with the simulation process, because in each simulation run, project sizes and targets were, in general, changed. More important, it was found that, on the basis of experience with the simulation models, the operating policies incorporated in them were sufficient for the purposes of the study.

The second model, which was built and run, analyzed the socioeconomic effects of farmer migration. This simulation model embodied a theory of farmer migration to newly developed irrigation areas in zones such as the Río Colorado (Hellman, 1972). The model is a system dynamics simulation model [Forrester (1968); for an application to water resource planning, see Hamilton, Goldstone, Milliman, Pugh, Roberts, and Zellner (1969)]. It deals with the interdependence of demographic phenomena, specifically migration, with investment strategies for irrigation infrastructure. The model is composed of three sectors: a demographic sector, an economic sector, and a water sector. Their interdependent structure produces the dynamic behavior of the system.

The central integrating element of the model is a "relative attractiveness" concept that embraces economic, social, and water-related indicators. Relative incomes, available opportunity, level of social infrastructure, and land distribution are considered as they affect migration decisions made by prospective farmers. In the model, a regional settlement promotion policy was found to be effective in accelerating initial migration to newly irrigated farming areas such as those proposed for the Río Colorado. Alternative investment phasing policies to balance water use with water availability were analyzed.

By focusing attention on an area larger than the Río Colorado basin and on the effects of social and economic management alternatives more general than those usually considered in basin planning, the dynamic policy model provided a valuable perspective on the planning problem. It was initially felt that the model could help in the definition of objectives and political constraints to be used in the screening model. The model was not used for these purposes, however, primarily because of delays in its development and lack of experience in using such models. Thus, its impact on the overall study was due primarily to its broadening influence on individual project members' thinking rather than to its quantitative results.

REFERENCES

COHON, JARED L., TOMAS B. FACET, ANDERS H. HAAN, and DAVID MARKS. "Mathematical Programming Models and Methodological Approaches for River Basin Planning." Ralph M. Parsons Laboratory for Water Resources and Hydrodynamics, MIT, Cambridge, Mass., January, 1973.

FORRESTER, JAY W. *Principles of Systems.* Cambridge, Mass.: Wright-Allen, 1968.

HAAN, ANDERS H. "A Screening Model for Water Resource Development: Stochastic Considerations" S.M. thesis. Department of Civil Engineering, MIT, Cambridge, Mass., February, 1972.

HAMILTON, H. R., S. E. GOLDSTONE, J. W. MILLIMAN, A. L. PUGH, III, E. B. ROBERTS, and A. ZELLNER. *Systems Simulation for Regional Analysis: An Application to River-Basin Planning.* Cambridge, Mass.: MIT Press, 1969.

HAMMOND, EDWARD. "Scheduling in Large Scale Optimization Models." S.M. thesis. Department of Civil Engineering, MIT, Cambridge, Mass., June, 1972.

HELLMAN, JAY JOHN. "Migration in a Developing Country: A Systems Study: The Stimulation and Retention of Agricultural Migrants." Ph.D. Thesis. Department of Civil Engineering, MIT, Cambridge, Mass., September, 1972.

THE AUTHORS

Jared Cohon is Associate Professor in the Program in Systems Analysis and Economics for Public Decision-Making of the Department of Geography and Environmental Engineering at the Johns Hopkins University. He received M.S. and Ph.D. degrees in Civil Engineering at MIT. His research interests are in systems analysis, particularly multiobjective programming theory, and its application to public decision-making.

Marcos M. Elinger is the Head of the Department of Applied Mathematics at the National Institute of Water Science and Technology, Argentina, and a consultant in water resource systems to the State Subsecretariat for Water Resources and the Ministry of the Interior in Argentina. He received his Agricultural Engineering degree from the University of Tucumán, Argentina, and worked as a Research Engineer in the Río Colorado study at MIT. His main field of interest is water resources systems planning and operation.

Tomas B. Facet is a consultant to governmental and private groups in Argentina. Until 1976 he was Professor of Operations Research in the Departments of Engineering and Management at the University of Cuyo. He did his undergraduate work in Operations Research and Economics in Argentina, and in 1975 he received M.S. degrees in Operations Research and Civil

Engineering from MIT. His research centers on the application of mathematical programming to water resource investment problems.

WALTER M. GRAYMAN is an associate in the consulting engineering firm of W. E. Gates & Associates, Cincinnati, Ohio. He did his undergraduate work at Carnegie-Mellon University and received the Ph.D. in Water Resources from MIT. His major research interests are in hydrologic and environmental modeling and geographical information systems.

BRENDAN HARLEY is president of Resource Analysis, Inc. He did his undergraduate work in Civil Engineering at University College, Cork, and received the Sc.D. in Civil Engineering at MIT, where he was also a faculty member. His principal professional interest is in mathematical modeling of hydrologic systems.

ROBERTO L. LENTON is currently Program Officer in Agriculture, Resources and Rural Development with the Ford Foundation, New Delhi. He did his undergraduate work in Civil Engineering at the University of Buenos Aires, and received the Ph.D. in Water Resources from MIT. A former member of the faculty of the Department of Civil Engineering at MIT, his principal professional interest is the planning and management of water resources.

DAVID C. MAJOR is currently Visiting Scholar at the United States Army Corps of Engineers' Institute for Water Resources. He did his undergraduate work in Economics at Wesleyan University, and received the Ph.D. in Economics from Harvard. The author of *Multiobjective Water Resource Planning* and the Co-editor for Social Sciences of *Water Resources Research*, he has taught in the Economics Departments at Harvard and the City College of New York as well as in the Department of Civil Engineering at MIT. His principal research interest is public decision-making.

DAVID H. MARKS is Professor and Associate Head, Water Resources Division, Department of Civil Engineering, MIT. He received the Ph.D. in Geography and Environmental Engineering from the Johns Hopkins University, and he did his undergraduate work at Cornell. His principal research interest is in the application of operations research to water resources and environmental planning.

EDWARD A. MCBEAN is Associate Professor in the Department of Civil Engineering at the University of Waterloo. He received his Ph.D. in Water Resources from MIT. He is also a principal in Edward A. McBean and Associates, Ltd., a Waterloo-based engineering firm. His principal research interests are the planning and management of water resources and environmental engineering.

JAVIER PASCUCHI is a senior staff member of the Institute of Water Economics, Law, and Administration in Argentina. He received his undergraduate degree in Economics at the University of Buenos Aires, and did post-graduate work at MIT and Harvard. He was formerly on the faculty of the School of Economics at the University of Buenos Aires and a consultant to the State Subsecretariat for Water Resources.

FRANK E. PERKINS is Professor and Head of the Department of Civil Engineering at MIT. He received his Ph.D. in Civil Engineering from MIT. His principal research interest is the computer modeling of physical processes for water resource planning.

JOHN C. SCHAAKE, JR., is Chief of the Hydrologic Services Division and Deputy Associate Director for Hydrology of the U.S. National Weather Service. Before joining the NWS, he was a member of the Civil Engineering faculty of MIT and was active in consulting practice. He received his Ph.D. in Sanitary Engineering and Water Resources from the Johns Hopkins University and did post-doctoral work with the Harvard Water Program.

JOSE LUIS SUAREZ is Professor of Microeconomics at the University of Buenos Aires and is engaged in private consulting. He received his undergraduate degree in Economics from the University of Buenos Aires, and he took graduate work at MIT. His principal research interests are in resource allocation in water resources and transportation.

JUAN B. VALDES is Associate Professor in the Water Resources Program at the Universidad Simón Bolívar, Caracas. He received his Ph.D. in Water Resources from MIT and did his undergraduate work at the Universidad Católica de Córdoba, Argentina. His major interests are the application of statistics and systems analysis to water resources and hydrology.

Dario Valencia is Professor at the Universidad Nacional de Colombia (Medellín) and until recently was vice president of this university. He did undergraduate work in Civil Engineering and graduate work in Mathematics at Medellín, and he received his S.M. and C.E. at MIT. His major interest is stochastic hydrology in water resources planning and development.

Guillermo J. Vicens is Senior Analyst/Project Manager at Resource Analysis, Inc. He received his Ph.D. in Water Resources and did his undergraduate work at MIT, where he also served on the faculty. His principal professional interest is in the development and application of hydrologic models.

INDEX

Note: for information on individual export/import diversions, irrigation areas, reservoirs, and power plants, see the pages listed under the entries for Development Sites, Export/Import Diversions, Irrigation Areas, Power Plants, and Reservoirs.